THE LAST FRONTIER

THE LAST FRONTIER

AMANDA SAYLE

CENTURY

LONDON MELBOURNE AUCKLAND JOHANNESBURG

Copyright © Hanna-Barbera (Live Action) Pty Ltd 1986

First published in paperback in Great Britain
in 1986 by Arrow Books Ltd

This hardcover edition published in 1987 by
Century Hutchinson Ltd
Brookmount House, 62–65 Chandos Place
London WC2N 4NW

Century Hutchinson Australia Pty Ltd
PO Box 496, 16–22 Church Street
Hawthorn, Victoria 3122, Australia

Century Hutchinson New Zealand Ltd
PO Box 40–086, Glenfield, Auckland 10
New Zealand

Century Hutchinson South Africa (Pty) Ltd
PO Box 337, Bergvlei 2012, South Africa

Taft Hardie presents a McElroy + McElroy Production
THE LAST FRONTIER
Starring Linda Evans, Jack Thompson,
Jason Robards, Judy Morris
Screenplay by Michael Laurence
Produced by Tim Sanders
Executive Producer: Hal McElroy
Directed by Simon Wincer
Director of Photography: Ian Baker

Printed in Great Britain by WBC Print Ltd, Bristol

British Library Cataloguing in Publication Data
Sayle, Amanda
  The last frontier.
  I. Title
  823'.914[F]   RR6069.A9/

ISBN 0–7126–1640–3
ISBN 0–09–951620–9 Pbk

— Prologue —

The afternoon sun poured down its full heat on to a vast sandy plain in central Australia. It was unlovely terrain. A flat, featureless landscape that seemed to stretch to infinity in every direction. The sparse vegetation stood out in stark contrast to the arid soil, whose colour was intensified by the dazzling light. Scrubby wasteland here and there gave way to areas that were dotted with white salt-pans or slashed with a dried-up river or gridded with dunes.

It was truly the dead heart of the continent.

Yet even here, life somehow went on. Blowflies buzzed. Mosquitoes droned. Insects crawled. A lone kite hung in the cloudless sky then swooped down in a graceful arc as it saw something below. Kangaroos dined off meagre fare. A pack of wild dingoes fought over the rotting carcass of a dead cow. Among the sandhills, tiny ants and trapdoor spiders engaged in their daily vendetta. Moths and butterflies flitted aimlessly.

A small marsupial mouse hunted for food on the plain, happily unaware of its impending fate. Wings flapping and talons lowered, the kite hovered for a moment then dived with awesome speed. Its sharp claws tore the life out of the mouse in a split-second and it carried off its prey in triumph.

All at once, a harsh noise crackled through the stillness. It was the fierce splutter of a light aircraft. A Cessna was flying low across the red plain, throwing its shadow on to the baked surface below. The dingoes looked up from their meal. The kangaroos paused to take notice. A goanna opened its hooded eyes. They waited until the aircraft had passed, then returned to more important things.

The Cessna flew on until it came to a range of mountains that switchbacked their way for miles with dark splendour. As the plane hummed on through the azure sky, something stirred below.

On the summit of the highest mountain was a human figure who seemed to be carved into the rock itself. A tall, solid, bronzed man moved slowly forward into the light and gazed upward. He watched the aircraft until it had disappeared from view, then he turned to survey the blood-red wilderness all around him.

Silence and isolation had been restored. He was satisfied.

He ambled back to his lair in the shadow of the rock.

— 1 —

Los Angeles International Airport was positively humming with activity. Although it was dusk, the various terminals were still working at full stretch as flights arrived and departed at regular intervals. Crowds of people filled the lounges or clogged the escalators or thronged the main concourses. Tearful farewells and joyful reunions took place on every side. The whole city appeared to be in transit.

It was organised pandemonium.

'Not so fast, Mom!'

'Yeah, what's the hurry?'

'Just keep up with me.'

'But the plane's not for *hours*.'

'Come on, will you?'

Kate Hannon headed purposefully along the passageway with a trolley loaded with luggage. The twins dragged their feet. While their mother might be anxious to press on, they were following with the utmost reluctance.

Kate knew it. She flung a command over her shoulder.

'Get a move on.'

'This bag is heavy,' Tina complained.

'Then give it to Marty. Carry his guitar instead.'

'No way!' the boy protested.

'I can manage,' Tina sighed. 'If only you'd slow down, Mom.'

'Sorry.'

Kate eased her pace a little. Like her children, she was tense and apprehensive about the new life on which they were embarking but she was determined not to admit it.

7

In rushing the twins along, she hoped to stop them from voicing any more dissent. The past week or so had been one long, continuous argument and it had left her drained. The time for discussion was over. The had made a commitment and she was going to honour it.

'How much further, Mom?'

'We're almost there, Tina.'

'Worse luck!' Marty muttered.

'What was that?' his mother challenged sharply.

'Aw, nothing.'

'Good.'

The trio threaded their way on down the busy corridor.

Kate Hannon was an alert, attractive woman in her mid-thirties with the kind of subdued beauty that is only enhanced by the passage of time. Fair hair hung to her shoulders and framed a round, open face that was lit by a pair of bright, intelligent eyes. For comfort during the long flight, she had chosen a check shirt and a pair of slacks. Even in her casual attire and with her features puckered into a frown, Kate could still make most men take note.

The twins had inherited her good looks though both were disguising it at the moment. Tina, in a shapeless top and baggy pants, wore a tormented expression that hid her natural radiance. Marty, in T-shirt and jeans, opted for a scowl that gave him an almost sinister look. Both the fourteen-year-olds were palpably unhappy.

Marty glanced across at his sister and hissed, 'Don't cry!'

Kate heard him but made no comment. She had vowed that she would not be drawn into another bitter wrangle with them. That vow was very soon put to the test.

'Billy coming to the airport?' asked Marty.

Tina stifled a sob and her brother immediately wished that he had not mentioned the boyfriend. He shrugged apologetically.

'He promised,' she murmured.

'Billy will be here,' he encouraged.

His concern for his twin was obvious. As her head drooped down and she fought off another sob, Marty tried to raise her spirits with a light joke.

'Cheer up, Tina. Look on the bright side.'

'*What* bright side?'

'We could be going to live on the moon.'

'It couldn't be as bad as the Australian outback!'

'That's enough!' Kate snapped. 'Both of you!'

She quickened her pace again and the children had difficulty in keeping up with her. Marty's flight bag slipped off his shoulder and he had to dive to retrieve it.

'Do we have to walk so fast?' he demanded.

'Yes.'

'Why? We have lots of time.'

'We already missed our plane,' his mother reminded him.

'Because of me!' Tina exploded. 'Why don't you say it?'

Kate took a deep breath and her voice throbbed with warning.

'Tina, I am not in the mood.'

'Don't fight,' Marty counselled.

But his sister had had enough. Stopping dead in her tracks, Tina let the bag that she was carrying fall to the floor. Tears now coursed down her cheeks and she let out a cry of despair.

'I'm not going!'

The others came to a halt and turned. Taut as a drum, Kate strove for self-control. It was exactly the situation she had feared. Mother and daughter stood there for several seconds in a wordless confrontation, heedless of the curious stares of the people passing by them. Marty was torn between sympathy for his sister and profound embarrassment.

'What?' Kate spoke with measured calm.

'I'll be all right. I'll stay with Billy.'

'Out of the question.'

'Why?'

'Tina,' her mother insisted, 'I am not putting up with any more of your nonsense.'

'It's not nonsense!'

'Pick up that bag.'

'I'm not coming to Australia.'

'Do as I say!'

'No.'

There was a brief pause, then Kate walked over to her daughter and delivered a resounding slap to her cheek. The noise echoed like a pistol-shot along the cavernous passageway.

Tina was more shocked than hurt. Marty was equally surprised. Neither of them could see that their mother was the one who was most upset by the incident.

'Mom,' Marty said in disbelief. 'You never hit us before.'

'Maybe that's been my mistake.'

Tina turned imploring eyes on her mother, already regretting that she had pushed her to it.

'I'm scared.'

After a moment's hesitation, Kate reached out to clasp the girl in her arms. She forced a tight smile, trying her best to reassure the children. And herself.

'Me, too,' she confessed.

They continued much more slowly on their way.

Twenty minutes later, having checked their baggage in at the airline desk, they were caught up in the chaos of the departure lounge. A sea of bodies ebbed and flowed all around them.

'I looked it up on the map.'

'So did I.'

'It was there – Larapinta . . .'

'Actually on the map of Australia.'

'Right in the middle.'

'I was amazed.'

Well-wishers had come to see them off. While Tina chatted to her girlfriends and Marty talked with the members of his band, Kate was having a final word with three of the people she would miss most. Judy, Fran and Mary were close and supportive friends, working women like herself who understood her problems and helped to cope with them.

Fran was intrigued by the name of Kate's new home.

'Where does it come from?'

'Larapinta? It's Aboriginal.'

'Wow!'

'Does that mean you'll be surrounded by those little black guys with bones through their noses?' said Mary uneasily.

'We do have some Aborigines working for us, I believe,' replied Kate. 'Quite a few, in fact.'

'One thing, anyway,' noted Judy. 'At least if you're on the map, you can't get lost.'

Mary was anxious. 'With two thousand square miles of your very own, you can get lost in your own backyard.'

'Your new home is bigger than LA,' observed Fran.

'It couldn't be,' disputed Judy.

'It is – but without the people.'

'That could be an advantage,' conceded Mary. 'I mean, just look at the crowd in here, will you? LA is a madhouse.'

'That's why we live here,' added Judy.

The women shared a brittle laugh.

Kate was glad that her friends had come to the airport and she felt an upsurge of affection for them, promising to write as soon as possible and pressing them to come and visit her in Australia.

Doubts then began to assail her and she had a moment of panic as she considered what she was walking out on. Her friends meant everything to her and they made life in Los Angeles, with all its difficulties, relatively happy and fulfilling. She was now about to cut off all her support systems. It was like starving herself of oxygen and she felt an intense pain shoot through her.

What if I'm making a dreadful mistake? she thought.

11

Suppose Australia doesn't work out for us? Am I really ready for a second marriage? Is he the right man?

Judy sensed her anxiety and put an arm around her.

'Hey – how're you feeling?'

'Optimistic,' said Kate.

But the wary look in her eye belied the word. She glanced across at the children and heaved an inward sigh. The twins looked more morose and resentful than ever. It was torture to her.

Marty was surrounded by a group of noisy teenage boys in garish clothes. He had helped to form the band and was its lead guitarist. Just as they were starting to develop their own individual sound, he was being dragged off halfway across the world.

Buddy spoke on behalf of the others.

'Let me know if your old lady comes to her senses.'

'Yeah.'

'Maybe she'll change her mind and decide to come straight back home to civilisation.'

'Hope so, Buddy.'

'We won't need to look for a new guitarist then.'

'Sure thing.'

Marty swallowed and tried to handle what was proving to be a very emotional occasion. Taking leave of his friends was even more dispiriting and agonising than he had imagined. The band was his whole world. It gave him status and definition, lifting him above the ruck of his schoolmates and holding out a promise of a bright future as a professional musician.

There was another vital gain. Girls. As a shy and inexperienced adolescent, Marty had found it very awkward to connect with the opposite sex. The band changed all that. Female fans mobbed them whenever they played. It did wonders for his ego and allowed him to make his first fumbling experiments with girlfriends.

Now it was all over. The sense of loss was excruciating.

Buddy brought out a small package from behind his

back. Embarrassment made him shuffle his feet and mumble his words.

'Anyway . . . this is from all of us, Marty . . . from the band.'

'Gee, thanks!'

Marty took the gift-wrapped six-pack of tapes and held it tight. He was genuinely touched but the present only made him feel worse. It had a finality about it and marked the end of his time with the band.

The others weighed in with best wishes and slaps on the back.

'Good luck, Marty!'

'Yeah – and keep practising that guitar!'

'Stay cool, man!'

'Come back soon. Okay?'

Afraid to meet their eyes, Marty kept his head down. He did not dare to show his true feelings and so he suffered in silence. Trying to behave like a man, he was cruelly aware of the fact that he was still only a boy inside. It all served to deepen his anger at his mother. What she was doing was unforgivable.

Can't she see it's killing me? he asked himself.

Tina stood nearby with a gaggle of her girlfriends. Though she smiled at their comments and answered their questions, she was not really concentrating on them. Her gaze kept straying across the lounge in search of Billy. Flying away from California was bad enough. To do so without seeing him once more would be prolonged torment.

Where *was* he? Come on, Billy, she thought. I love you. I need you.

Daisy showed an interest in the travel arrangements.

'Tina, may I see your ticket?'

'Why?'

'I just wanna look, that's all.'

Tina shrugged and handed the ticket over before looking around again. Hundreds of faces but not the one she longed to see. Her heart constricted. Time was running out.

Beth put a sympathetic hand on her arm.

'Maybe Billy got caught in traffic.'

'Yeah . . .'

'Maybe he was taken ill,' Beth suggested. 'Maybe he went to the wrong terminal. Maybe he made a mistake about the time of your flight. There's *lots* of reasons why he hasn't made it yet.'

Tina thought of one of them and it made her shiver. Maybe Billy didn't want to come.

The idea took root in her mind and bored away like a red-hot corkscrew. Billy was everything to her. In the six months they had known each other, she had moved from being a gawky teenager into a sophisticated young woman. She loved him so deeply that she simply could not comprehend a life without him.

Billy was wonderful. Four years older than her, he had left home and set up on his own. His maturity and independence thrilled her. He was an adult and he had chosen her. Tina revelled in the fact that it made the other girls jealous. It made her number one. Gave her an edge. Enlarged her.

And it was no brief infatuation. Billy was committed to her. They planned to live together as soon as she was old enough to leave her family. All they wanted was to be together for ever.

He had sworn that he would be at the airport.

Don't let me down, Billy, she screamed inside.

While Tina scanned the lounge with mounting fear, Sandy, a plump, precocious fourteen-year-old with high hopes of becoming a *femme fatale*, fastened hungry eyes on one of the members of Marty's band.

'God!' she exclaimed. 'Will you look at that cute little Davey. I want his body!' What she got instead was a sharp dig in the ribs from Daisy. 'Well, he's gorgeous,' she argued.

Beth grabbed Tina's camera from her.

'Everyone bunch up,' she ordered.

Tina shook her head. 'No, Beth . . .'

'Aw, come on . . . Everybody – please!'

The other girls formed a quick line with Tina in the middle but she was in no mood to be photographed. She pouted and lowered her head. Beth peered into the viewfinder and gave the signal.

'Now!' she called. 'Pretend you're happy!'

Smiles appeared magically on most faces but Tina promptly hid hers behind the magazine she was carrying. The camera clicked and it was all over. Their last time together.

Sandy realised something and emitted a wild shriek.

'I forgot my brace!' she wailed. 'I smiled. Oh no! I'll look like I'm out of the *Rocky Horror Show*!'

'You do, anyway,' Daisy mocked.

Beth quickly returned Tina's camera and took her hand.

'Don't be mad at me,' she begged.

'I'm not, Beth.'

'Am I still your best friend?'

'Always.'

Tina hugged her with an element of desperation.

High above their heads, the public address system crackled into life. A female voice boomed across the departure lounge and cut through the sustained babble.

'Announcing the departure of Qantas Flight Twelve non-stop to Sydney, now boarding through gate 127 . . . Would all passengers travelling on Qantas Flight Twelve now proceed to Gate 127 . . .'

Time was up. Still no Billy. Tina shuddered.

Her life-blood seemed to be ebbing away.

'Well,' Kate decided. 'This is it, I guess.'

'Goodbye, honey,' said Judy, getting her kiss first. 'And don't worry about a thing. He's a great guy. It's gonna be swell.'

Kate nodded bravely then submitted to a flurry of farewells as the others embraced her. Marty and Tina gave final sad waves to their respective friends then filed through passport control with their mother.

There was no turning back now.

15

They might not see Los Angeles again for a long time.

As they walked along with the other passengers, Kate Hannon reflected on the enormity of the risk that she was taking. On the strength of a whirlwind courtship, she had married a comparative stranger and agreed to follow him to Australia with her children.

Kate was not just taking on board a husband. She was setting out on a whole new life. The sense of adventure had inspired her at first. Misgivings now took over.

Guilt made her fling some hard questions at herself.

Am I doing the right thing? Okay, I'm entitled to make such an important decision for myself, but should I change the children's lives so completely? Why make them so miserable? Los Angeles is the only home they've known and they love it. Am I failing them as a mother in tearing them away? Am I being cruel? Insensitive? Plain selfish?

Why am I putting *my* happiness before theirs?

Kate tried to convince herself that it was for their benefit as much as for hers. They would be part of a proper family from now on and they would be living in exciting surroundings. The twins would be bound to respond. They would soon adapt.

She stole a look at Marty and Tina. Both were grim and resigned as they plodded along beside her. Now, her children hated Kate for what she was doing to them. Australia *had* to succeed. It was the only way that they would ever forgive her.

Kate found herself praying that it would all work out. Everything was now at stake. It was costing them all they had simply to make the journey. They could not afford to come back. It was a one-way trip.

Los Angeles suddenly seemed such a warm, safe, comforting place to be and pangs of remorse troubled her. She had turned her back on it in favour of something that she now saw in its true light.

It was fantasy. An amalgam of hope, dream and ambition.

They were on a journey into the unknown.

— 2 —

The Qantas 747 taxied slowly along the runway in the darkness, its lights flashing and its wheels squishing over the moist tarmac. Inside the aircraft, seat belts had been fastened and the passengers were watching the flight crew as they went through the obligatory safety routine. A baby cried. An old lady adjusted her hearing aid so that she could catch what was being said. Towards the rear, two children bickered over which one of them should have the window seat.

After swinging around in a half-circle, the plane came to a gentle halt and waited for clearance from the control tower. The flight crew now took their seats and strapped themselves in. They did not have long to wait. There was an explosion of sound as the engines roared, then their full thrust was unleashed. The jumbo jet shot forward at breakneck speed for a short while and then soared upward with irresistible power, climbing into the black sky, levelling out, then altering its trajectory once more so that it could surge even higher.

When the signal lights went off, the passengers undid their safety belts and made themselves more comfortable. The baby had stopped crying. The old lady's hearing aid was turned down. A dual smack solved the problem of which child should get the window seat.

The flight to Australia was airborne.

Kate Hannan was surprised at the amount of noise and movement. There was a loud buzz of conversation and the aisles were already in use. She hoped that it would not be like that all the way to Sydney. The children were sullen and preoccupied. Marty had unwrapped his present and was examining the tapes. Tina was staring out through the glass at the myriad lights of Los Angeles, wondering why Billy had failed to turn up at the airport and feeling almost suicidal.

Under other circumstances, the twins would have been bubbling. If they had been going to Australia for a holiday, they would have been filled with anticipatory delight and bent on enjoying every second of the flight. As it was, they were withdrawn and dejected. Both of them looked utterly betrayed.

Kate tried to rally them with another token smile. 'Okay?'

There was a long pause. She leaned in closer. 'Marty?'

'I guess so,' he grunted.

'What about you, Tina?'

But her daughter refused to speak. Face pressed against the window, she continued to peer out even though Los Angeles and her romance with Billy had vanished completely.

In the long term, Kate told herself, they would all be happier and more integrated in their new country. Sacrifices were inevitable – she had made several herself – but they would all be worth it in the end.

Or would they? Supposing that she had made a dreadful error? Suppose that her instincts had misled her and set her up for a cruel disappointment? Supposing that neither she nor her children could bear life in the Outback? Kate went quite dizzy for a moment. It was all too painful to contemplate.

When her head cleared, she saw one of the cabin stewards coming down the aisle towards her. The young woman was carrying a tray of drinks and handing them out to passengers as she passed. Kate sat up with a start. In a twinkling she was reminded of the day when Tom Hannon came into her life.

Incredibly, it was less than a month ago . . .

*

Late night in a downtown restaurant in Los Angeles. The place was packed. The customers were noisy and the staff kept constantly on their toes. It was an unpretentious establishment with Formica tables and plastic chairs and modest décor but the food was good, the prices very reasonable and the service quick. In the hour before it closed at midnight, it was always bursting at the seams.

One of the waitresses sidled up to a colleague at the counter.

'Table Eight.'

'What?'

'Male Caucasian. Early to mid forties. About a hundred and eighty pounds. *Alone*. Can't keep his eyes off you.'

'Judy,' said her friend. 'Don't you ever give up?'

'Not me, honey,' Judy replied, subtle as a foghorn. 'If *I* was getting the attention he's giving you, I'd be over there like lightning.'

'What about your husband?'

'What about him!'

Kate grinned. Judy was the person who made the job at the restaurant bearable. She was a big, buxom, vivacious woman with an inexhaustible interest in the opposite sex and its many possibilities. Even when she was rushed off her feet, Judy missed nothing.

'He's real cute,' she opined.

'Keep your mind on your work.'

'From outa town, I'd say. What d'ya think?'

'I haven't had time to notice him.'

'Well, he's sure noticed *you*, sister!'

Kate could not resist turning around for a look. She found herself held by warm, kind, appraising eyes that gazed directly into hers. Judy's estimate of his age and weight had been fairly accurate. He was a lean man with a weathered handsomeness that spoke of a life spent largely out of doors under a hot sun. His jacket was smart but right out of fashion. He was not American.

The customer at Table Eight stood out from the others like a non-actor who has wandered on to the stage by mistake and got caught up in an unfamiliar play. Yet he was not fazed by it all. On the contrary, he looked very relaxed and in control. There was a quiet strength about him that was instantly appealing.

'Just my luck!' Judy moaned.

'What?'

'He's in your section.'

Kate tore her eyes away from the stranger and checked her watch. Other priorities declared themselves. She put a hand on Judy's arm.

'I have to call home. Cover for me.'

'I will if you get Dr Peterson to fit Danny in this week before he loses all his second teeth. The way he eats candy, he'll be the only twelve-year-old on the block with dentures.'

'I'll try, Judy.'

'I want more than "try". I'm talking about my son here.'

Judy gave a lecherous smirk and stared over at the customer.

'Oh boy! Just let me at him!'

She sailed off to take the man's order and to vamp him while she was at it. He was mildly amused but he was not deflected from the main object of his curiosity. While talking to Judy, he watched Kate intently as she collected a tray of food from the counter, took it across to a table, unloaded the two plates then flitted off towards the door at the rear of the dining area.

A slow, deliberate smile spread over the man's voice.

'What's her name?'

'Judy,' announced his waitress. 'And I'm not married.'

Kate, meanwhile, scurried out to the public telephone in the corridor. The booth was no more than a small awning fixed to the wall and it offered no privacy. People were moving to and fro all the time and the hubbub from the restaurant was quite loud.

Lifting the receiver, Kate inserted money into the slot and dialled a number. She waited impatiently as it rang out. A voice finally spoke on the other end of the line. It sounded sleepy.

'Yeah?'

'Marty? Did I wake you?'

He yawned. 'Sort of. I went off in front of *Miami Vice*.'

'What did I tell you about watching TV so late?' she chided. 'You have school tomorrow.'

'I know, Mom.'

'So you should be in bed. Now.'

'I was just going.'

'You do that,' she insisted. 'Where's Tina?'

'Oh, uh . . .' Marty cleared his throat. 'In the bathroom.'

'Well, I want to talk to her.'

'Can't I take a message?'

'No. Please go and get her.'

'But I think she's in the bath.'

'Don't lie to me, Marty,' shouted Kate, realising that he was covering for his sister. 'Tina is not there, is she?'

'Yeah. I told you.'

'Then get her. This instant.'

An embarrassed silence. 'I can't, Mom.'

'No – and we both know why, don't we? You can call Billy's place and tell her that I want her home at once! Got it?'

'I got it.'

'I am very angry, Marty, you tell her that. I'll be home soon and I expect to find you both asleep when I get there.'

'You will, Mom,' he promised.

'We'll talk about this in the morning.'

Kate hung up and was plagued by all the old fears once more. She knew that she should be there to look after her children but she simply had to have an evening job to swell the family income. Like so many other women in the same situation, she was trapped. It was galling.

When she got back to the counter, she was still blaming herself for neglecting the twins. Sick with worry, she picked up her order book and flicked through it, trying to force her mind back to her work. Judy arrived beside her with a tray in her hands. She sensed trouble.

'Bad?'

'The usual.'

'Well, you would go and have twins!'

'Twice the anxiety.'

'Put the fear of death into them. It's what I do with Danny.'

'That's not the answer, Judy,' Kate sighed. 'How can you expect children to do what you ask them when you're never there with them? They need reassurance.'

'Don't we all?'

'It's so frustrating! If only I didn't have to work nights.'

'There is one way out, honey. Find yourself a sugar daddy to pick up the tabs.' Judy cackled. 'Of course, you'd still have to work nights now and then but you'd see a helluva lot more of your kids.' She handed the tray to Kate. 'Come on – back on the treadmill. Table Eight.'

'Okay.'

Still distracted, Kate wended her way through the tables until she reached the customer. He scrutinised her face and was aware of her change of mood since she had come back into the restaurant.

Kate lifted up a plate and offered it to him.

'Roast beef sandwich?'

'Thank you,' he said with a smile. 'That was fast.'

She set the plate down in front of him and went to pour him some coffee. He stopped her with a raised palm.

'I ordered white tea.'

She heard the twang in his voice this time and realised that he must be Australian. Kate made an effort to concentrate.

'That's tea with milk?'

'Yes.'

'Australian?'

'Sorry?'

'New Zealand, maybe?'

'Whatever you have is fine.'

Kate laughed and her tension eased at once. He was baffled.

'I wasn't asking about the tea,' she explained. 'That accent. Are you an Australian?'

He grinned self-consciously, happy that they were connecting at last and keen to make the most of his opportunity.

'Oh, yeah,' he said. 'I'm here visiting my sister. She lives in San Diego. She's married to an American.'

'We get a lot of Australians through here.'

'Does that bother you?'

'No, I rather like them.'

She removed his empty water glass and put it on her tray. His eyes followed her hand and his grin broadened.

'I see you don't wear a wedding ring.'

'Here we go again!' she murmured.

'Does that mean . . .?'

Politely but firmly, Kate gave him her standard reply.

'The service is fast. LA is fast. I'm not.'

His face crumpled with embarrassment and he was angry with himself.

'I apologise,' he said with evident sincerity. 'That was very clumsy. I'm a little out of practice.'

'At picking up waitresses?'

'No. Of course not. That is . . .'

Their eyes met. His were transparently honest. Kate broke away.

'I'll bring your tea.'

Tom Hannon watched her as she made her way back to the counter. Everything about her fascinated him. He liked her appearance, her voice, her manner and her graceful movements. He even admired the way she had put him down when he had spoken out of turn. Needing to share his thoughts with someone, he turned to the man at the next table.

'That's a pretty woman,' he confided.

'Uh?' The man gave him a blank-eyed stare.

'Really something, isn't she?'

Tom was grateful he had chosen that particular restaurant.

After the stragglers had been shown out, the tables were cleared, the lights switched off and the place closed up for the night. Along with the other waitresses, Kate went into the back room and changed quickly out of her working uniform. Her children still monopolised her attention and she was anxious to get back home to them as soon as possible.

She headed for the door and called out a farewell.

'Good night, Judy!'

'See you tomorrow, honey! Oh, and don't be too hard on them.'

'What?'

'Your kids. Remember that *you* were fourteen once.'

'That was a hundred years ago.'

Kate let herself out into the street and felt the warm night air hit her. When a figure stepped out of the shadows ahead of her, she knew at once that it was the handsome Australian. She was not surprised to see him there. What did astonish her was the fact that she did not seem to mind.

Her striking good looks were a mixed blessing. They might be the envy of her female friends but they did tend to expose her to a lot of unwanted interest at the restaurant. Some men appeared to think that the waitresses were there for the asking, and Kate was all too used to finding over-friendly customers lurking outside for her. She had learned to dispatch such wolves with a few curt phrases.

Those phrases all deserted her now. What was it about this man that made him so different?

He confronted her with an easy smile and introduced himself.

'I'm Tom Hannon.'

'Hi.'

24

'And you're Kate Adamson.'

'How do you know that?'

'I asked your friend.'

'Oh.'

'Judy was very helpful.'

'It's been nice meeting you, Mr Hannon,' she said, dismissively. 'I hope you enjoy your trip back to Australia. Goodbye.'

She tried to move past him but he blocked her way.

'There's a lot of strange types about,' he remarked. 'I thought I'd wait and . . . escort you to your car . . .'

He stood back and she walked past him. Tom fell in beside her and they strolled in silence along the sidewalk. When Kate eventually spoke, her tone was noncommittal.

'It's at the auto shop. Everyone in this town has car karma.'

He stayed beside her for a couple of blocks until they reached the bus stop. Tom was about to say something that he had carefully rehearsed when the bus arrived. They got into it and found that nearly all the seats were taken.

The bus seemed to contain a microcosm of the whole city. Faces of all ages and all nationalities were crammed in together. Late-night people with late-night expressions of boredom, fatigue, indifference or sheer despair. One old man reeked of alcohol. Two black youths chewed gum. A Mexican woman bit into some kind of sandwich. A Korean was singing softly to himself as he looked at the world through glazed eyes. More than one passenger was asleep.

Kate took a seat next to a middle-aged woman in a flowered dress. Tom managed to sit directly behind her and had to content himself with gazing at the back of her head for a while. Then he noticed her reflection in the window and studied it closely.

She was glad of his company and yet strangely nervous about it. As the bus rumbled on through the downtown streets, Kate tried to work out why she had such ambivalent feelings. She had not really wanted the man to take

25

her home and yet she had done nothing to prevent him. Part of her wanted to ignore him but another part of her was gripped by curiosity.

Who was he and why had he singled her out?

Looking much calmer than she felt, Kate turned her head slowly towards the window. She saw his reflection now and watched him watching her. Their eyes locked once more and then he smiled. Kate swung her head away.

Tom Hannon could wait no longer. Leaning forward so that he was almost touching her hair, he told her what he had been wanting to say all night. The words tumbled out of him in hesitant bursts and he was not at all discomfited by the fact that other people could hear them.

'I'm forty-three years old. My wife died five years ago. I have two daughters. I breed cattle on my own place, two hundred miles south-west of Alice Springs . . . in central Australia.'

He paused for breath. Kate had tensed slightly.

'I'm going home in a few days,' he continued. 'In the meantime, I'd be very grateful of your company. I'm not the kind of man that puts the hard word on a woman the first time he takes her out, so you've nothing to fear on that score.'

He paused again. She remained immobile.

'It's just that I haven't seen much of California,' he added reasonably. 'Having come all this way, I want to get my money's worth out of the place. Look around a bit. See the sights.' There was a beat as he ran his tongue over his lips. 'Anyway, maybe you'd like to think about it?'

Kate's eyes strayed to the window again and she met his gaze. It was entirely without guile or threat. His words came straight from the heart. Tom Hannon was obviously not shooting her a line.

The woman next to her had listened to it all with cynical interest. She gave a little shrug. Kate tried to suppress a smile as amusement momentarily got the better of her nerves.

26

Nothing more was said. When the bus stopped for the fourth time, Kate got up from her seat and headed for the exit. Tom was at her heels. They were soon walking alone along an empty street, their footsteps echoing on the hard stone and their shadows striding ahead of them under the harsh glare of the overhead lights.

Ultimately, it was Kate who broke the silence.

'Does "putting the hard word" on someone mean what I think it does?' she asked.

Tom was thrown and took some time to recover.

'Probably.'

Unexpectedly, she roared with laughter and his hopes soared. He grinned happily. He was making progress after all.

'I live right here,' she said.

'I see.'

'Time to say good night.'

'Oh.'

'Thanks for seeing me home.'

'My pleasure.'

They had stopped outside an apartment block. Kate searched in her handbag for her key and told herself that she ought to walk straight out of his life before any complications set in. She had enough on her plate without taking on an anonymous Australian. Logic told her that the relationship could go no further.

But it was instinct that did the talking.

'I must be crazy,' she decided. 'I'm divorced . . . I have two children also – twins – a boy and a girl, fourteen years old. I work as a dental receptionist during the day and wait table three nights a week so, as you can see, I don't have much time for socialising.'

She turned to face him. They were very close to each other.

'If I go out with you, just what do you expect from me?'

Tom's gaze was as honest and unflinching as before.

'It'll be up to you, Kate.'

Something about him compelled trust. Logic was still

27

insisting that she had no room for him in her world but she discarded its advice. Tom Hannon had a quiet integrity that was at once refreshing and reassuring. He had none of the phoney charm of the men who usually tried to date her.

'You'll have to teach me some more Australian expressions.'

'I'd be delighted to. Tomorrow?'

'Why not?'

'I'll pick you up right here. Just tell me when.'

Kate almost blushed. She felt rather foolish that she had misled him about where she lived and hoped that he would put it down to natural precaution on her part. Now that she had agreed to see him again, she was ashamed at not having told the truth.

She pointed to the apartment block across the road.

'Actually, I live over there. Apartment Twelve. I'll be ready by nine-thirty. See you in the morning.'

Before he could reply, Kate ran swiftly across the road and disappeared through the door to the block. Tom Hannon stood there and beamed. When a cat cried on a nearby fence, he walked over to stroke it and soon coaxed a purr out of the animal.

'Puss,' he whispered, 'I'm gonna marry that girl.'

He had never been so certain about anything in his life.

— 3 —

High above the Pacific Ocean, the Qantas 747 hurtled on through the darkness like a shooting star. The relentless drone of its engines was muffled by the unforgiving blackness of the night sky.When the aircraft hit some mild turbulence, it rocked gently for a few moments then steadied itself and flew on.

The passengers in the economy section did not even notice the brief discomfort. Many of them were already asleep, their legs wrapped in blankets distributed by the flight crew. Others were watching the movie that was being shown simultaneously in the different sections of the plane. With the cabin lights dimmed, the flickering screens exerted a mesmeric power.

Marty was annoyed with himself for enjoying the movie so much. Intent on hating the journey, he was irritated when he got carried away by what was happening on screen. The movie was helping to defeat time and to subdue his resistance to the whole Australian venture. It rankled.

Tina had no such problems. Her resistance was stronger than ever. When she looked at the screen, all she could see was Billy. First love is always special but with her it had developed into an obsession. All her hopes for the future had been built on her relationship with Billy and he had vowed that they would be together for the rest of their lives. At a stroke, their cherished plans had fallen to pieces. She was left with nothing. Not even the memory of a farewell scene at the airport. Tina closed her eyes as fresh tears began to flow.

Kate was all too aware of her children's feelings. They exuded misery and resentment. It was part of the price she had to pay for her decision to leave Los Angeles. The twins might be embittered now but Australia would win them over in time. They would come to appreciate that it meant a better future for all of them. Marty would soon forget about his days with the band and Tina would learn that she could, in fact, survive without Billy.

They would all live happily ever after.

This, at least, was the theory. Kate was enough of a realist to know that it might be very different in practice. There was one immense consolation. She would not be alone. Her new husband would be beside her all the way.

Tom Hannon made anything possible.

A dance sequence came up on the screen and it triggered off another memory. Kate removed her headset so that she could not hear the soundtrack of the movie.

Her ears were suddenly filled with other rhythms . . .

Drumbeats stirred the blood. Vividly coloured feathers vibrated and shimmered in the blinding sunlight. Pounding feet. Clapping hands. Pulsing music that seemed to reach right into the soul. The Mexican dancers twisted and turned on the cobblestones, their magnificent headdresses bobbing away, their spectacular costumes swirling and their ornate jewellery jangling noisily. The frenetic pace of their display was exhilarating.

When they reached the climax of their routine, the applause was loud and sustained. The spectators had been absolutely enthralled.

'That was fantastic!' Tom Hannon announced.

'I thought you'd like it,' Kate said.

'It's as good as being in Mexico itself.'

'Yet it's right on my doorstep.'

Olvera Street was its usual blaze of colour. Set in the heart of bustling downtown Los Angeles, it is the part of the city that most emphatically proclaims its Spanish origins. The street has been restored as a Mexican market-

30

place and – despite some examples of grotesque commer-
cialisation – it is truly picturesque.

Vendors were hawking everything from miniature som-
breros to velvet paintings that glowed in the dark. Stall-
holders competed with raucous cries. Homemade tortillas
were on sale. Tourists haggled over souvenirs. Cameras
were busy on all sides. Music played. Dancers danced.
Cheers were raised.

Olvera Street was very definitely alive.

Tom and Kate walked hand in hand through it all.

'Thanks!' he declared.

'For what?'

'Bringing me here.'

'You wanted to see all the sights.'

He stared directly at her and his eyes twinkled fondly.
'I'm looking at the best sight of all right now.'

'That doesn't say much for the others.'

'You'd put the Sydney Harbour Bridge in the shade.'

She smiled in acknowledgement of his compliment.

Kate was enjoying his company enormously. Tom was
natural and unforced in everything he did. She had never
met anyone so ready to respond with such pleasure to
each new experience. Wandering around the marketplace
had filled him with an almost childlike glee. He was in his
element.

'Where would you like to go now?' she asked.

'I leave that to you, Kate.'

'How do you feel about ships?'

'Why?'

'You'll see.'

The *Queen Mary* lies at permanent anchor in the dock at
Long Beach. Once a floating palace belonging to the
Cunard Steamship Line, she is now a luxury hotel and
major tourist attraction.

Tom Hannon moved around with his mouth agape.

'They must have spent an absolute fortune on it!'

'How the other half lives,' mused Kate.

'It's so *big*. When exactly was it built?'
'1936.'
'I just hope I look that good when *I'm* fifty!'

Tom's curiosity was inexhaustible. He led her all over the ship, pointing out details that caught his attention and asking a hundred questions. Kate found his enthusiasm infectious. When they came to the ballroom with its sumptuous décor and air of vanished splendour, Tom's eyes widened in astonishment.

Before he could stop it, an exclamation shot from his lips.

'Starve the lizards! Now I've seen the bloody lot!'

It was the same wherever they went. Tom's interest did not flag for an instant. He was the ideal person to take around Los Angeles. Everything was a source of uncomplicated fun to him.

'Hey! These are Charlie Chaplin's!'
'I know.'
'Never realised his feet were so small.'
'You learn something new every day,' she teased.

They were on the forecourt of Grauman's Chinese Theatre, examining the sets of footprints left in the concrete by famous Hollywood stars. Tom was overwhelmed to see so many great names.

'These are Clark Gable's,' he said reverently.
'They all came here sooner or later.'
'And there's Robert Mitchum's.'

He moved to another set and eased his right foot into the print. It was a perfect fit and it made him chuckle with joy.

'Quick, Kate. Come over here.'
'I can't right now.'
'But I've got the same size shoe as James Stewart. Look!'
'Sorry. My heel is stuck in Ginger Rogers.'

Tom went to her rescue and freed her gently. She gave him an involuntary kiss on his cheek by way of thanks. It made his whole face light up. He waved a hand expansively across the forecourt.

'See if you can get your heel stuck in someone else.'

Each time they went out together, they grew steadily closer. They came to know each other's likes, dislikes, moods and individual quirks. Aware of the deepening relationship between them, they did nothing to impede it. For both of them, it had become a time of wonderful discovery.

The afternoon they spent at Anaheim was typical.

'What would you like to see, Tom?'

'Everything!'

'But that would take a whole week.'

'So? We stay here a week.'

'What about my job?' she asked with a laugh.

'All I know is that this is the best damned holiday I ever had and I mean to enjoy it to the full!' He slipped an arm around her waist. 'You're getting something out of it as well, aren't you?'

'Oh, yes!'

Disneyland enabled them to recapture their youth again.

Kate had been there before with her children but she had never been able to relax. The responsibility of looking after them had taken the edge off her own pleasure. Now it was different. She just surrendered to the whole experience and revelled in it.

Though she had lived in Los Angeles for many years, she had never really been able to take advantage of all that it had to offer. Being a working mother had deprived her of so much. The days spent with Tom Hannon taught her to see the city afresh. She felt that she had been somehow liberated.

For him, too, it was an endless delight. He was a man who had put in years of unremitting toil on his ranch and soldiered on in the face of many setbacks. Suddenly, he was off duty. He could let himself go for once. Tom Hannon did so with a vengeance.

'Wheeeee!'

'Tom!' she screamed. 'We'll fall off!'

'Not while I've got hold of you.'

Descent in a Matterhorn bobsled was a thrill a second.

'We made it!' she said with relief when they reached the bottom. 'I never thought we'd get down in one piece.'

'Let's have another go.'

'But I was frightened to death, Tom.'

'So was I – that's why I want to do it again.'

'You'll have to hold me tight, then.'

'I'd worked that bit out for myself.'

Kate smiled but warning bells had begun to sound inside her head. She was getting too fond of Tom Hannon and letting him get far too fond of her. The closer they became, the more painful it would be when he went out of her life and back to Australia. It was time to cool it, she decided. This would be their last time together.

The reception area at the dental surgery was at one end of a large, well-appointed modern waiting room. Dressed in her white uniform and with her hair pinned up smartly at the back, Kate sat behind the desk and dealt with some paperwork. A few patients were lounging in easy chairs, flicking idly through the magazines that had been set out on low smoked-glass tables. Hygienic silence ruled.

It was shattered by the telephone. Kate picked up the receiver automatically and spoke into the mouthpiece.

'Dr Peterson's surgery . . .'

'I'd like to make an appointment,' said a man's voice.

'Certainly, sir. When would be most convenient?'

'How about tonight?'

Kate recognised Tom's laugh and chided him pleasantly. 'Tom Hannon, you've got to stop calling me at work.'

'Why?'

'Because you'll lose me my job, that's why.' She glanced up at the patients, who studiously avoided looking at her, then she continued in a whisper. 'Don't do it again, please. It's . . . awkward.'

34

'What did you think of yesterday?' he pressed.

'Tom . . .'

'We went down the Matterhorn three times,' he reminded her.

'I know. And I had a wonderful time.'

'Best day so far for me.'

'I'm glad.'

'So when do I see you again? Tonight?'

Kate braced herself. The parting of the ways had come. 'No, I can't,' she said firmly. 'I told you that.'

'What about tomorrow?'

Out of the corner of her eye, she saw Dr Peterson coming out of his surgery with a female patient. It was time to bring the call to an end. And the relationship. Her whisper hoarsened.

'Tom, I have to go.'

'Not before you give me an answer,' he insisted.

'I'm sorry. I work tomorrow night.'

'Take the evening off.'

'I can't afford to.'

'In that case,' he warned mischievously, 'I'll come to the restaurant and haunt you from Table Eight.'

'Don't you dare!'

Kate put a hand over the telephone as Dr Peterson ushered the patient past the desk, she tried to terminate her own conversation.

'Goodbye, Tom.'

'Where shall I pick you up tomorrow?'

'Look,' she said briskly, 'we had some great fun together but it has to stop. You've got your life to go back to and I've got mine here. Why don't we move this whole thing into a more comfortable space and just be friends.' She thought of something else. 'And, by the way – thanks!'

'What time tomorrow?' Tom asked, as if he had not heard a word that she had said.

Kate decided to bid him farewell and put the telephone down but her voice betrayed her. Instead of making it clear that it was all over, she heard herself capitulating.

'Eight o'clock.'

'I'll be there.' He hung up at the other end and she followed suit.

Kate sat there and reviewed the conversation with a blend of irritation and pleasure. She was annoyed that she had been unable to hold out against him and yet glad that she would be seeing him again. Tom Hannon had brought a touch of colour and romance into her rather humdrum existence. It was worth remembering that.

He was due to go home soon and would fly out of her world for ever. She decided that she might as well get full value out of the fleeting affair while it lasted. It had boosted her morale tremendously and turned Judy green with envy.

Why not? she asked herself with a shrug. I like him. He's a nice guy. After some of the slobs I've known, he's just about perfect. Why throw it away before I have to? I'll stick with it.

Her employer came up to the desk.

'Everything under control, Kate?'

'Yes, Dr Peterson.'

'Good,' he replied with a knowing smile. 'Send the next patient in, please.'

Kate snapped back into her role as a receptionist.

'Mr Lucas. Would you go into the surgery now . . .?'

The sushi bar was a victim of its own popularity. Not only was it packed to capacity but there was a long queue of people waiting for seats to be vacant. The place was exotic, dimly lit and throbbing with energy. Behind the bar, Japanese cooks sliced the raw fish with practised hands then prepared a variety of sauces. Japanese waitresses shouted orders through to the kitchen in their native language and unseen kitchen staff yelled back. The din seemed quite natural and was an accepted part of a unique atmosphere.

Tom Hannon sat at the counter with Kate. Unlike her, he found the noise and the sense of crush rather distracting.

He was used to wide open spaces and was never at ease in a crowd. Also, he wanted to be in a more intimate setting with Kate. The sushi bar was too public.

It had been Kate's choice and she was completely at home. She felt a pang of sympathy as she watched the staff rushing around to keep pace with the demands of the customers. It was a treat for her to be taken out for a meal instead of having to work in a restaurant herself. She had picked the bar because of its superb food and its ethnic idiosyncrasies. The general clamour did not disturb her in the least. It was her normal environment.

A plate was set in front of each of them. Their meal was served on a bed of rice and garnished with a rich aromatic sauce.

Tom had a worried frown as he scrutinised it.

'Aren't you going to try it?' she invited.

'Oh, yeah.'

He put a small amount on the end of his fork and sampled it.

'Well?'

'Raw fish, uh?' he grunted.

'Uh huh. You like it?'

'It's certainly . . . different.'

She laughed at the pained expression on his face.

'Tom, don't you have sushi bars in Australia?'

'Not where I live.'

'Of course,' she said. 'You're hundreds of miles from the coast.'

'We've got a fish 'n' chip shop in Glenwarra,' he volunteered.

'A *what*?'

'Fish 'n' chips. They come wrapped in newspaper.'

It was her turn to pull a face. The idea sounded revolting. 'You're kidding.'

'Nothing like it, Kate. Especially with lots of salt and vinegar.'

'Ugh!'

'It'd be a great cultural experience for you.'

'Think I'll give it a miss.'

Kate was hungry. She began to tuck into her meal with relish and washed it down with sips of wine. Tom simply toyed with his food. He waited for a moment when the sound level diminished slightly.

'Kate, I do appreciate this.'

'But you haven't eaten anything.'

'Not the meal,' he explained. 'I was talking about you. I'm very grateful to you. Taking time off work. I know how it is when you've got kids to think about.'

Kate shrugged. 'Well, I don't do it too often. But I'm allowed to escape every once in a while. Besides, I'm having a nice time.' She flashed a grin and tried an Australian accent. 'Real beaut!'

'Ripper!'

They laughed happily. Kate wanted to learn the new word.

'What's that? Say it again.'

'Ripper?'

'Yes. You mean – as in "Jack the Ripper". Ugh!'

'Nothing like that. It means "terrific", that's all. This is a ripper sushi.'

Her laughter increased and he felt his love swell in his heart. 'And I thought they spoke English in Australia,' she said.

'No,' he teased. 'It's a whole different language. Like here.'

She lifted her plate and threatened him playfully with it. Their faces were close together and his eyes were smiling.

'Kate,' he said, casually. 'Any chance of meeting your kids?'

Taken completely by surprise, Kate sat there nonplussed and relied on instinct to give him his answer.

'Yes, Tom. I'd like that. Very much.'

— 4 —

When it came to taking photographs, Tina was a real perfectionist. She moved around the room, experimenting with various angles then made a series of adjustments to her camera so that she got everything exactly as she wanted. The three of them were seated at the dining table, bunched closely together and trying to hold on to frozen smiles. The wait seemed to be interminable.

Marty was the first to feel the strain.

'Get a move on, Tina!'

'You can't hurry a photograph,' she argued.

'It takes you *hours*.'

'Care and attention always pay off, Marty Adamson.'

'Big deal!'

'Ready, everybody?'

'Hooray!' he jeered.

'Hold it right there!'

Tina pressed a switch and the flashbulb went off.

While the photographer wound on the film, the others relaxed. It was Saturday night and Tom Hannon was on his first visit to the apartment. Though the place was small, it was impeccably clean and very comfortable. Kate's touch was in evidence throughout.

He also admired the way she had brought up her children. They were bright, lively and well-behaved. More to the point, they obviously liked him. Tina would not have offered to take a photograph unless she had wanted to and Marty was clearly the sort of youth who was very selective about the adults he favoured with his conversation.

Tom Hannon had somehow passed the test. They approved.

Kate was at the head of the table. She signalled to Tina.

'Now come and finish your dinner before it goes cold.'

'Okay,' said the girl, resuming her seat.

'I'd like a copy of that snap when it comes out,' Tom requested.

'We'll send you one,' Kate promised.

Now that the photographic session was over, Marty showed some pride in his sister's talent. He turned to Tom.

'Tina's a camera freak. She's won two competitions.'

'Marty!' she protested.

'That's wonderful!' Tom congratulated.

'Only at school,' she explained.

'Still,' he rejoined, 'it's an achievement. Well done!'

'Thanks.'

Kate offered the serving pot to the honoured guest.

'Tom? Some more?'

He shook his head and patted his stomach contentedly.

'I don't think I could manage another morsel, Kate. That's the best meal I've had since I've been in California.'

'It's the best meal *we've* had for ages,' Marty observed. 'You must come again, Tom.'

'Your mother is an excellent cook.'

'When I have the time.'

Kate and the children continued to munch away while Tom watched. It was good to be part of a real family once again. He felt more relaxed than he had done for a very long time.

'Tom,' Marty asked, 'were you born at Larapinta?'

'Yes. And my dad, and his before him. Now my two girls. That's four generations of us.'

Tom reached inside his coat for his wallet.

'I saw a movie on TV that was shot in the Outback,' Marty remembered. 'They call it the "last frontier". Right?'

'Some call it that.' Tom took out some photographs and handed them to Kate. 'Those are my girls.'

Kate looked down with interest at a picture of two teenage girls on horseback. One was grinning at the camera while the other was grimacing. Both were screwing their eyes up against the glare of the sun. A plain stretched out behind them.

Tom used his index finger to point out his daughters.

'That's Zoe – she's fifteen.'

'They're both very pretty,' said Kate.

'The one pulling a face is Emmie – she's just turned thirteen.'

Kate studied the first photograph carefully before passing it on to her own children. She could see a resemblance to Tom in both of his girls and it pleased her. He watched her throughout and tried to gauge her reaction.

'I suppose they've been riding horses since they were babies,' Kate said.

'Yep.'

'You must be very proud of them, Tom.'

He beamed. 'Well, you could say that.'

'Do they have koala bears where you live?' Tina wondered.

'Afraid not.'

'What about crocodiles?' Marty asked.

'It's semi-desert out there.'

'They're good photos,' Tina decided, giving her expert opinion.

'Not up to your standard, though,' Tom returned.

Marty was staring at the older girl. He tried to sound cool.

'Zoe's kinda cute . . .'

'The voice of experience!' Tina mocked.

There was more than a grain of truth in her good-humoured taunt and it shattered his pose at once. He flushed and quickly changed the subject to cover his confusion.

'Do you know IN-X-S, Tom?'

'Sounds like some kind of cattle brand.'

'How about Midnight Oil?'

'You've lost me, Marty.'

'They're rock bands,' Kate explained.

'That let's me out,' said Tom.

Tina rolled her eyes upwards for Marty's benefit and her brother smirked. Tom noticed the byplay between them and was amused.

'I'm afraid I'm a bit of a square.'

'That makes two of us,' Kate admitted. 'Shake.'

She offered her hand and Tom shook it warmly.

'Mom's musical taste is crummy,' Marty announced. 'I mean, she actually likes Elvis!'

'What's wrong with him?' Kate challenged her.

'Yes,' supported Tom. 'Even I've heard of Elvis Presley.'

'He's *ancient*!' Marty decreed with contempt.

Kate and Tom could not help laughing at this arrogant dismissal of the pop star. Tina leapt to her feet and grabbed her camera.

'This one's to cement American–Australian relations!'

'I think we've had enough,' Kate decided. 'Don't you, Tina?'

'Last one, Mom. I promise.'

'It'll only take another half-hour,' Marty teased.

'Closer,' ordered the photographer. 'Move in closer.'

She pushed Tom in towards her mother so that their shoulders were touching. Unaware of what it presaged for their future, Tina took the photograph.

'Great!'

'That sums up the evening I've had here as well.'

'Been lovely to have you, Tom,' said Kate.

'Yeah. You're an okay guy,' Marty declared. 'For a square.'

Tina groaned. 'Elvis Presley! My God!'

Kate was gratified. She had wanted the dinner party to be a success and it had been just that. Her children had liked their guest enough to let him know it. From their response, Kate understood a little more clearly why she was so fond of Tom Hannon.

He was his own man.

When the meal was over, the children vanished into thin air before they could be involved in the washing-up. Kate did not mind that they had slipped out to their regular Saturday night appointments. It meant that she had some time alone with Tom. She liked having him in her home.

They adjourned to the kitchen and got to work. While she washed up, he dried. They made a good team.

'They're nice kids, Kate,' he began.

'Thanks.'

'You've done a terrific job on them.'

Kate was about to accept the compliment in silence and leave it at that but something about him demanded honesty. Taking a deep breath, she told him the truth.

'I get so afraid for them sometimes.'

'Why?'

'LA is such a violent city to grow up in and I'm not always there to protect them.' She extended her open palms in a gesture of hopelessness. 'When they need their mother, I'm usually out working somewhere. Trying to make ends meet.'

'Don't blame yourself.'

'I'm all they've got, Tom. That's what worries me the most. I'm their last line of defence.' She dipped the last plate into the hot soapy water and washed it absent-mindedly. 'What if something should happen to me? It's a terrifying thought.'

'Nothing *is* going to happen to you,' he reassured her. 'Besides, those kids look as if they can take care of themselves pretty well. You deserve some credit for that, don't you?'

She nodded. 'I guess so.'

Tom asked the question he had been saving up for days.

'How old were they when your husband walked out on you?'

Kate's face clouded over immediately. She took time to answer.

'Two years,' she said. 'I had no money, no job, no prospects. And there were three mouths to feed. I don't know how we got through those early years, Tom. It was a nightmare.'

'You came good, Kate,' he noted. 'You're a survivor.'

She smiled, handed him the plate then dried her wet hands.

'Tom . . .'

'Yes?'

'Tell me about your wife,' she said abruptly.

He was taken aback. 'My wife?'

'What was she like?'

Tom Hannon rubbed a finger across his chin while he searched for words. Affection came into his voice.

'Well, she wasn't a kind of feminist woman . . . but one of the old-fashioned kind. I reckon it's a sad house where the hen crows louder than the rooster.'

Kate made no comment. She waited for him to continue.

He shrugged. 'I guess that makes me a bit of a chauvinist but I like a woman to need me. There's a rightness to it.'

For a long moment, their eyes fused.

Tom put the plate down and took her in his arms. He kissed her full on the lips and she responded warmly, pushing hard against his strong, firm body and caressing his back. When he broke away, he held her by the shoulders and blurted out his thoughts with gruff tenderness.

'I love you, Kate. Will you marry me?'

She stared at him in blank amazement, stunned by his proposal and bereft of words. The suddenness of it all had taken her breath away. It was something that had simply never occurred to her. Kate had taken it for granted that her fling would be over when he went back to Australia. She had great difficulty adjusting to the idea of marriage.

'I don't want to rush you,' he continued, 'but I have to

be home at the end of the month. So – think about it, will you?'

'Tom . . .'

'Don't give me an answer now. Think about it. All right?'

At a complete loss for words, she nodded her assent.

He kissed her again and she went into his arms, feeling safe and wanted as he hugged her tight. Tom cupped her chin and smiled down at her.

'"Kate Hannon" . . . it's got a sort of ring to it.'

'Tom,' she reasoned, 'we hardly know each other.'

'I know enough.'

The emotions that she had held in check for days now came bubbling to the surface. Tears welled in her eyes and her heart was a mallet against her ribs. She fastened her lips impulsively on his and explored his mouth with her tongue, relishing the taste and smell of him, thrilling to his touch as his hands ran all over her body.

He moved back his head long enough to ask a question.

'What time will the kids be back?'

Then he was kissing her all over again, one hand playing with her soft, downy hair and the other stroking her breast. He kissed her lips, her chin, her cheeks, her forehead, her ears and her neck in a frenzy of longing. Kate then eased his face gently away and took him by the hand to lead him to the bedroom.

It was in darkness but the spill of light from the passageway threw a glow of welcome across the double bed. They moved to the centre of the room and he embraced her again before starting to pull off his jacket. She stopped him with a raised palm.

'No, Tom. Let me . . .'

Kate had an overwhelming urge to please him, to yield up to him the things that she had held back from the other men who had passed through her life. Those affairs had been brief and mechanical, an escape from boredom, a way of reminding herself that she was a woman. But she had only been going through the motions.

45

When her husband walked out on her, Kate was shattered and the trauma of it had remained with her ever since. It meant that she had never been able to trust any man properly or give herself wholly to him. Tom Hannon was different. This time it was for real.

Standing behind him, she teased his jacket off slowly, inching it down his arms so that each tugged movement was a separate pleasure, biting at his earlobes with gentle teeth. His shirt came next, unbuttoned leisurely and then taken off him with exquisite care to reveal a lean, muscled torso with fine brown hairs on his chest.

Kate now turned her attention to his shoes. Making him sit on the edge of the bed, she ran a hand up and down his leg as she eased his feet out of his shoes. As she removed his socks, she brushed his bare feet with her lips, making him groan in delight and reach out for her. She parried his arms.

'No, Tom.'

'I *want* you, Kate!'

'There's no hurry.'

Her hands went up his legs and she undid his belt in the same studied way. She could see that he was ready for her and she let her hand rub the full length of him as she unzipped his fly. His trousers came off after minutes of delicate foreplay.

Kate reached for his briefs, white slips that set off the tanned body that lay before her. She stroked him through the material at first then bent down to nibble at him for a few seconds, stirring with satisfaction as she felt his hardness grow and throb. With excruciating slowness, she pulled his briefs right off and dropped them to the carpet.

Tom Hannon was now stretched out naked before her.

He was all man. Roused, loving, lustful. He was beautiful.

She kicked off her shoes and stood before him. Unzipping her dress, she slipped her arms out then let it fall to the floor with a soft rustle. Kate was wearing nothing but a pair of red panties. She smiled invitingly as Tom's eyes roamed hungrily over her body.

Shoulders of gleaming softness. Long, slender arms. Firm, full breasts with raised nipples set in dark pink aureoles. A slim waist above generous hips. Thighs that made him sit up on the bed with wonderment.

As Kate turned around and took off her panties, his patience snapped. He jumped to his feet and grabbed for her with wild need. It had been four years since he had slept with a woman and fourteen since Kate had last wanted someone enough to trust him.

They fell on the bed and kissed away their frustrations in a riot of passion. He was ardent but considerate, taking care not to hurt or startle her. As his lips burned on hers, his hands caressed her breast and his fingers traced a circle around her nipple until it swelled to its full extent. When he finally touched it, tremors of delight ran through her and she dug her nails into his back.

Tom worked his way down her neck, kissing every inch of it with gentle lips before taking her nipple into his mouth. Kate felt her pleasure intensify until it was almost too much to bear.

She pushed him on to his back and traced a meandering path of butterfly kisses all over his chest and stomach. Tom moaned with pure joy when she bent over and licked him with teasing slowness. When he could hold out no longer, he lifted her off him, turned her over and spread her thighs, sliding into her with a ramrod strength that made her swoon. His back arched and fell with increasing speed and power and his mouth found hers in a kiss that contained every ounce of their love and commitment.

His joy rose to a crescendo and released itself in a starburst of such irresistible force that it touched off her own climax so that they floated together on a magic carpet of sheer ecstasy. They seemed to go on and on and on, as new surges of pleasure lifted them higher and took them faster.

47

It was minutes before either of them had breath enough to speak.

'Thank you . . .' he said.

'Thank *you*.'

'Kate . . .'

'Just hold me,' she whispered.

They lay entwined in each other's arms, sprawled on the double bed in companionable silence. Both were deliciously shocked by it all. Neither of them had expected it to happen yet neither had regrets. In making love so freely and expressively, they had shown how they felt about each other and were very content.

'We must wash dishes together more often,' he said.

'Shhh!'

She put her head on his chest and rested her leg between his so that she could lie on him. He stroked her hair and kissed it, inhaling its fragrance again and sighing quietly.

Kate nestled into the memory. Their lovemaking had all the excitement of novelty with all the reassurance of familiarity. She wanted Tom in a way that she had never thought would be possible for her again. He had awakened her and she in turn had roused him from an enforced slumber.

She leaned up on her elbow to look at him again, enjoying the sight of his body, stroking his thigh, responding to his smile.

He chose his moment to return to the proposal.

'Yes or no?'

'That's unfair.'

'Why?'

'Because you have me at a disadvantage.'

'That was the idea.' He laughed and pulled her to him. 'Kids need a balanced family life. They miss a father figure. You've said that yourself.'

'I know.' He raised a questioning eyebrow. 'Tom . . . it's a big decision to make.'

'*I* made it when I saw you that first night at the restaurant.'

'It's different for me,' she said softly. 'I need more time. Please, Tom. Just be patient for a little while.'

There was a boyish earnestness in the way he looked at her.

'As long as I live, I'll never let a single, solitary thing hurt you, Kate.'

She could read his heart and knew that he spoke the truth.

Reality intruded like a cold shower. 'God!' she exclaimed. 'What's the time?'

She angled his wrist so that she could check his watch. It was already past eleven o'clock. Kate was galvanised into life.

'Tom, the children'll be home soon.'

He sighed and made a move to rise. Kate held him a moment longer. She kissed him once more on the lips to show her profound gratitude.

'It's strange . . . I feel so comfortable with you.'

'Is that good or bad?'

'Good.'

'In that case . . .' He tried to ease her back on the bed.

'Get up!' she ordered, resisting.

'Yes, Mrs Hannon.'

Tom was right. It did have a ring to it.

Marty and Tina sat side by side on the divan with perplexed faces. He had returned from a practice session with his band while she had spent the evening with Billy. Neither of them had expected their mother to be waiting up for them with what she described as important news.

Wearing her dressing gown, Kate stood in front of them and looked from one to the other. Her face was positively glowing.

'Well?' said Marty. 'What gives?'

'Can't you guess?'

'No.'

'Tom asked me to marry him.'

The twins were dumbfounded. Kate tried to ease the

shock by explaining it to them in a little more detail.

'We've seen a lot of each other while Tom has been in California and we somehow clicked. I know it's sudden.' She gave a laugh. 'For me, too. But I think, deep down, I wanted it to happen. Tom's a wonderful man. And he likes you both very much. He told me.'

She knelt down so that her face was level with theirs. Her hands reached out so that she could touch them.

'It's going to be fine, I promise,' she continued brightly. 'It's a chance of a whole new life – for the three of us.'

The children exchanged a worried look.

'How do you mean?' asked Tina.

'Well . . . we'll be going to Australia to live. On Tom's cattle ranch.'

It was a complete bombshell. They sat there quite motionless.

'For the next few years, anyway,' added Kate. 'When you're older, you can come back to the States if you wish.'

Panic seized both of them. It burst out in a flurry of questions and arguments. Kate was under attack.

'Why can't he come and live here?'

'Why can't he buy a ranch in California?'

'Don't *we* have a say in it?'

'Yeah – why didn't you tell us this was on the cards?'

'How can you love a guy you hardly know?'

'Do you really *want* to live in a hole like Australia?'

Kate waved her hands in the air to calm them down. 'Hold on, hold on,' she said. 'One at the time.'

'Ask Tom to come and work here in the States,' Marty urged.

'Yes!' agreed his sister.

'Oh, I couldn't do that. I wouldn't expect it.'

'But why do you have to *marry* him?' Tina probed. 'Can't you just see each other? You could go and visit him.'

'Sure,' her brother agreed. 'You didn't need to marry Alan.'

'It's not the same, Marty,' Kate argued.

50

Tina took over. 'You mean with Alan it was just sex?'

Her mother winced slightly but gave her a candid reply. 'It was a little more than that. When you're older, you'll understand.'

'Don't bank on it,' she muttered.

'Australia!' Marty was disgusted.

Kate tried to lift them by injecting some enthusiasm into her voice. She slapped her hand on her thigh for effect.

'Hey, come on now! It's not so terrible, is it? You know, people even say that Australia is very much like America. But because there's fewer inhabitants, there's space to grow. Not like here. What was it you called it, Marty? "The Last Frontier." Imagine we're pioneers, taking off on a great adventure into unexplored territory. Isn't that exciting?'

She searched their faces for a flicker of response but found only fear. Marty and Tina were horrified at the whole idea.

'Anyway,' Kate murmured, 'you'll get used to it. I know you will. You need a little time.' She could think of only one more thing to say. 'I love you.'

All that remained was a long, empty, forbidding silence.

The San Diego Freeway was as busy as ever when they drove south. Kate was at the wheel of her car, having collected it from the auto shop that morning. She and Tom were joking lightly about the meeting that lay ahead of them, both trying to hide their nervousness. They were going to break the news to Tom's sister and they were not quite sure how she would react.

Getting married was not as straightforward as it seemed.

'Did you tell the kids last night?' asked Tom.

'Yes.'

'How did they take it?'

'Not too bad at all,' she lied. 'They'll come round to it.'

She swung the car into the outside lane and accelerated.

Standing on an ocean bluff, the house commanded a fine view of the sea. The garden stretched on down almost to the cliff's edge. As they stood near a cluster of palm trees, they could watch the foam-capped waves rolling in towards the sandy shore. It was a restful scene though it carried with it a hint of danger and menace.

Molly Winters was a wealthy, middle-class San Diego matron, married to a successful real estate man. Fourteen years away from her native country had turned her, outwardly, into a typical American but there was still a faint echo of her Australian accent and she was both unable and unwilling to let go of her early roots. When she stood next to her brother, the family likeness was quite unmistakable. Both had the same hard, seasoned, indomitable look.

Kate made a real effort to get on with her. While Tom shared a beer with his brother-in-law, Frank, the two women strolled down to the end of the garden. Kate had the sickening sensation of having been examined and found wanting.

Like the sea below them, Molly's voice came in surging waves. She was nothing if not forthright.

'I'm an American now but, like Tom, I was born at Larapinta so I know what I'm talking about. It's a vast wilderness and only the strongest survive there.' She turned a steely eye on Kate. 'And it's especially hard on the women.'

'I see.'

'I don't think you do – yet.'

'What exactly is wrong with the place?'

'Everything,' emphasised Molly. 'The isolation and the loneliness can really get to you. Then there are snakes, dingoes, insects and all the other natural hazards that come with the territory.' She warmed to her theme. 'They're in the middle of the worst drought in living memory in central Australia right now. It hasn't rained for four years. Cattle are dying every day. Tom flew here to borrow $200,000 from Frank and me so he can drill more wells.'

52

She spelled it out for the other woman. 'Because without water, he can't survive.'

Kate took a moment to assimilate it all. Molly could see that she was stunned by the revelations and she took an almost perverse pleasure in the fact.

'I gather Tom hasn't mentioned any of this.'

'No. Not yet. But I'm sure he will when he's ready.'

'Tom was afraid he'd scare you off.'

'I don't scare easily.'

'Wait till you see Larapinta.'

'I'm looking forward to it,' said Kate bravely.

'It's no place for children. They'll hate you for taking them out there.'

'That's my decision.'

'In the hot weather, it's hell on earth.'

Molly was about to go into gruesome detail about the terrors of the Outback but Kate had already heard enough. She stopped the older woman before she could get into her stride.

'You don't want me to marry him, do you?'

'It's all happened much too fast for my liking,' Molly explained coldly.

'Thank you for being so blunt.'

'Marriage would be a terrible mistake for both of you.'

Kate held back an angry retort and spoke with measured calm.

'Molly, I understand how you feel,' she said. 'But I happen to love Tom and nothing you say can change my mind.'

The two of them stared each other out for several seconds.

It was a brief and informal ceremony held in a small wedding chapel. Tom Hannon and Kate Adamson stood before the Justice of the Peace as he went through the marriage service in a flat, nasal voice. The bridegroom wore a lightweight suit that did not quite fit him and he smiled proudly throughout as if a great honour were about to be conferred on him. He felt as if he were floating on air.

The bride looked radiant in a peach-coloured suit with matching accessories. Pinned to the lapel in a haze of love-in-a-mist was a single rose, its creamy petals flushed with a delicate pink. Her hair shone like silk under the fluorescent lighting and her face was a study of pure joy.

Dr Peterson was very happy for his receptionist. He knew about the countless struggles that Kate had been through. Though he was sorry to lose her from the surgery, he was delighted that she had at last found someone who could provide all the things that had been missing in her life for so long.

Judy was there with her husband, and so were Fran and Mary. All three women shared Kate's buoyant optimism, each of them deeply moved by the occasion. Like Kate herself, the friends were carried away by the romance of it all.

What could be more wonderful than to meet, fall in love with and marry a man in such a short space of time? That the couple would be flying off to an idyllic existence in a distant continent only served to heighten the magic. It was the stuff of dreams.

Judy's loud whisper introduced a more realistic note.

'And to think it all started with a roast beef sandwich on Table Eight!'

The other witnesses were less contented with the ceremony.

Frank and Molly watched with basilisk disapproval, their cold eyes seeing nothing but the worst possible outcome. Marty and Tina were suffering an ordeal, their minds tormented by the implications that the marriage would have for them.

The official soon reached the climax of the service.

'I pronounce you man and wife . . .'

Mr and Mrs Tom Hannon were filled with elation.

Led by Judy, the witnesses came forward to surround

54

them and shower them with best wishes. Even Frank and Molly offered restrained congratulations. Marty and Tina remained apart, viewing it all with grave misgivings.

Kate caught sight of them and a dark cloud momentarily obscured her sun. Then Tom was kissing her and the rays of sunshine returned. She was in her husband's arms and everything was all right again.

Ecstasy bore her gently away.

— 5 —

The captain's voice was bright and cheerful over the cabin speakers.

'Ladies and gentlemen, soon we'll be starting our descent into Sydney. We should have you outside the terminal in about twenty minutes or so. On behalf of the crew, we hope you enjoyed your flight and look forward to your travelling with Qantas again. Thank you and good luck!'

There was a sudden buzz of interest. With their destination now so close, passengers began to get themselves ready and pack everything away in their hand luggage. Some of them were only just coming awake after a lengthy sleep. When they lifted the blinds from the windows, they recoiled from the early morning glare.

Australia was welcoming them with a glorious day.

'Wake up, Marty.'

'Uh?'

'And you, Tina. We're almost there.'

'Oh . . .'

The twins had dozed off during the later stages of the journey but the rest had not weakened their hostility in any way. They rubbed at their eyes and tried to stretch their aching limbs in the cramped space. Tired herself, Kate nevertheless tried to sound breezy and confident for their benefit.

'The flight didn't seem *that* long, did it?'

'Yes, it did,' Marty moaned.

'I feel lousy,' said Tina.

'We'll soon be landing in Sydney,' Kate told them. 'The fresh air will do us all a power of good.'

Cabin stewards were coming down the aisles with trays of drinks. Even after several hours on duty, they remained pleasant and courteous. Their uniforms seemed to be as smart as when the plane left Los Angeles.

'Orange juice?'

'Thanks,' said Kate, accepting the plastic cup.

'I bet you two would like some.'

'Yeah.'

'Thanks a lot.'

The steward handed Marty and Tina a cup each and then moved on.

Kate turned to the children and gave them a warm smile. In an attempt to lift their spirits, she raised her plastic cup in a toast.

'Happy landings!'

The twins responded in hurt silence then sipped their drinks.

Kate put the cup to her lips and went off into another reverie. Her mind travelled back in time to a very precious memory. . .

It was early morning. The bedroom was strewn with packed suitcases that were waiting to be closed. Champagne was poured into a glass already half-filled with orange juice. A second glass was topped up as well.

Tom Hannon was in his dressing gown. Kate was still fast asleep in her bed. He gazed down at her with longing and thanked his lucky stars for the decision to come to California. Meeting her had turned a jaded widower into a delighted husband.

He sat on the side of the bed and leaned over to kiss her gently on the forehead. She came drowsily out of her slumber and reached for his hand before brushing it with her lips.

'I like sleeping next to you, Tom Hannon.'

'Good – because you'll get plenty of practice.'

'That suits me.'

'And me.' He looked at her fondly and touched her

cheek with the back of his hand. 'What did you think of the honeymoon?'

'Far too short.'

'But while it lasted?'

'Ripper!'

They laughed. He kissed her and gave her one of the glasses.

'Time to shake a leg, Mrs Hannon. This is the big day.'

'I know,' she said, controlling a yawn. 'I was awake for hours, wondering if I've packed everything.'

'Scared?'

'Not really.'

'That's my girl!'

He clicked her glass in a toast.

'To the future!'

'I'll drink to that, Tom.'

They sipped together then she rested her head against his chest. As he talked, he stroked her hair gently and nuzzled against it.

'I want you to love the Outback like I do, Kate. It's got a kind of magic. The land's a living thing. You can hear its heart beating. At night, you wouldn't believe there could be so many stars in heaven . . . Time doesn't exist any more.'

'I want to love it, Tom. I really do.'

At that precise moment, she had never felt closer to him.

Restored by the drink and refreshed by a quick shower, Kate Hannon went bouncing into her daughter's bedroom with a cheery greeting.

'Oo-oo! Wakey, wakey!'

The words died on her lips. She was thunderstruck.

Tina was not there.

The bed had been stripped and the coverings folded neatly before being stacked on the bottom. Drawers had been pulled out and emptied. The wardrobe had been ransacked. All the make-up and lotions had vanished from the top of the dressing table. Posters had gone from the walls. On the floor were some clothes that had evidently been abandoned during the sudden departure.

Kate stood in the doorway and wilted. There was a dull ache in the pit of her stomach. Her happiness had now evaporated. Tina's flight was an act of revenge against her. Kate knew that she had driven her daughter to it and the thought filled her with profound sadness. The empty room was like an accusation.

A note was propped up on the bedside table.

Kate raced across and snatched it up.

The car screeched to a halt outside a rather dilapidated apartment block in Venice. While Tom stayed in his seat, Kate got out, slammed the door and hurried towards the building. She went in through the main entrance and ascended the uncarpeted stairs, her heels clacking on the bare wood. Paintwork was fading everywhere and there was a general air of neglect about the place. Naked light bulbs dangled overhead. A musty smell hung about.

Kate went along a corridor until she found the apartment that she wanted. She knocked hard. She heard voices inside the room then the door inched open. The anxious face of an eighteen-year-old youth appeared in the crack.

'Hello, Billy,' she said, reining in her temper.

'Oh . . . hi.'

'I've come for Tina.'

'She's not here.'

'Please don't lie to me.'

'Tina left some time ago. You missed her.'

'If you don't mind,' Kate insisted, 'I'll just step inside and see for myself . . .'

She pushed the door open but Billy blocked her way. He was a tall, moodily handsome young man with the unkempt look of someone who had left home too early and was caring for himself with only minimal success.

'Excuse me, Billy . . .'

Her acid politeness made him stand aside for her. Kate

swept into the room then came to a halt. Tina was cowering in the corner.

'Get your things!' her mother ordered.

'No!'

'Tina . . .'

'I want to stay with Billy.'

Kate was in no mood to argue about it. Stalking into the bedroom, she grabbed two cases and came back out again. She stuck one case under her arm, holding the other in the same hand. This left her other hand free to grab her daughter's wrist and pull her towards the door. Tina struggled defiantly but Kate was far too strong.

'Do something, Billy!' cried the girl.

'Leave her alone, Mrs Adamson,' he said, blocking the door again. 'Tina's place is here with me. She's going nowhere .'

He stood there with a combination of bravado and wariness.

'Out of our way, Billy,' Kate warned.

'No, Mrs Adamson.'

'The name is Mrs Hannon now,' she stressed in icy tones. 'My husband is waiting for me in the car. Would you like to discuss this matter with him?'

There was a long eye-to-eye confrontation then Billy gulped and backed down. He was angry with Kate for humiliating him in front of Tina and he semaphored his apologies to her as she was dragged out.

'Billy!' she screamed.

'Don't worry, Tina!' he called after her. 'I'll find a way somehow. We'll be together.'

He watched them clump down the bare boards and out through the front door then he punched his fist with the other hand.

The fresh air did not lessen Tina's resistance. She did all that she could to break free and Kate had to tighten her grip. They moved along in front of a brightly coloured mural that served as an ironic counterpoint to the black rage in front of it.

'Young lady, you have lousy timing!'

'I *had* to be with him!'

'How could you do something like this?' Kate hissed.

'It's different for you.'

'How?'

'I'm leaving all my friends,' Tina blubbered. 'I'll never see them again.'

'You'll make new friends in Australia.'

'I don't *want* to make new friends!'

'That's not the right attitude.'

'You don't understand,' she wailed.

Kate swung her round and pinned her to the wall.

'Of course I do.' Kate was emphatic. 'Don't you think I know what you're both going through? It's not all for me, Tina. I'm doing it for you and Marty as well. I want something better. I want us to be a real family for the first time in our lives and all I'm asking is that you give it a chance. *Please!*'

Tina replied by trying to make run for it but Kate held her firm. Hauling her daughter unceremoniously to the car, she dropped the suitcases, opened the rear door, bundled Tina in, threw the luggage after her, then jumped in beside her and pulled the door shut.

'Drive us back, Tom,' she said. 'I'm needed here.'

Thick crowds milled around in the departure lounge at Los Angeles International Airport and ruled out any hope of a quiet moment together. Tom Hannon took his wife's hands in his and squeezed them.

'Don't be too hard on Tina,' he counselled. 'They're being uprooted and they're feeling the shock.'

'I sympathise, Tom,' she replied. 'After all, I'm being uprooted as well. I tell them that.'

'They'll get over it in time.'

A sudden impulse made her put her arms around him.

'Oh, I wish that we were flying home with you now.'

'So do I, Kate.'

'It might make things a bit easier.'

'Look at it this way,' he said reasonably. 'Me going on ahead means that I can break the news to my girls face to face and get them used to the idea before you and the twins arrive.' He grinned amiably. 'What would Zoe and Emmie think if I rolled up with you three in tow?'

'They'd have the surprise of their life.'

'Exactly. It'll give us both a bit more time to sort things out with our kids. Okay?'

Kate nodded. She accepted the wisdom of what he was saying but she was still reluctant to let him go. It wounded her to have to part with Tom so soon after their marriage. It seemed unnatural.

'Don't worry,' he soothed.

'Will you be there to meet us, Tom?'

'I'll be at Sydney Airport a week from today with the biggest bunch of flowers I can find. Will that do, Mrs Hannon?'

'Is it a promise?'

'It's a promise.'

And he sealed it with a long, clinging farewell kiss.

Kate Hannon could still feel his lips on hers when the Qantas 747 touched down on the runway at Sydney. The jolt brought her out of her daydream and she saw that they had safely arrived. A week apart from Tom had seemed like a year but it was finally over. Her fatigue fell away from her as she thought about what lay ahead.

'Will all passengers please remain in their seats . . .'

There was a slight delay as the plane was boarded by a team of officials with large aerosol canisters. They went up and down the aisles and sprayed their disinfectant everywhere.

'What did they say it was for?' Marty asked.

'Pest control,' said his mother.

'Watch out, Tina,' he joked.

It was the first time he had laughed since they left. Kate saw it as an encouraging sign. Marty's juvenile sense of humour might have some practical use after all.

When they were finally allowed off the aircraft, they made their way to Immigration and went through all the formalities. The children were rocked by the information that they would become Australian citizens. Tina was outraged.

'But I'm an *American*!'

'This is your home now,' Kate argued.

'I don't want to be an Australian.'

'We don't have much choice, Tina.'

'Why didn't you warn us about this?' Marty protested.

'I hate this country already,' his sister added.

'We'll talk about it later,' said Kate.

It was one more source of friction between them.

They went to the baggage hall and waited for their luggage to appear on the carousel. Marty now came into his own, pouncing on their bags as they were whisked past and hauling them off with skill. Kate was grateful for his help. She put everything on a trolley and pushed it towards Customs.

After their bags had been searched and they had been questioned, they were permitted through. They came into the arrival hall with a sense of relief and found themselves facing a metal barrier. A solid knot of people stood behind it, waiting for friends or relatives to arrive, scrutinising every face that came through the door.

Kate and the twins walked the length of the barrier with their eyes raking the crowd. When they could not pick out Tom, they decided that he must be at the back somewhere and strolled on round into the hall itself. They now conducted a more thorough search.

But they still could not see Tom Hannon.

Isolated in the middle of a crowd, they stood there and waited as happy reunions took place all around them. Jet lag had sapped their strength and frayed their nerves. Now they were marooned in a strange land. Even the children were eager for a sight of Tom Hannon's kind face. But it did not materialise.

Kate suddenly felt very vulnerable.

'What's happened to him?' asked Tina.

'He'll be here.'

'When, Mom?'

'Give him time.'

'Boy!' Marty sighed. 'What a welcome!'

'There he is!' Kate exclaimed.

'Where?'

But she had already left them to go running towards a man near the barrier. Tom's back was to her and she could see that he was holding a bunch of flowers behind it. He had kept his promise.

Her joy was stillborn. It was not her husband.

A young woman came through the doors and the man hailed her. They embraced warmly then he gave her the flowers. Kate now saw that he was not really like Tom.

A premonition troubled her. Something had gone wrong. She trudged sadly back to the children again.

'What now?' Marty grunted.

'We wait,' said his mother.

'How long for?'

'Until Tom comes.'

'Supposing he doesn't?' Tina wondered.

'He won't let us down,' Kate assured her.

Her tone was calm but her mind was in a turmoil. Throughout a long, lonely week she had kept herself going with the conviction that her husband would be at the airport to give them the kind of welcome that would sweep away any lingering doubts. Kate had been counting on him. She needed the feel of his arms and the inspiring strength of his love.

But Tom Hannon was not there.

Her mood began to swing like a pendulum between anger and fear. Tom was late. On purpose. He wanted her to realise that he was not at her beck and call. At bottom, he was like Australians were supposed to be: indifferent to their wives, treating them with disdain, offhand and discourteous. Tom might not even come himself. He would send someone else and forget about the flowers.

It's not true, Kate told herself. Tom *isn't* like that. He's kind and considerate. He knows how important it is for him to be here, to make it easier for me and for the kids, to ensure that our very first experience of Australia is a happy one.

Perhaps he was different at home. In Los Angeles, he could afford to be more attentive and romantic. Kate would not have responded to any other kind of courtship. Now he was on his own patch, he had reverted to his true self, a man whose main priority was to run a ranch and whose time for the niceties of marital life was limited.

Yet even as her anger rose again, it faded once more into concern. Kate remembered his proposal and the spontaneous love that had followed it. His commitment to her was total.

Tom Hannon was the most solid and reliable man she had ever met. Only a very special reason could have prevented him from meeting them as arranged. With stomach turning, she began to speculate about what that reason could be.

He had been unavoidably delayed en route. He had been taken ill or involved in an accident. Some disaster had occurred at Larapinta and he had been detained there. His children had raised such violent objections to his marriage that he was having to stay with them to calm them. Fear etched deep lines in Kate's brow.

The cleaner pushed the electric polisher around the hall and tried to put a sheen back on a surface that had been dulled by the passage of many feet. It was afternoon and the place was empty apart from the three figures at the far end. The noise of the machine thundered away, then the cleaner switched it off and took it away.

Kate sat with the twins amid the luggage. They had been there for hours. While she glanced desultorily at a magazine, they picked at a sandwich apiece. With the noise problem gone, she made a decision.

'I'm going to ring Tom's ranch!'

'What if he's not there, Mom?' asked Tina.

'Then his daughters will be. They'll know what happened.'

Kate went into the telephone booth and sorted out some coins. Finding the number in her address book, she then dialled the operator and asked to be put through to Larapinta in the Northern Territory. She listened to various clicks and bleeps as the connection was made then she heard the number ringing.

It continued to ring for a long time.

'Sorry,' said the operator's voice. 'There's no one answering at Larapinta. Would you like to try later?'

Bewilderment turned Kate's face into a mass of frowns. 'But there *should* be someone there. Zoe and Emmie . . .'

'Mom,' Marty interrupted. 'Why don't we just stay put? He'll turn up.'

'Yeah,' Tina agreed. 'Let's hang around here.'

'We can't,' their mother explained. 'Our tickets are to Glenwarra.'

'Are you still there?' asked the operator.

'Yes.' Kate spoke into the telephone again. 'Sorry. I can hear you.'

'There's no reply on that number.'

'Could it be out of order?'

'I checked. It's fine.'

'Oh. Thank you.'

Tired, hurt and depressed, Kate hung up and came out of the booth.

'Maybe he got the wrong day,' Marty suggested.

'No.'

'Maybe we should just go back to the States,' Tina urged.

'If Tom's not here,' Kate decided, 'we have to go on.'

Marty was worried. 'By ourselves?'

'We've come this far on our own,' his mother reminded him. 'A little further won't kill us. Off we go. Time for some action around here.'

She jollied them along but her brain was still swimming. Where was Tom? What had gone wrong?

Glenwarra Airport was a remote and God-forsaken spot in the Outback. The terminal building was really no more than an ugly, squat, iron-roofed shed and the runways were dirt landing strips. It was a far cry from the sophistication of Sydney.

When the small twin-engined plane came into land, it taxied noisily towards the terminal then jerked to a halt. Two men wheeled steps into position outside the door of the aircraft.

A handful of passengers disembarked. Kate and the children were the last to leave. They stepped out into the furnace of the afternoon and had to shield their eyes from the glare. As they descended the steps, they felt as if they had arrived on an alien planet. Through the shimmering heat haze, all that they could see around them was parched brown landscape that was broken up in the distance by a line of rugged hills.

'*This* is Glenwarra!' Tina complained.

'No,' replied her brother. 'It's the end of the Earth.'

Kate did not hear them. She was too busy scanning the terminal building for a sign of her husband but she was out of luck once more. He was definitely not there.

Her anxiety deepened and her mouth went dry.

The Stenning Arms Hotel was a typical Outback pub with wide verandahs and a hitching rail. A group of men, some black and some white, had congregated outside to drink beer and pass the time. A dog slept on the dirt road. Flies buzzed incessantly.

The patrons looked up with lazy interest when a woman and two children arrived outside the pub. All three newcomers were perspiring from the effort of carrying their heavy luggage. They were obviously intimidated by the sight that greeted them on the verandah.

Kate put down her bags and told the twins what to do.

'Stay right here. Keep an eye on the luggage.'

'You're going in there *alone*?' Marty gasped.

'Neither of you is old enough to go into a bar.'

'Do you think it'll be safe, Mom?'

'There's only one way to find out, Marty.'

Watched by a cluster of impassive faces, Kate went up the step and through the entrance. It was darker and cooler inside but much noisier. The bar was a haven for the locals, a liquid fridge for a bizarre collection of men. Some stood at the counter and argued, others sat at tables and played cards, one was fast asleep on the staircase, two more were engaged in arm-wrestling.

Work at the restaurant had accustomed Kate to many aspects of human behaviour but she had never encountered an atmosphere quite like this. There was a weird, listless quality about it all.

She leaned across the bar and shouted above the din.

'I want to get to Larapinta before dark!'

The licensee was a burly man with a slow grin. He ambled across to her and rested both hands on the top of the counter. Kate checked a name on a piece of paper while he assessed her frankly with his eyes.

'The bus driver told me to see a man,' she continued. 'A charter helicopter pilot called Nick.'

'You'd be jokin', wouldn't you?' he returned.

'What?'

'Y'won't get a Stenning to take you to Larapinta.'

'Why not?'

'There's a feud bin goin' on between the Hannons an' Stennings f'r donkey's years.'

Kate stared at him in total disbelief. The news was a blow.

'A feud?' she repeated then spelled the word. 'F-E-U-D?'

'Yep.'

'Oh, God!' she sighed. 'Is there anyone else?'

'Not till tomorra.'

'Tomorrow?'

'Or the day after, maybe.'

'What do we do until then?'

'Stay here,' he invited. 'We'll fit you in somewhere.'

A few men had drifted over to stand beside her by now.

'She can have my room,' said one of them lecherously. 'As long as she don't snore and don't mind sharin'.'

Crude laughter went up and even less tempting offers were made. The coarse male banter helped Kate to reach a decision.

'Where do I find Mr Stenning?' she asked.

'Outside,' the licensee replied, jerking a thumb towards the door.

'Outside? On the verandah?'

He chuckled richly. 'No. Out there an' to yer right. You'll find 'im on top of that hill y'can see. 'E's often up there. Buggered if I know why . . . but the Stennings're a law to themselves. They own this pub and they damn near own the town.'

'I'll go and speak to him,' Kate announced.

The licensee drew a schooner of beer then slammed it down on the counter in front of a customer. He grinned tauntingly at Kate.

'I'll bet you five dollars 'e'll say "no".'

She managed a half-hearted smile then backed away towards the door. The licensee called after her with a snigger in his voice.

'If you're thinkin' of goin' after 'im, I'd wait till a bit later, when it's cooler!'

Kate ignored the advice and went straight out through the door. An apprehensive Tina was waiting for her. Marty was chatting to a group of men further down the verandah.

'Mom,' she whispered in alarm. 'They're Aboriginals!'

'They won't hurt us, Tina.'

'But they look so frightening.'

Marty broke away from the men and came back. He had obviously enjoyed his talk and was now quite excited.

'Say, those guys are buffalo hunters! I didn't know they had buffalo here. There's thousands of them up north.'

Kate was glad that her son had at last shown some real interest in Australia but she did not want to discuss it on the verandah. Being the centre of attention was very upsetting. Some of the bold looks she was getting went well beyond simple curiosity.

'I'm hungry,' Tina whined.

'You're always hungry,' her mother said fondly.

'Did you find out where the pilot is?' Marty asked.

'Yes – up there.'

'Where?'

Kate pointed to the hill over to the right.

'He's sitting up on top just waiting for us to come calling.'

'Why is he up there?' Marty wondered. 'Wow! This is one crazy country!'

They gathered up their things and moved off wearily.

A battered flat-top truck rumbled over the uneven track then screamed to a halt in a cloud of red dust. Kate and the children got out and unloaded their luggage. When she had paid the Aboriginal driver, he waved a wrinkled black hand at them and drove off. They were suddenly left alone in a wilderness, at the base of a rocky hill in the Flinders range. It was an eerie sensation.

Kate looked up at the craggy hillside that loomed above them. It was quite daunting. She shook her head and mumbled to herself, 'Mr Stenning must be a nut. Probably runs in the family.'

'What?' Marty asked.

'Nothing.'

'Can I come with you?'

'No, honey. Stay with your sister.'

'Why do I have to miss out on the fun?'

'Climbing that hill will *not* be fun, Marty.'

Tina surveyed the flat red desert all around them. 'Hell must be just like this,' she declared.

'Only not quite as hot,' added Marty, now sweating profusely.

'Don't wander too far,' Kate warned.

'We won't, Mom,' said Tina.

'Good luck!' Marty called.

'I may need it.'

Kate Hannon gritted her teeth then started the long climb to the summit and to her first meeting with Nick Stenning.

— 6 —

Curiosity soon got the better of the children and pushed their other concerns into the background. The sandy plain that surrounded them was not as empty and forbidding as it at first appeared. When they explored the area at the base of the hill, they were soon rewarded with some fascinating sights.

'Quick, Marty! There's an ostrich.'

'I think it's an emu.'

'Who cares? I want a shot of it.'

Tina pulled out her camera and clicked away as the bird strutted along not far from them. Other subjects soon claimed her attention.

'Wow! Kangaroos!'

'Just look at 'em hop!'

'There are dozens of them!'

Marty nudged her and pointed to something in the middle distance.

'See what I see?'

'Are those *camels*?' she gasped.

'Yeah. Roaming wild. Want me to go catch a couple so that we can saddle 'em up?'

Tina laughed and took a picture of them. Australia was turning out to be fun. Billy was temporarily forgotten as she searched for more photographic material.

'This grass is scratching my legs,' she complained.

'Spinifex.'

'What?'

'That's what it's called. Spinifex – or porcupine grass.'

'How do you know?' she asked, greatly impressed.

'Tom told me,' he said airily.

They walked on past a sandhill and did not see the large, deadly western brown snake that was sunning itself there. Tina had spotted another emu and was determined to get closer for her next photograph. With Marty at her heels, she hurried forward.

Suddenly they were stopped dead in their tracks.

'Aaaagh!'

Her scream was a mixture of surprise and terror.

Without warning, a prehistoric lizard had erupted out of the mulga right in front of them. It was almost six feet long, covered in hard scales and flicking out a long forked tongue. Tina went into her brother's arms for safety but there was no danger. The creature was as startled as they were and it scuttled away at speed.

Marty recovered his self-possession and said with bravado, 'I guess we showed *him* who's boss!'

The children continued on their way more carefully.

Kate Hannon battled her way up the curving side of the hill in the fierce heat. She used the guide chain to haul herself up even though it burned her hands. The steepness of the ascent soon took its toll. Her muscles were aching, her breathing was laboured and perspiration had broken out all over her.

But she did not give up. She was determined to find the man who could fly them to Larapinta and she made light of the physical discomforts. She reached the halfway mark and paused for a few minutes. The sun was painting the whole mountain range with vivid colours and turning the plain below into a red carpet. There was a savage beauty in the whole scene that touched Kate.

Her first priority, however, was to get to the top of the hill. Summoning up all her strength, she set off again. Flies bombarded her and prickly heat added to her problems but she drove herself on regardless. Her husband was in serious trouble somewhere. She sensed it. Kate simply had to get to the ranch, at whatever cost.

The second half of the climb was even more taxing than the first. Searing pain attacked every limb and reduced her to a slow crawl. Her hands were blistered by the chain. Her eyes were stinging. The dryness in her throat was like a sharp metal object.

Exhaustion had all but conquered her by the time she got within reach of the summit. Sheer will-power took her over the last few torturing yards. Kate was dripping with sweat, caked with dirt and throbbing with fatigue. But she had made it.

Gulping for air, she stood there and looked around. There was no sign of life anywhere. The summit was deserted. She felt the first stirrings of wild anxiety.

'Mr Stenning?' she called.

Her voice echoed in the empty space. Was it all a grotesque hoax? Had the licensee sent her to the top of the hill for a joke? Frustration began to gnaw away at her. Were all her efforts in vain?

Kate put her last ounce of strength into her plea. 'Mr Stenning!' she yelled. 'Hello! Is anyone there?'

Her voice carried across the whole plain. Silence ensued.

Then a figure seemed to rise out of the rock itself. Nick Stenning, silhouetted against the sun, was angry at the intrusion.

'What do you want?' he snarled.

'Are you Nick Stenning?'

'Why?'

She shielded her eyes but still could not see him properly. 'I have to reach Larapinta before dark . . . my children and I. They told me your helicopter was for charter.'

There was a long pause as he considered her request.

'Sorry,' he decided. 'Find someone else.'

He turned away abruptly and settled down in the rock again, merging with it so that he was almost invisible. While he nestled down in the shadows, she was still exposed to the fury of the sun.

Accumulated worry, tension, fear and anguish con-
joined inside her and started to boil. Kate exploded and
the words came tumbling out of her like molten lava.

'Look, I don't care about your stupid feud!' she shouted.
'It's no concern of mine. I've travelled halfway around the
world with my children . . . to the ends of the earth. And
I'm tired, too tired for you to tell me "no" after I've
climbed this – this rock . . . in this stinking heat, to find
you . . . I'll be damned if I'll accept it.'

The effort had drained her and she was now swaying
to and fro. Another surge of rage stiffened her resolve and
brought more defiance.

'My kids and I have got to get to Larapinta. Not
tomorrow. Tonight. You hear me? Tonight, Mr Stenning!
And, hopefully, before it gets dark. So would you mind
telling me just what the hell you intend doing about it?
And don't you dare tell me "no" again. Just don't you
bloody dare!'

Kate struggled to regain control of herself. She used the
back of her hand to wipe a mixture of sweat and tears
from her face then concentrated on maintaining her balance. Her legs were like jelly and her body felt like a ton
weight.

Nick Stenning rose slowly out of the rock again and
ambled over to her. He came from darkness into light
and stood right in front of her. Kate could not help her
involuntary reaction to his powerful physical presence.
There was something almost overwhelming about his
maleness. It disturbed her.

He was about her own age, lean, wiry and nut brown
from a constant acquaintance with the sun. Tough and
uncompromising as the wilderness all around him, he
seemed to belong, to be part of it.

His clear blue eyes ran blatantly over her face and body
as he assessed her. There was amusement lurking in his
gaze.

'I've been away a couple of weeks,' he said brusquely.
'What's your connection with Tom Hannon?'

75

Kate tilted her head and met his bold stare without flinching.

'I'm his wife.'

The light vanished from his eye as if it had been snuffed out by a cold wind. Despite the heat, Kate shivered.

'Be ready to leave in an hour from the airport,' he ordered. 'And don't be late.'

Resenting his arrogance, she replied with taut politeness. 'Thank you.'

Kate swung on her heel and began the difficult descent to the ground. Nick Stenning remained motionless. His face devoid of expression, he watched her struggle away.

The bar at the Stenning Hotel was busier and noisier than ever and the licensee was serving beer as fast as he could pull it. The din subsided slightly as a figure came in through the door. Everyone turned to see who it was.

Kate fought her way through the crowd. Dirty, exhausted and with her wet clothes sticking to her body, she came up to the bar counter and planted herself in front of the brawny licensee.

'You owe me five dollars,' she challenged.

He looked at her in comic surprise. Other voices chimed in.

'Go on, mate. Pay up.'

'You lost the bet.'

'Give the lady her money.'

The licensee opened the till and handed her a five-dollar note.

'Thank you,' she said.

Kate was about to leave when she noticed the full schooner of beer that stood in front of the man next to her. The temptation was too great. Her thirst was now overpowering. Grabbing the glass, she lifted it to her lips and quaffed at least half the contents. She thumped it down again before the startled owner.

'Next time – my shout. See you . . .' Her tone was apologetic.

She made her way back to the door through the bemused drinkers.

The licensee spoke for them all: 'Stone the bloody crows!'

With its blades whirring away, the helicopter flew across the vast desert panorama. Nick Stenning was at the controls, piloting the craft in dogged silence. Marty sat beside him, watching the plain unfold below and wondering how much further they had to go. Kate was directly behind them, cradling Tina's head in her lap and trying desperately to fend off sleep herself.

Nick remained remote, withdrawn, uncommunicative. Marty undid his seat belt so that he could lean forward to get a better view. He had to shout above the combined roar of engine and blades.

'How come it all looks so dead?'

'Drought,' replied Nick.

'How do the animals live?'

'Most don't. It's hard on stock.'

'Is there no water at all?'

'Below ground. You have to sink wells.'

'What about Larapinta?'

'What about it?'

'Will we be able to take a shower there?'

Nick angled his head around and glared darkly at the boy. 'Do that seat belt up!' he snapped.

'Sure, sure . . .'

'Don't bother Mr Stenning, Marty,' his mother advised coolly. 'We'll find out all we need to know soon enough.'

She stared angrily at the back of Nick's head but she bit back what she really wanted to say to him. It was no time for her to vent her spleen. Silence was the wiser alternative.

*

It was late afternoon when the helicopter at last began to lose height. Sunset was lavishing new colours on the landscape. Shadows lengthened and hues deepened. There was an austere loveliness to it all.

Nick Stenning jabbed a grubby forefinger at the window.

'There's Larapinta . . .'

Marty and Kate peered down eagerly and Tina awoke to get her first glimpse of their new home. As the helicopter flashed past, they saw a long iron roof on which white letters had been painted against a background of dull red.

Larapinta.

It stood out like a beacon to all approaching from the air.

The sun was now dipping below the horizon. Nick brought the helicopter down to land on a dirt strip and sent up a cloud of red dust. He switched the engine off and the blades gradually lost their frenzy. The dust below began to settle.

Nick opened the door and jumped out. He started to unload the luggage. Very tentatively, Kate and the children alighted. They looked across at the rambling weather-board farmhouse a couple of hundred yards away. It was grim, silent and dark.

Even Nick was uneasy at the apparent desertion. He frowned.

'*This* is Larapinta?' Kate asked.

'It's the Hannon place,' he grunted. 'Looks a bit quiet. I'd better help you across with your things.'

Her temper flared. She had put up with far too much of him as it was and she did not want to prolong their time together by a second.

'That's won't be necessary,' she announced firmly.

'It's no trouble.'

'We'll manage.'

'Suit yourself.'

She had his money ready and handed over the notes.

'Perhaps you'd like to count it?'

'You have an honest face,' he mocked.

'I don't like you, Mr Stenning,' she said evenly. 'I hope we don't meet again.'

He flashed a rare smile and his eyes came alive again.

'You never know your luck.'

He climbed back into the helicopter while Kate and the children gathered up their luggage. Marty was clutching his beloved guitar, Tina was dragging a large suitcase along and Kate herself seemed to be weighed down with baggage.

They staggered on through the gathering dusk. Nick looked up with genuine concern at the seemingly empty homestead. He was unhappy about the idea of leaving them there alone but he reminded himself that it was not his problem. There was nothing that he could do to change the situation. He shut the door and strapped himself into his seat.

Kate and the children stumbled across open ground as their bags got heavier and their arms weaker. The plaintive howl of a dingo echoed across the plain and startled them. They got another fright when the helicopter started up behind them with a sudden roar. Kate glanced back over her shoulder in time to see it lift off into the deep purple sky.

Nick Stenning flew swiftly away. He did not look back.

The three lonely figures moved on to the dark house, each of them wondering what they were about to find. A feeling of lifelessness seemed to pervade everything. It was as though the occupants had left very suddenly and abandoned the place to its own fate.

The house was colonial in style, old and sturdy with a tin roof. Wired verandahs kept out the swarms of flies that plagued the area all year round. A series of outhouses telescoped from the house and ran on down to stables and a barn.

There were several large water tanks, and off in the distance, a huge feed shed stood against the darkening sky. All around them, the land stretched away for mile after tedious mile of scrub.

Here was true isolation and a deep, black silence.

Marty and Tina turned to their mother for reassurance. She put down her luggage and rested a hand on each of them, striving for a warm smile that just would not come.

'Did you know it would be like this, Mom?' asked Tina.

'No, I didn't.'

'The windows are all boarded up.'

'Those are shutters. Maybe they close them at night.'

'Jesus!' said Marty. 'What a creepy joint!'

They nervously mounted the steps that led to the open porch. Kate rapped her knuckles on the door. The sound reverberated across the whole landscape and the lone dingo howled its response.

She knocked again but there was still no reply. When she tried the door, it swung inwards with a creak. Kate led the way inside. They came into a large room that was shrouded in darkness.

'Tom!' she called. 'Tom Hannon!'

Still no answer. They conversed in half-whispers.

'Marty,' instructed his mother, 'find a light switch.'

'Okay.'

'I knew we shouldn't have come!' Tina moaned.

'And don't *you* start again, young lady,' Kate warned.

Marty groped his way to a wall and located a light switch. When he tried it, nothing happened. He clicked it on and off.

'It just won't work, Mom.'

'Oh, that's right,' she recalled. 'Tom said they have a generator for electricity. We'll have to find that.'

Marty bumped into a table and made out a shape on it.

'Here's a lamp!' he said in triumph. 'All we need is matches.'

'I don't have any,' Kate replied.

Tina casually took some book matches from her pocket and threw them across to her brother. The implication shocked her mother but she made no comment. It was hardly the ideal moment to tackle the girl about the dangers of smoking.

'There's no one here,' Tina hissed.

'I'm sure there's a perfectly good explanation,' Kate said hopefully. 'There has to be.'

Marty lit the oil lamp and turned up the wick, bathing the whole place in a warm glow and enabling them to see that they were in the living room.

Big comfortable armchairs stood opposite a bulky sofa but the rest of the furniture was missing. Curtains and paintings had been taken down. Ornaments had gone. One complete wall was covered in wooden shelving that held a stunning array of books, some leather-bound, some paperbacks, none of them very new.

A private library of this size seemed such an incongruous thing to find in the middle of the Outback.

'What's going on?' Marty asked.

'I don't know,' Kate admitted, bewilderment replacing fear. 'Give me the lamp. We'll take a look around.'

With the light guiding their way, they went out into a narrow passageway. Kate opened a door and peeped into what was obviously the main bedroom. They reacted in surprise. The spacious and once lived-in room was now virtually empty apart from the king-size iron bed that stood at its centre.

When they came to the kitchen, they lit two more oil lamps and set them where they could shed most light. The large country-style room gave off the same feeling of desertion, of life having been dramatically interrupted.

A modern electric range dominated one wall, while another was adorned by an ancient fuel stove. Kate busied herself by checking the cupboards for food, directing her mind to immediate practical matters. She found tinned meat, fish and beans. A drawer in the sink unit yielded up an old-fashioned tin-opener.

'What's *that*?' Tina was examining the stove with patent distaste.

'What does it look like?' Marty retorted.

'It's an old stove,' explained Kate.

'Yeah, but how does it work?'

'You burn wood in it, Tina.'

'My God!' she exclaimed. 'People still use stuff like that?'

'Out here they do,' Marty explained.

'No central heating?'

'Only in the daytime.' He added, 'It's called the sun.'

Kate deposited the tins on the table and became brisk.

'I'm in no mood to tangle with a generator before Tom gets back,' she decided. 'That means we'll have to use old Bertha here for the cooking. I want you both to go out and find some wood.'

'Where?' Tina protested.

'There must be a wood heap or something close to the house.'

'Sure, Mom,' Marty agreed. 'Come on, Tina . . .'

'It's dark out there,' she said.

'Take a lamp,' Kate suggested. 'But leave the matches.'

The girl's eyes connected briefly with her mother's. She could see that there was going to be further discussion about her possession of the book matches. It made her blush slightly.

'Let's go,' said Marty.

'Be careful,' Kate urged. 'Watch where you're going.'

'We will, Mom . . .'

They went out cautiously through the back door.

As soon as she was left alone, Kate became aware of the true depth of her fatigue. She had to hold on to the table for support. Despair lapped at her and set her mind racing.

Where the hell are you, Tom Hannon?

She had maintained a show of calm for the sake of the children but her inner panic now took over. Had Tom lied to her? Was he simply stringing her along for the fun of it? Did he, in fact, exist? Was she really married to someone called Tom Hannon or was the man whom she had met in Los Angeles some kind of confidence trickster?

Ideas that would have seemed incredible a week ago now took on the lustre of possibility. To fend off her doubts, she reminded herself that she had met his sister, who had ratified all the details about Larapinta. But Molly had opposed the marriage bitterly and told Kate so to her face.

Why? What did the woman know that made her try to drive a wedge between Kate and Tom? Was there something wrong with her brother? Some mental problem? Some secret illness? What were they both keeping from her?

Kate slumped into a chair and clenched her fists in anger.

Stop humiliating me, Tom Hannon! I've had enough!

Another thought attacked her. Why had he been so eager to come on ahead to Australia? What other husband would want to leave his wife so soon after their marriage? Tom could have brought her with him and then gone on alone to Larapinta to prepare his daughters. There was something very sinister in the delay. What had he come on ahead to do?

Please, Tom. Say something before I go mad!

Kate was dizzy with pain and apprehension. She made an effort to steady herself. The tins had to be opened. Shaking her head to rid it of torment, she reached for the first tin and jabbed the point of the opener into its lid. As she tried to work the implement round the edge of the tin, it slipped from her fingers and dropped with a clatter to the floor.

Her control went and she hurled the tins after it. Then she fell across the table and beat it with her fists, drumming out her agony and crying like a lost child who cannot understand what is happening.

Save me, Tom Hannon! Where *are* you!

Like all the other rooms in the house, the children's

bedroom was stripped of almost everything. They dragged in two mattresses and set them up on the floor with sheets and blankets. It was not the most dignified way to spend their first night in Australia but they were past caring now.

Tina dozed off even as her mother tucked her in.

'Good night, Mom . . .'

'It will all look different in the morning, you'll see.'

'If it's not,' mumbled Marty, 'can we go home?'

'*This* is home now, honey.'

Kate bent over to give Tina a kiss then went over to Marty. Both mother and son realised the significance of it. She did not usually kiss them good night at home. The crisis had thrust them back in time and made them babies again, infants in need of maternal comfort and reassurance.

'Will Tom be here in the morning?' Marty whispered.

'I hope so,' she sighed. 'Go to sleep now.'

'It'll be okay, Mom,' he said, nestling down under the blankets. 'I know it will.'

She gave a tired smile, appreciating his attempt to cheer her up. After turning their lamp down, she crept out of the room and along to her own. The big iron bed looked more forlorn than ever.

It was an omen.

Kate had found a small table to set beside the bed. Her lamp was burning bravely on it. She reached for her suitcase and lifted it on to the bed. When she opened it, she rummaged inside for a few moments before she brought out a photograph of Tom.

It had been taken in Olvera Street only weeks ago, showing a very happy man beaming at the world. Memories were awakened and Kate felt soothed at once. She propped the photograph on the table so that she could see it easily, then she put her case back on the floor. The day had finally come to an end.

Still fully dressed, Kate lay down wearily on the top of the bed. Her eyes remained fixed on the photograph as

84

she reminded herself of the man, his goodness, his vows, his love.

'I trust you, Tom Hannon,' she said faintly.

She was still looking at his face when she fell asleep.

— 7 —

Headlights from several vehicles sliced through the darkness to illuminate the narrow dirt airstrip at Cutta Cutta. They acted as beacons to guide the helicopter as it slowly descended out of the black sky, its whirring rotor blades flashing in the light and shattering the silence with brutal effect.

There was something bizarre and unreal about the whole scene. It was somehow larger than life. So were most things at Cutta Cutta.

Caught in the light, Meg Stenning waited on the edge of the airstrip with shadows dancing across her expressionless face. She was a handsome, shapely country-woman who scorned make-up and who chose britches and a man's shirt as her normal attire. Vitality oozed from her but it was offset by an underlying hardness.

She was all woman but there was nothing soft or feminine about her. Meg seemed to glory in her toughness. Like all the Stennings.

Resentment smouldered in her eyes as she watched. There was a happy defiant tilt about her head and her jaw was set. She was unhappy about her brother's visit and she was not going to pretend otherwise.

When the helicopter landed, the motor cut out but the blades continued to circle madly for a short while. Before they had stopped rotating, Nick Stenning jumped out of the machine and walked away from it towards his sister. The vehicles which had lit the runway now started up and drove away. Only the moon provided light.

Nick and Meg met each other in the enveloping darkness.

'Evening, Meg,' he began.

'You're late.'

'I came, didn't I?'

'Worse luck!'

'You always did give me a warm welcome,' he mocked. 'I was summoned. Why?'

'Dad will tell you.' Rancour showed itself in her face and in her voice. 'This is between you and him!'

Nick Stenning wheeled away from his sister and headed towards the blaze of light in the distance. His stride was unhurried.

Against his will, he had come home again.

A figure emerged from the massive house and stood on the verandah as Nick approached. Silhouetted in the lighted doorway, the man cast a giant shadow across the yard.

It was symbolic.

Ed Stenning was a king in his own domain, a legend in the land. As his son drew closer to the great homestead where he was born and raised, Ed turned and went back inside without acknowledgement or greeting. The door banged shut behind him.

Nick paused in the darkened yard and looked up at the sky. A cloud drifted across the moon and extinguished its light. He took a deep breath to fortify himself against the confrontation.

Then he entered the house.

The study was a large, impressive, richly furnished room where the king held court. Ed Stenning stood in front of a huge fireplace and waited. Above the mantelpiece was a full-length portrait of the man, an imposing figure bestriding a vast, red-brown landscape.

Ed Stenning himself was smaller in stature than the portrait led people to expect. He was strong, forceful and straight-backed, with cobalt blue eyes in a tanned leather face. The habit of command had left its indelible mark on him.

Nick entered the room without ceremony. Tension rose instantly. It had been a long time.

Ed's gnarled features broke into a semblance of a smile.

'Welcome home, Nick.'

His son made no reply. He went straight to the drinks cabinet and poured himself a large whiskey. Then he glanced around the study with cynical amusement. It had not changed.

His father watched him and kept his feelings well-masked.

'How've you been?'

'Don't your spies keep you informed?'

Ed bridled. 'You change your attitude or this won't work.'

'Cheers, Dad!' Nick saluted him with his glass then sipped from it. He returned his father's level stare in a long, silent tussle.

Ed decided to come straight to the point. 'I'm about to buy another property.'

'Why? I'd have thought you owned enough by now.'

'This is different.'

'Yeah? Who's the victim?

Ed glowered but he would not be shifted from his course. There was too much at stake for it to be thrown away in a display of temper. Containing his ire, he made his offer.

'I want you back to work the place.'

All the acrimony that kept father and son apart was encapsulated in that moment. Ed fought against it and his tone became more jocular and expansive.

'Your future's here, Nick. It always was. Gallivanting around the Outback in a helicopter's no life for a son of mine.'

'That's up to me.'

'You could do so much better for yourself. Stennings belong at the top and that's where I want to put you.'

Nick sipped his whiskey and remained very sceptical.

'This sudden fatherly concern's a bit out of character, isn't it?'

'What do you mean?'

'You drove me away, Dad.'

'Oh, no!' Ed protested vehemently. 'Don't blame me for the years you've wasted. It was your decision not mine.'

'And, of course, you had nothing to do with it?'

His father's jaw was thrust out. He was not giving any more ground in the battle that had consumed their lives. By the same token, Nick was standing by his own position.

'I hoped you might have improved,' Ed growled.

'Have *you*?'

Another impasse. Neither dared to speak.

The older man moved swiftly to the drinks cabinet and helped himself to a brandy. He sampled it and then paced the room before turning once more to his son. Manufacturing another smile, he stated his case without preamble.

'I didn't bring you here to rake over old ground. There's been enough of that. The past is dead. It's the future I'm concerned about.'

Ed crossed to a gigantic wall map which showed the extent of the Stenning cattle empire. With Cutta Cutta and all its other land, it represented a very large slice of central Australia. Adjoining it was a much smaller area – Larapinta.

The old man's wrinkled finger tapped it.

'There,' he announced. 'A lifetime dream – about to be realised.'

Nick was aghast. '*Larapinta?*'

Ed swept his hand impressively across the marked portion on the map and pride made him swell.

'All Stenning land. A kingdom *I* created. And now, finally, Larapinta will be part of it.'

Nick turned away in disgust and drained his glass. With

surprising agility, his father crossed to the desk and seized something from it. He came to wave it in front of his son.

'Look at this!' he demanded. 'I had my own water survey done on Larapinta . . . Under Hannon land is an entire lake. All the water we've ever needed! This drought is killing me. But Larapinta water means new life.' His face was now aglow. 'Well?'

The men stood face to face. Neither of them noticed that Meg was lurking in the shadow just outside the open door and listening to every word that was being said.

'Well?' Ed repeated.

'Not interested.'

'Do you realise the chance you're turning down? You bloody fool!' hissed Ed.

'Land-grabbing isn't my style. Give it to Meg.'

'The place is *yours*.'

'She's the son you always wanted.'

Nick put down his glass and started to the door. His sister had now retreated and he did not see her as he stalked out. Ed went after him and tried to call him back.

'You don't know what's happened. At least hear me out.' But his son was deaf to his plea and strode on.

When Nick reached the front door, Meg was already there, holding it open for him. She spoke with controlled, malicious, icy calm.

'Don't come back, Nick. We don't need you.'

He stormed out without a backward glance.

Meg Stenning slammed the door after him with a sense of finality.

It had worked out exactly as she hoped.

Sunrise at Larapinta household brought an affirmation of life. Birds sang, chickens clucked and a horse whinnied in the stables. The countryside was already turning from grey to gold. A new day had come.

An old dust-covered truck rattled across the plain and pulled up with a squeal of brakes outside the house. Seated behind the wheel was Deirdre Shackleton, a cheery square-faced countrywoman in her fifties with a ruddy complexion and a wiry frame. Travelling with her were two young teenage girls who looked very subdued.

They got out of the truck, then noticed that the front door of the house was ajar. The girls shrank back and the woman took charge.

'Leave this to me.'

She reached back inside the truck and pulled out a rifle from beneath the seat. After checking that it was properly loaded, she moved cautiously towards the verandah with the girls behind her.

She was more than ready to shoot if need be.

A sixth sense woke Kate Hannon in the main bedroom. The lamp had gone out now but there was enough sunlight filtering through the cracks in the shutters to dispel the gloom. As her eyes began to focus, she gave a start.

Three complete strangers were staring down at her.

One of them was pointing a gun at Kate.

When she had recovered from the initial shock, she smiled and sat up. Relief flooded through her as she looked at the two girls.

'You must be Zoe and Emmie . . .'

They stared at her in total confusion. It was unnerving.

'Where's Tom?' Kate asked. 'Isn't your father with you? We missed each other at the airport.'

'Who are you?' Zoe asked accusingly.

'I'm Kate.'

She was taken aback by the question and even more hurt by their reaction to her answer. They had evidently never heard of her. Kate swung her legs over the edge of the bed and stood up.

The older woman lowered the gun and moved in closer.

'There's a bit of confusion somewhere,' she said. 'We've come to see to the horses – didn't expect to find anyone here. I'm Tom's neighbour – Deirdre Shackleton. The girls are staying with me.' There was an ominous pause. 'It's obvious that you don't know . . . Tom's dead.'

The news hit Kate like a hammer blow and she had to hold on to the bed. She was completely dazed. The unbelievable had happened.

Tom was dead. Her whole world had collapsed.

The other woman spoke quietly but her words seemed to pound at Kate's ears and make her head ring with pain.

'It was a shock to everyone. He rang from the airport, sayin' that he was on his way. Had a surprise for us all. Flying his Cessna.' She gave a little shrug. 'When he hadn't turned up by nightfall, we sent out a search party. We found the plane – and Tom inside it. We buried him three days ago.'

Tears glistened in the eyes of the two girls as they were forcibly reminded of their father's tragic accident. They stared fixedly at the woman who had just spent a night in his bed.

Kate felt as if she had been plunged into a nightmare. Nothing was real any more. Everything she touched fell to pieces in her hands. She was consorting with demons who found new and more subtle ways to torture her. Wherever she turned, there was more agony.

All her strength seemed to ebb away and she felt a great emptiness inside her. Her whole body was trembling.

'Who are you?' asked the older woman.

Kate did not even hear the question. Her mind was numb.

'Who *are* you?' repeated the other.

Kate had to struggle to manage an answer. 'I'm his wife.'

Incredulity registered on the three faces. It was their turn to reel with shock. Deirdre Shackleton put a consoling arm around each of the girls.

Kate looked down at a double bed that seemed to mock her with its emptiness. The deserted house was an all too accurate metaphor of her situation. She could stand it no longer.

Running out of the room, she blundered her way to the front door and went out into the yard. By the time the

92

others had reached the verandah, Kate was marching blindly away from the property and into the barren land that surrounded it.

There was no direction to her steps. She walked across the red dust with the sun striking her head. Her grief was like a torrent inside her and it kept her striding on.

Her sense of loss and desolation was unbearable. It was as if some malignant joke had been played on her. She had given up everything to come to a new country for a fresh start with her husband. She had gambled it all on one throw and she had lost.

Australia had been an endurance test to her from the moment that she arrived, but she had put up with it for Tom's sake, believing that he would soon come along and make everything right. He had been her light at the end of the tunnel and now it was extinguished.

Kate was lost, alone, vulnerable. All hope had gone.

'As long as I live, I'll never let a single, solitary thing hurt you, Kate.' His voice echoed through her brain with cruel irony.

'As long as I live . . .'

Her despair turned to hysteria and she broke into a run, charging off across the sand as fast as she could, trying to shake off the demons who stalked her, flailing her arms wildly as if fending them off and closing her eyes to shut out the sight of the wilderness all around her.

She ran till her lungs were bursting and her legs were columns of fire, then she tripped, stumbled and fell head-long to the hard ground. This was Larapinta. The place which had brought her all the way to Australia. The land that had betrayed her and robbed her of everything.

Kate clutched at the soil with angry fingers and her rage produced a primal scream that cut through the silence like a knife.

'Tom!'

Her hands continued their attack until blood ran from her fingers and strength left her. She lay prostrate on the ground and whispered her last words to the ghost of her dead husband.

'I can't go on . . . I can't go on . . .'

The family cemetery stood some distance from the house at Cutta Cutta. It was no more than a small collection of gravestones surrounded by a low iron fence and sheltered from the sun by a large gumtree. Weeds had sprouted up among the headstones and there was an air of neglect about the whole place.

Nick Stenning came in through the gate and walked somnolently to a graveside. He stared down at the weathered headstone and read the name that was engraved there.

OLIVIA STENNING – born 1929 – Died April 4th, 1962
Beloved wife of Edward Stenning
Mother of Nicholas and Margaret

Anger and sorrow rose up in his heart at the same time and he turned away to contend with them. When he faced the grave again, he knelt down and began to pluck at the weeds with strong hands.

Ed Stenning watched him from the verandah of the house with growing emotion. A man of granite, his eyes filled unexpectedly with tears of pain as old memories returned to haunt him.

He had lost a wife – and a son. Both were dead to him.

Nick finished the weeding and stood up again.

Someone else came into the cemetery and walked up behind him.

'You can't let go, can you? . . . Of a woman who's been dead for twenty years.'

He swung round to face Meg. Her eyes were cold.

'Well,' she said sneeringly, 'you live with your ghost . . .'

Nick went past her and headed back towards his helicopter.

*

94

The large iron bed still stood at the centre of the main bedroom. The place was bare, uncluttered, lifeless. Kate Hannon lay on the bed fully dressed and stared at the ceiling. The photograph of her husband was still on the table beside her but it had curled slightly in the heat.

She did not move or blink. Kate was now beyond tears. Her whole future had been smashed in a plane crash in the desert. She was a woman in limbo. Waiting for life to return.

Night spread its dark cloak over the plain once more. The Larapinta homestead was a lonely outpost under a dome of stars. A light was on in the living room and another, in the children's bedroom, was soon switched off. Only one sign of life remained.

Attracted by the light, insects bounced against the flywire door. Down in the stables, the horses snorted and shifted about uneasily. An occasional howl rang out across the plain.

Kate heard none of it. She was seated immobile in an armchair in the living room directly below the electric light. Her unseeing eyes stared at the floor. Grief ate hungrily into her soul. Her mind was smouldering. Her body was numb. She was in mourning.

An hour passed and then she got up. Moving listlessly to the telephone table, she picked up the directory and glanced at the instructions inside the front cover. Then she picked up the receiver and slowly dialled a number.

Insects continued to buzz and beat at the flywire door.

The operator's voice was bright, female but distant.

'What number are you calling?'

'Yes,' mumbled Kate, 'I want to place a call to California . . . person to person . . . to Mrs Molly Winters . . .'

The bulb in the ceiling began to flicker and fade.

'You have a number?' asked the operator.

Kate looked up in alarm then gasped as the light went out altogether. She was suddenly immersed in total darkness. Fear made her drop the telephone and it swung crazily to and fro on its lead.

'Hello, caller. Are you still there? What number did you . . .?'

Hearing nothing but her own panic, Kate groped her way across the room, banging into various objects. When she felt the table, her hand closed gratefully on the matches. The match soon burned down and she blew it out as the flame licked her hand.

A second match guided her into the kitchen and a third helped her to find the kerosene lantern. She managed to get it alight before the match guttered. The lantern had an evil smell but its beam gave her courage. She went quickly to the children's bedroom.

Anxious and flustered, she went across to her son.

'Marty . . . ?'

But he was fast asleep. By the light of the lamp, she could see his pale, exhausted face, now so childlike again. Kate wanted his help with the generator but she did not have the heart to wake him. It would be unfair. Marty needed his sleep.

Kate straightened up and calmed herself. She was the adult. It was time to start behaving like one. She retreated quietly from the room, determined to sort out the problem on her own.

She came out on to the verandah, hesitated for a moment and then stepped down into the yard. As she carried the lamp in front of her, she moved in a small envelope of light. The sheer volume of the black starlit space above her was menacing. She felt frightened. Defenceless. Humbled.

But she had something to do and she pushed herself on.

The horses were still restless down in the stables and their snorts and whinnies disturbed her. She reached the generator shed and pushed back the door on its squeaking hinges. By the glare of the lamp, she confronted a sullen pair of beasts – the diesel engine and electrical generator.

They mocked her with ignorance. She shone the light

back and forth over their dusty, oily armour without a clue about what she had to do. Her frustration seethed inside her.

'Damn you!'

Anger brought a touch of self-assertion but it did not last. As she worked her way around the machines, Kate got caught up in a thick cobweb and lost her nerve. She lashed out with an arm to fight herself clear then withdrew quickly from the shed.

Tom Hannon would have known what to do.

She missed him more than she would have believed possible. His death had created an aching void in her. He was gone for ever. Her sadness welled up in her with such force that she felt quite faint. It took her a full minute to collect herself.

The horses were more unsettled than ever and insects were now swarming around the light. She had been defeated by the generator, and the vast blackness of the night was imposing its own threats. The house suddenly seemed like a haven and Kate hurried back to it.

She mounted the verandah, yanked open the door then froze.

The bottom of the flywire was torn.

Kate was certain that it had been secure earlier on. It would not have kept the insects at bay otherwise. Now it had a gaping hole in it, as if something or someone had forced an entry.

Terror clutched at her and made her tremble. Then she remembered the children. If they were in danger, she had to save them. Creeping warily, she opened the door, went in and made her way to the kitchen.

As soon as she entered, she knew that she was not alone.

Kate went quickly in search of a weapon. Pulling open a drawer, she grabbed a carving knife and held it out in front of her. Sweat was trickling down her face by now. Her heart was thumping and she was breathing stertorously.

A menacing growl cut through the air.

She swung the lamp to illuminate the larder door. It was ajar.

Kate could stand it no longer.

'Marty!' she yelled.

The larder door at once banged open and a pair of dingoes came out, their eyes glittering in the light and their fangs bared. As Kate let out a loud shriek of horror, they scampered to freedom.

Kate shuddered. She felt utterly humiliated.

Marty's anxious voice called from the bedroom.

'Mom! You okay?'

'I'm here!' she shouted. 'It's all right!'

Then she broke into frightened, angry sobbing.

The danger was not over. They were still exposed. She rushed out to the flywire door and saw that the gap had been widened by the sudden exit of the dingoes. Kate slammed the inner door against the invaders. Frantic with disgust, she pushed home the bolts.

Still half-asleep, Marty came blundering down the passageway in his pyjamas. He was apprehensive and disoriented. Tina came behind him in her nightie, fear turning her face white.

Kate set down the lamp and almost fell into the chair.

'Mom?' whispered Marty.

'What happened?' asked Tina.

Kate gathered them in her arms and held them very tight.

'Oh, God!' she sighed.

— 8 —

The mid-morning sun exploded out of a clear blue sky and dropped its heat on to the parched land that rolled away to the horizon like a red ochre carpet.

A solitary eagle soared lazily overhead as it waited for its next prey to appear. Down on the ground, a grasswren was building its domed nest in the crown of a spinifex clump. Kangaroos grazed nearby on the sparse patches of mulga and witchetty bush that dotted the sweeping plain.

In the distance, a small spiral of dust heralded the approach of a vehicle. Its rasping noise soon banished the silence. The kangaroos lifted their heads and remained as motionless as statues. As the vehicle headed towards them, they suddenly came alive again and went bounding away to escape the intruders.

Deirdre Shackleton sat comfortably behind the driving wheel of her flat-top truck as it bounced its way over the rough dry ground. Kate was beside her, hanging on grimly and marvelling at her companion's ability to ride out the bumps so easily.

Marty and Tina were seated behind them, gripping the sides of the truck for safety, intimidated by the strangeness of the landscape and its quality of other-worldness. As the front wheel explored a hollow, the children were thrown a few inches into the air.

The driver let out a cheerful cackle. 'Hold on to your hats!'

The truck increased its speed and left an even larger cloud of dust in its wake. Kate raised her voice to compete with the engine.

'I didn't get a chance to thank you properly, Mrs Shackleton.'

'What for?'

'Mending the flywire on that door for us.'

'Oh, that was nothing,' said the other woman dismissively. 'All it needs is a hammer and a few tacks. You'll soon learn to do that kind of thing for yourself.'

'Yes,' Kate agreed. 'I'll have to, won't I?'

'Must have been a nasty shock for you, though.'

'It was terrifying. I never realised that they could get into the house itself.'

'Dingoes. Wild dogs. Been here long before any of us white people.' The driver shook her head philosophically.

The flatness of the plain was now broken up by undulating dunes that were clothed in hummock grasses. Larapinta territory looked so bleak and inhospitable, Kate found it hard to believe that it supported any stock.

Deirdre Shackleton seemed to read her thoughts.

'It's tough going. Two years ago, there were over ten thousand head of cattle on Larapinta. Now it's half that number. Water-holes dried up . . . and only one bore that's left working.' She glanced at Kate. 'Out here, water's more precious than gold.'

She jabbed her foot down hard on the accelerator and the truck went careering across the plain at full bat with its three passengers clinging on desperately.

A windmill marked the site of a sub-artesian bore. In the shadow that it threw across the ground, the structure provided the venue for a life-and-death battle between a large python and a kangaroo rat. The snake, inevitably, was the victor. With leisurely calm, it settled down to ingest its meal.

The truck pulled up no more than ten yards away, its occupants quite unaware of the drama that had just taken place. They stared up in silence at the windmill, immobile in the still air, quite defunct. A short distance away was a big dry hole that had once been an operative dam.

Scattered over a hundred-yard radius were the rotting corpses of several steers.

Kate and the children were horrified by the sight. They had never been so close to such a scene of appalling desolation. Deirdre Shackleton saw their distress and felt a wave of sympathy for them – forlorn strangers thrust into a world they neither knew nor understood.

Kate's voice held a whispered echo of the past.

'Tom said the land's a living thing,' she remembered. 'He said you could hear its heart beating sometimes . . .'

'It's true,' confirmed the older woman, her eyes panning the landscape with grudging affection. 'The land doesn't belong to us. We belong to it.' She called back to the children. 'Why don't you kids stretch y'legs?'

'Great!' said Tina.

'Come on!' Marty urged.

Grateful to get out of the truck, they jumped down to the ground and stretched their aching limbs. Tina held her camera and glanced around apprehensively. Marty was more adventurous.

'Let's go explore some.'

'If I see another of those lizards, I'll die.'

'Stick close to me. I'm not scared.'

'Okay, Marty.'

They wandered off across the cracked ground.

Kate got down from the truck herself and strolled a few yards away from it. As she gazed at the barren landscape, she felt more alone than at any time in her life. She had been robbed of her happiness in the most brutal way and left with nothing.

Deirdre came and stood beside her, intuitively sensing what she was going through and wanting to offer some help.

'Thinkin' about Tom?'

'Yes.'

'Did you love 'im?'

The bluntness of the question jolted Kate. She looked deep into the other woman's eyes. Something seemed to pass between them. Deirdre's manner softened and she nodded, now satisfied.

'Tom was a good mate.'

'I understand.'

'I reckon you do,' replied the other with a wry smile. 'But you'd every right to tell me to mind m'own business.'

The ghost of a smile touched Kate's lips. 'I realise I must've come as quite a shock.'

'Yep. Tom went to America to get himself some cash not to go shopping for a new wife.'

'He didn't exactly go shopping, Mrs Shackleton.'

'I'm sure. Just happened. One of those things.'

'That's about it.' Her face darkened. 'I do feel sorry for Zoe and Emmie. It's bad enough losing their father like that without having me foisted on them.'

'Been rough on them an' no mistake. But they can go on stayin' with Ralphie an' me till we manage to contact Tom's sister . . . She and her husband are in America somewhere.'

'San Diego. I met them.'

'Good. You can give a hand to track 'em down.'

'I've tried to ring Molly once already.'

'We need to sort out something permanent for those girls.'

'I know.'

'They can't just hang around here.'

'Neither can we.' A sigh escaped her lips. 'I can't help feeling that we're trespassers.'

'Rubbish!'

'This whole place seems so foreign to us.'

'That's the Outback for you.' She used a hand to brush away a fly then became serious. 'I don't suppose you've been able to give much thought to what you're gonna do?'

'Not really.'

'What do your instincts tell you?'

'Go home.'

'I'd do the same in your boots.'

'There's just one problem, Mrs Shackleton. We don't have any money.'

Kate turned away and walked sadly across to the empty dam. The other woman was pensive. It was a few minutes before she went off to join her companion.

They looked together into the great dry hole that once held water.

'How many wells does Larapinta have?' Kate wondered.

'Once it had an even dozen. And each one cost between twenty-five and fifty thousand dollars . . . dependin' how deep you hafta drill.'

'It's a fortune!'

'Cattle need water.'

'Is there no other source?'

'Not when the creeks and dams go dry. You depend totally on sub-artesian water.' She hunched her shoulders. 'It's all there is. Till it rains.'

'And when will that be?'

'You tell me. We been waitin' four years already. On the other side of those ranges' – Deirdre pointed her finger – 'is the Stenning ranch. They own Cutta Cutta. Old man Stenning rules over three thousand square miles of the best cattle country in the Territory. He's like a king out here.'

'What sort of man is he?'

'Bit of a bastard but we all pay homage outa habit.'

'That pilot who flew us here . . .' recalled Kate. 'His name was Stenning.'

'That's Nick. None too sociable.'

'He was downright rude.'

'The Outback never turned anyone into a gentleman,' noted the other. 'Nick used to be the crown prince. Then he fell out with his old man.'

'Why?'

'Don't know. But it turned Nick Stenning into the black sheep of the family.'

Kate Hannon recalled her first meeting with him on the summit of the hill. It had been an abrasive moment and she had found his manner repulsive. Yet now she was thinking about him, wondering why he had left home to become an outcast.

She hated everything about the man, but he stayed in her mind for a long time.

Kate could not understand why.

Behind the boundary wire that divided Larapinta territory from the Cutta Cutta ranch, a gleaming new Land Rover stood on a sandy rise. The Stenning logo was emblazoned on both doors with striking effect.

Brown and weather-beaten, Ed Stenning sat in the passenger seat and trained his binoculars on the four tiny figures moving about in the distance beside a dead waterhole. He grunted with satisfaction and lowered the glasses to reveal eyes that could see for a hundred miles.

With a grim smile playing around his mouth, he looked across at Meg, who was seated behind the driving wheel. Denied the feminine influence of a mother for most of her life, she had grown up very much in his mould. She did not need to be told what her father was thinking. It had her complete approval.

Something caught her attention and she directed him to it. Dark clouds had started to form on the horizon. Ed was untroubled by them. He raised his binoculars again and resumed his surveillance.

Tina soon tired of photographing the empty landscape and the heat was now really punishing. She kicked some sand aimlessly.

'It reeks here. There's nothing to do.'

'Yeah, I know. Kinda weird.'

'Nothing to look at. Not even the sound of a car going by. It's the pits, Marty. And it's like being in an oven.'

'We'll be going home soon.'

'Am I glad about that!'

'Back to the guys.'

'Home to Billy.'

Marty thrust his hands into his pockets and became reflective. 'I sure feel sorry for Mom.'

'Me, too,' admitted his sister, her tone softening.

'We mustn't rush her, Tina.'

'What do you mean?'

'She may need time to work through it,' he explained. 'Mom pinned everything on coming out here to Tom. He was a nice guy. She must have loved him a lot to make a decision like that.' He took his hands from his pockets and folded his arms. 'All I'm saying is . . . well, do you remember how you felt when you had to leave Billy?'

'It was awful! I thought it was the end of the world.'

'But Billy is still alive and waiting for you in LA.' He bit his lip and turned away. 'Tom is dead. Mom will never see him again.'

Tina nodded. 'We'll give her time. All she wants.'

Deirdre Shackleton looked up at the darkening sky and felt the first small gusts of wind. A frown corrugated her brow.

'We better get straight back.'

'Why?' asked Kate.

'Looks like a dust-storm blowin' up.' She yelled to the children. 'Kids! Come on! Dust-storm on its way!'

Tina and Marty stared at the strange clouds and backed away nervously, then spun round and ran quickly towards the truck.

'What exactly is a dust-storm, Mrs Shackleton?' Kate wanted to know.

'You'll see. Get in!'

They clambered back into the truck and the older woman gunned the engine. It throbbed into life immediately.

'By the way,' she added. 'My friends call me Auntie Deir.'

They traded a smile and Kate was pleased. She had been accepted. Auntie Deir was the best thing that had happened to her since she had come to Australia. She knew instinctively that they could be good friends.

'Let's get goin'' then!' shouted the driver.

The truck lurched forward. Kate glanced anxiously through the back window and was relieved to see that Marty and Tina just managed to climb aboard as the vehicle picked up speed. Trying to stay ahead of the storm, Auntie Deir created a dust-cloud of her own as she drove madly in the direction of the homestead.

Behind them near the windmill, unruffled by all the commotion, the python was basking in the sun. The kangaroo rat was now an obscene bulge in its normally smooth length.

The wind hit the Larapinta homestead with great force, rattling every door, window and roof. Chickens complained noisily in their pen and the horses registered their protest in the stables. Dust was stirred up in thick eddies and thrown against the buildings.

Well conditioned to such freak storms, Zoe and Emmie ran around the outside verandah to close and bolt the shutters. The wild hysteria of the blast increased and red dust whirled everywhere.

Zoe stood on the edge of the verandah and gazed out past the barn, now an indistinct blur in the gathering gloom. She tried to pierce the blanket of dust and catch a glimpse of the truck.

'Come inside,' said Emmie.

'They should be here by now.'

'Auntie Deir will know what to do.'

'*She* will,' commented Zoe with a slight sneer. '*They* won't.'

The girls went back into the house and closed the door firmly behind them before starting on the important job of blocking up every crack and opening that they could find.

Emmie worked beside her sister and did her share willingly.

'You don't like them very much, do you?' she said.

'I don't like them at all.'

'Why not?'

'They don't belong, Emmie.'

'I know.' She pondered. 'The lady is not too bad, though.'

Zoe took a much harsher view altogether.

'I don't want her for *my* mother!'

Now invisible in the whirlblast of red dust, the flat-top truck battled its way along, bouncing and rattling over the hard ground so violently that it seemed about to part from its axles.

Kate was in great discomfort but at least she was sheltered inside the cab. Wrapped up in a tarpaulin in the back of the vehicle, Marty and Tina were thrown about like bags of chaff. The drive was a real ordeal.

Overhead, a monstrous cloud of dust obliterated the sun and hurled a dark shadow across the land. The wind intensified its fury and pressed down on the truck like a giant hand.

Before they knew what was happening, the engine stalled and the vehicle ground to a premature halt. Cursing loudly, Auntie Deir tried the ignition several times but to no avail. Out of sheer irritation, she struck at the steering wheel with her fist and connected with the horn. Its plaintive beep was drowned by the howl of the wind.

'Damn and blast it!' she bellowed. 'This is all we need!'

'Anything I can do?'

'Pray!'

Auntie Deir hopped out of the truck and went round to the front to heave up the bonnet. Kate went with her for moral support and the twins soon joined them to see what was going on. Within a matter of seconds, all four of them were coated in a shrieking red curtain that wound itself round them and wiped them completely from view.

The dust-storm raged with irresistible venom.

*

At the Larapinta homestead, the wind continued its vicious attack. Though the girls were doing their utmost to keep it at bay, it was still gaining entry through tiny cracks, tugging at the shuttered windows, blowing down the chimney, rising through the floorboards.

Caught in the draught, Emmie gave a shiver.

'I've never known it as bad as this.'

'It'll pass,' said Zoe, trying to reassure her.

'I wish Dad was here.'

'Just do what he taught us.'

'How are we going to manage *without* him?'

'Don't stop, Emmie. There's still plenty to do.'

They scrunched up pieces of newspaper and used it to fill gaps in the boarding. Old clothing was used to stuff into larger openings but the wind somehow managed to keep coming in.

'Just listen to that *howl*!' said Emmie.

But Zoe could hear another sound as well. A low, mechanical, grinding noise that seemed to be getting closer all the time. When her sister heard it as well, they moved instinctively together. Alarm streaked their faces as the sound, distorted by the wind, seemed to surround the whole house.

A blurred shape moved slowly across the yard like some strange monster. Plastered in dust, its eyes glowed angrily and it let out a deep growl before coming to a halt in front of the verandah.

Marty and Tina leaped off the back of the truck immediately and ran for cover with the tarpaulin still over their heads. Inside the cab of the vehicle, Kate and Auntie Deir were caked with red dust from head to toe. The older woman lowered the window, spat manfully then quickly wound up the window again.

'I feel like I swallowed half the Simpson Desert.'

'You okay?'

Auntie Deir wiped her mouth on her sleeve and grinned. 'It'll take more than a dust-storm to kill me.'

'You did wonders with that engine.'

'I got it working, that's all that counts.'

'I could never do something like that.'

'You'd learn, Kate. I had to.' She indicated the house. 'You'd better get inside.'

'Aren't you coming in?'

'No, I'm gonna make a run for it.'

'In *this*?'

'I'll take my chances.'

'Why not wait till it blows itself out?'

'Might take hours. I've got a sick husband at home and I don't like leavin' 'im alone too long.'

Kate gestured helplessly in the direction of the homestead. 'What about . . . Zoe and Emmie?'

The response was premeditated, almost too offhand.

'I wondered if you'd let them stop with you over-night? They'll be no trouble. I'll pick 'em up tomorrow.'

'I don't mind – but will they?'

'Probably.'

Kate needed only a few seconds to reach her decision. 'Okay.'

She waved her farewell, got out of the truck and closed the door tight behind her. Auntie Deir released the brake and eased the flat-top forward, her headlights jabbing at the impenetrable curtain of dust. As she glanced in her rear-view mirror, she could just make out the figure of Kate standing near the verandah with the storm swirling all around her.

Auntie Deir smiled. She hoped that her plan would work.

Left alone, Kate ran swiftly to the front door and let herself in. The twins were waiting inside with Zoe and Emmie. The two sisters looked up at Kate in a questioning silence.

'She'll be back for you tomorrow.'

There was a tense moment as the full realisation hit

them that they would all be under one roof together for at least the next twenty-four hours. None of the children seemed pleased.

There was still work to do, however. Whatever their differences, they had to unite against the common enemy who was beating at their door.

Emmie was the first to speak. 'Everything's gotta be blocked up so the dust can't get in.'

'We can help,' Marty volunteered. 'Show us what to do.'

Emmie ran to a window and gathered up some rags to poke into the narrow gap along one side of the frame. Marty went with her then looked back for his sister.

'Come on, Tina.'

'Oh, sure . . .'

She went over to join them as fast as she could.

Zoe remembered something and let out a shriek.

'The horses!'

'I'll go with you,' offered her sister.

'No – you stay here.'

Zoe charged off past Kate and out through the front door. Before his mother could stop him, Marty sprinted off after Zoe and went out into the storm. Kate opened the door wide.

'Marty!'

Her voice was muffled by the cry of the wind, which now brought piles of dust in through the opening. Kate slammed the door shut once more and leaned against it. Her eye fell on the chimney. Another cloud of red dust came surging down it like a fall of soot.

The house was being invaded.

The wind outside had now reached such a pitch of anger that it almost blew Zoe and Marty off their feet. Most of the horses were already in the stable but a few were still loose in the corral, whipped into a frenzy by the lash of the storm, bucking and whinnying for all that they were worth. It would not be easy to lead them to safety.

Zoe dived in through the fence, grabbed the bridle of the first horse and tried to calm it by stroking its neck.

'Whoa, Shah. Whoa, boy. Easy now . . .'

But the animal shied and she had difficulty holding it.

'Can I help?' asked Marty.

'No.'

'You'll never get that horse in on your own.'

'Go away!' screamed Zoe. 'Go away!'

Marty elected to lend a hand, needing to prove something to her and to himself. Climbing in through the fence, he went up behind Zoe and tried to reach over her head towards the horse. The animal suddenly reared up with great force, tearing the girl's hand from the bridle and sending her crashing to the ground.

The horse hovered over her. Marty darted forward and pulled her clear in the nick of time as the thrashing horse came thudding down to miss her by inches.

Zoe scrambled to her feet with her eyes blazing.

'Will you keep out of my way!' she yelled. 'You're only frightening them more.'

'Sorry . . .'

Hurt and intimidated, Marty backed up against the fence.

Visibility was coming and going, dictated by the clouds of red dust that ripped at their faces, blinding and choking them, blanketing everything in sight.

Fifty feet away, a strong gust ripped the tin roof from one of the outbuildings and send it spiralling into the air. More havoc was being wreaked in the barn.

Murmuring reassurances, Zoe edged near to the horse again.

'Whoa, Shah. Steady, boy. I won't hurt you. Easy now . . .'

She made a grab for the bridle then led the animal, running, down to the stable and the relative comfort of its loose box.

The other horses continued to trot wildly around the corral, buffeted by the storm and totally confused.

Marty could not resist the challenge.

Picking up another bridle from the fencepost, he moved out into the middle of the circling horses and picked one out. Leaning into the wind, he tried to throw the leather over the animal's head but he met with no success.

A freak gust of wind blew across the corral and disturbed the horse even more. It reared up with a loud neigh and knocked him flying. Marty lay on the ground with the animal above him.

Zoe reacted with speed. Seeing what had happened, she risked life and limb by running straight at the horse and waving her arms at it. Though it reared again, it backed away and Marty was safe.

She helped him to his feet. Somehow she seemed to understand his impulse to prove himself. Zoe was no longer angry with him.

In the single look exchanged between them, the first of the barriers between the two sets of children was subtly breached.

— 9 —

The house remained in a state of siege as the storm waged its war outside. Though it was only afternoon, the lights had to be switched on to combat the gloom inside. Noise, draught and dust maintained their assault. It was relentless.

The four children were seated around the kitchen table, hunched together in a shared refuge. Kate had washed her face though her hair was still filthy. She stood at the working surface and prepared a meal for them, conscious of the unease that existed between Tom Hannon's children and her own.

Tina was struggling to retain her outward composure but she was terrified by the ferocity of the storm. Marty, too, was frightened by the constant wail and the creak of the rafters. Even the two sisters were exhibiting a slight nervousness.

Zoe pulled herself together and tried to soothe Marty.

'Dust-storms don't last long. There's nothing to be scared of.'

He nodded his silent gratitude.

'We're not scared,' insisted Tina with a hint of defiance.

She glared at Zoe for a moment then a strong gust of wind hit the house and sent a shower of fine dust cascading from the ceiling to sprinkle their heads and the table. Tina's bravado faded.

Zoe looked across at Kate and put a blunt question.

'When are you leaving?'

'I haven't really decided yet,' Kate replied calmly. 'And a lot will depend on what your aunt wants to do.'

'I guess you two'll be going to live in the States as well,' observed Marty. 'You'll like it.'

Emmie gaped. 'The States?'

'Doesn't your aunt live in San Diego?' he said.

The reality of their situation hit the two girls like a sudden blow. It had obviously never occurred to them that they might have to leave their native country. They sat there in shocked silence. Kate watched them with growing compassion. They were devastated.

There was a long, embarrassed pause. Marty wished that he had not mentioned America and he chided himself for plunging Zoe into such patent misery. He groped for words of comfort but he had no time to voice them. The light bulb started to flicker then it went out altogether.

'Not again!' Kate sighed.

'I'll go, Mom!' Marty announced.

'We'll manage with lamps,' she decided. 'We'll sort the generator out when the storm is over.'

Oil lamps were lit and set on the table. Dust particles came down from the roof. The wind's lament was unceasing. The house groaned in complaint.

Kate poured out some cups of tea and handed them round. Tina examined it with suspicion.

'What is it?'

'Tea.'

'Ugh!'

'Try it, Tina.'

'Don't we have coffee?'

'Try it,' Kate urged. 'I had a good teacher.'

Zoe seized on the oblique reference to Tom Hannon.

'You didn't love my father,' she asserted. 'How could you?'

'Zoe —'

'You only knew him for two weeks before you got married. I bet you thought he was rich, didn't you? That's why you went after him!'

Kate was stunned by the accusation. She backed away. Marty came to her rescue. 'It wasn't like that, Zoe!

Your old man and Mom really liked each other.' He glanced at his sister. 'We liked him, too.'

In the electric silence that followed, Tina moved to place a protective arm around her mother's shoulders, Zoe glared at them and Emmie began to sob quietly. Marty felt very uncomfortable.

Kate stepped forward to confront the two sisters.

'I knew your father had money problems before we got married,' she explained calmly, 'and I don't intend touching a single cent of his estate. I'll be contacting friends back home . . . they'll lend us the money for our return fares. Until that happens and until your futures are decided, we'll be staying on here at Larapinta . . . We don't have much choice.'

She sat down opposite them and leaned in close. Sincerity burned in her eyes and the girls could see that she meant what she said.

'I'd really like it if you'd stay on, too, and help us keep the place running till it's time for us to go. It appears that the men who worked here left after the funeral.' She gave a shrug. 'We're city people, I'm afraid. We don't know anything about caring for animals and mending generators and all the rest that's involved.'

Kate smiled sadly as she thought about Tom Hannon and what he planned for them all. Her heart went out to his two daughters whom he had loved so much.

'I know this is a very trying time for you both. It is for all of us. But your dad wanted us to be a family. For his sake, we could at least try being friends for the time that's left. Couldn't we?'

Zoe and Emmie regarded her through blank eyes. They were carefully weighing up what she said.

The storm ended as suddenly as it had begun. An unnatural stillness followed. Dust covered everything like red snow, turning the whole Outback into an eerie tapestry. No wind, no turbulence, no sound. The sun resumed command and made the whole scene glisten.

Kate Hannon did not stop to admire the view. Grateful that the crisis was at last over, she went straight to the bathroom and took off all her soiled clothes. The dust had got right through to her skin and left blotches all over her. Kate's fair hair was now a flame-red mass.

She stepped into the old-fashioned cast-iron bath to take a shower. When she turned on the taps, there was a single gurgle of protest and then cold brown water started to trickle down from the rose. Even this was welcome to her. She stood beneath the water and let it run all over her face and head.

It slowly revived her to cope with the toil that awaited.

Nick Stenning pulled the tarpaulin away from his helicopter and sent a shower of red dust down to the ground. The storm had caught him before he was able to get his machine to cover and he had had to improvise. The rotor blades were filmed with dust but the rest of the helicopter had escaped. It now gleamed in the sunshine and its metal panels began to warm up.

Slapping the machine familiarly like a rider patting a horse, he opened the door and climbed inside. As he fastened his seat-belt, he recalled the last time that he had flown and thought about his three passengers. Concern nudged him again. A dust-storm was a trial for even the most hardened bush people. He found himself wondering how Kate and the children had managed.

His mind played with another memory. He was sitting in the shade of a dark rock on the summit of a hill when a woman came looking for him. The effort of reaching him had clearly exhausted her. She asked for help. When he told her to find someone else, she refused to take his rejection and railed at him wildly.

Nick's lips parted in a nostalgic grin.

Then he started up his engine and took off. The helicopter ascended in a cloud of red dust until it reached clearer sky.

He was still grinning as the machine swung away in the sky.

Her hair still damp from the shower, Kate set about the preparations for dinner. A change of clothes had freshened her at once but she was already feeling the heat again. When she opened the refrigerator, she enjoyed the blast of cold air that came out. She found some food then shut the door firmly.

Tina came bursting into the kitchen, holding her hand to her mouth as she coughed. She went straight to the sink and spat into it.

'Ugh!'

'Are you okay, Tina?'

'I must have swallowed dozens!'

'What?'

'Flies!' She grimaced. 'Horrible things!'

Kate was amused. 'In that case, you probably won't need dinner.'

'Mom!'

'I was only joking.'

'Well, it's not funny!' protested the girl. 'Flies carry all kinds of disease. I could die!'

Kate smiled indulgently then crossed over to give her daughter a smacking kiss on the cheek. She stood back to appraise her.

'You look fine to me.'

'I don't feel fine.'

'Honey, I hate to say this but – to use an Aussie expression – you're becoming a bit of a whinger.'

She put comforting arms around Tina and pulled her close.

'It's a difficult time for all of us,' she said quietly, 'and the only way we'll get through is by pulling together. Stop thinking about yourself, Tina. I *know* you didn't want to come to this country and that you loathe everything about it.'

'Not everything . . .'

'Try to consider others. How do you think Zoe and Emmie must be feeling right now?'

'Pretty lousy, I guess.'

'They lost their mother, they lost their father, now they've lost their home.' Kate looked down at her. 'Imagine what it must be like for them. Poor things are completely bewildered.'

'Yeah. Then *we* dump ourselves on them.'

'Exactly. You just count your blessings, young lady.'

Tina brightened. 'Starting with Billy.'

Kate stepped back from her and nodded. Her tone altered. 'You and I must have a chat about Billy some time,' she warned.

'Why?'

'Because I'm not altogether sure he's a good influence on you.'

'I *love* him, Mom!'

'You're only fourteen,' Kate reminded her. 'I don't want you growing up too fast.'

'What are you on about?'

'That book of matches, for a start.'

'Oh . . . yeah . . .' Tina shifted her feet and looked guilty.

'We'll discuss it properly when we get a chance,' her mother promised. 'Meanwhile, keep your chin up. It's only for another couple of weeks.'

'A couple of *weeks*!'

'There's a lot to sort out.'

'But what do I *do* all that time?'

'Make the most of it,' Kate suggested. 'Take photographs for the kids at home. It's not many Americans get the chance to come to Australia. To this part, anyway. This is the heart of the country. Tom told me that . . .'

'Everything will be great once we're home in California.'

Doubts ambushed her mother. Her features darkened. 'I hope so,' she said.

'I'll get my camera.'

Tina kissed her lightly on the cheek then headed for the

living room. Something stopped her and she paused in the doorway.

'By the way, what's a whinger?'

'Someone who never stops complaining.'

Surprise showed. 'Is that *me*?'

'Now and again.'

'Sorry, Mom. I'm trying.'

'Try harder.'

Tina thought about it for a moment, then asked, 'Mom, how do people *live* without TV?'

'I don't know, honey,' Kate replied with amusement. 'It must be hell for them.'

Tina went out. Her mother's smile faded. Tom Hannon kept her company while she began to get the meal ready.

Zoe sat in front of a small pedal organ and played a selection of old melodies. Emmie accompanied her on the recorder with fluctuating success. It was as if they were grinding their way through a practice. Neither of them seemed to be getting any pleasure from the music.

Kate and the twins sat in the living room and listened. It was now evening and they were relaxing after their dinner. The impromptu concert had an air of unreality to it and seemed to increase the division between the two groups, as though the Americans were uninvited guests who were there on sufferance to witness something that was part of normal, everyday life at Larapinta.

Concentration soon wavered. Kate's mind was on Tom again, wishing that they had all been united harmoniously into one family. Tina grabbed a book and buried herself ostentatiously in it.

Marty suffered the most. As a self-appointed music pro, he found the performance very difficult to bear. The music itself was absurdly out of date and he winced at every sour note. In the end, he could take no more and he made an unobtrusive exit to the verandah.

The music followed him out there but he soon blocked it out. Taking out his Sony Walkman, he slipped on the tiny headphones, pressed a button and listened to a rock group instead. Pounding drums and plangent electric guitars soon filled his ears. He was reminded of his own band. Los Angeles now seemed such an enormous distance away.

Feeling very homesick, Marty sat down on the step and gathered up a handful of stones and threw them aimlessly across the darkened yard. There was a bark of interest as the ranch dog stirred in the shadows but the boy heard only the rock music. The first time he became aware of the dog's presence was when it padded along the verandah and nuzzled up to him.

His arm encircled the dog. He suddenly felt lonely and depressed, a teenage boy without a real identity of his own yet, uncertain and unsettled about his future.

'Helly, Bluey!' he said, patting the dog. 'Good boy!'

In this moment of desolation, he hugged the animal for comfort.

The long and punishing day had finally caught up with Kate and she lay sleeping in an armchair in the living room. She had said good night to the children, sat down for a rest and drifted off immediately. The room was now silent and deserted. Night brought coolness.

'Oh dear . . .'

She opened her eyes with a start and looked around. Annoyed that she had fallen asleep in the chair, she hauled herself to her feet and stretched. The light went out with a click.

'Damn!'

Kate groped her way across the room to the switch and flicked it to and fro. Nothing happened. It was as if the generator were waging some sort of vendetta against her. Her body sagged.

Then she heard a door opening in the passageway outside. A circle of light approached the living room. It was Zoe, an apparition in a white nightgown, holding an oil lamp. She came in and stood in front of Kate.

'The generator switches itself off every day between two and five, and again from ten till six in the morning,' she explained in a polite whisper.

'Oh, I see.'

'It's because diesel fuel is so expensive.'

About to leave, she hesitated in the doorway then walked back into the room. Zoe put the lamp down on the table and looked across at Kate. It was the girl's way of trying to atone for her harsh words earlier on, Kate realised, and appreciated the gesture.

'Thank you for letting me know, Zoe.'

'That's okay.'

'And thank you for the lamp.'

'Good night . . .'

The girl went swiftly back to her own room.

Warmed by the brief exchange, Kate reflected for a moment. She hoped that it signified an improvement in relations between the two halves of the Hannon family.

Zoe's consideration was gratifying. It was something to build on.

Auntie Deir threw another handful of meal at her chickens and then stepped back as they clucked around her feet. She cursed them good-humouredly and let herself out of the pen. Feeding them was one of her last chores for the time being. With her husband so ill, she had taken the running of the farm squarely on to her own shoulders and that meant handling the small jobs as well as the big decisions.

Wiping her hands on her skirt, she stumped back into the house.

There was a telephone in the kitchen. She picked it up and dialled the number that she knew by heart, tapping her fingers with impatience on the table as she listened to the ringing tone.

Eventually, there was an answer at the other end of the line.

'Hello,' said a tired voice. 'Who is it?'

'Kate?'

'Is that you, Auntie Deir?'

'Good morning!' said the older woman cheerily. 'Did I wake you?'

'Yes.' A yawn confirmed the fact. 'How are you?'

'Fit as a flea.'

'You got back safely then?'

'Of course. I've been driving through dust-storms for thirty years and more. Never found one yet that got the better of me.' She settled down in a high-backed wooden chair. 'Still, how are you?'

'Okay, I think.'

'You don't sound too sure about it.'

'I'm not.'

Auntie Deir cackled. '*I* feel like that most mornings.' She moved the receiver to her other hand. 'How are the kids?'

'Still asleep?'

'You obviously made out yesterday.'

'Zoe and Emmie were very helpful. They showed us exactly what to do and we all mucked in.'

'I just knew they would!'

'What time are you coming for them?'

'Actually, that's one of the things I'm ringing about,' explained Auntie Deir. 'Would you mind if the girls stayed with you for a bit longer? It'd help me out ... with Ralphie being crook.'

She sensed a reluctance, then Kate's voice came on again.

'Fine.'

'Are you sure?'

'Yes. No problem.'

Kate was hiding her reservations well. Auntie Deir smiled.

'Good,' she continued. 'Now for the main reason I gave you a call. We're having a barbie.'

'A what?'

'A barbie. Don't you people have barbecues in America?'

Kate laughed. 'Oh, is *that* what you mean?'

'Yeah – a barbie. And you're invited.'

'Am I?'

'On Sunday at our place. It's open house. People comin' from all over. Tom's friends.'

'I don't know, Auntie Deir,' said Kate as she considered the idea of a public gathering. 'I'm not sure I could cope.'

'Rubbish! You're the guest of honour.'

'But why?' Kate asked in surprise.

'They're all keen to meet you,' her friend explained. 'Not every day we see a new face out here. We like to be sociable. Besides, people are anxious to do their bit for you.'

'I don't follow.'

'They'll kick in for your fares home.'

'But they don't even know me,' Kate argued.

'They knew Tom – that's enough. A barbie is a way we have of raisin' money out here. Give people plenty to eat and drink and there's no tellin' how much they'll slip into the hat.'

'I couldn't accept charity,' Kate said.

'It's not charity!' Auntie Deir retorted. 'They're doin' it for Tom Hannon. So am I. Don't you disappoint us.'

'Auntie Deir . . .'

'See you on Sunday. Bye.'

She hung up before Kate could say any more.

It was all fixed.

Ed Stenning rode on horseback to the top of a hill that overlooked a huge rolling rust-coloured plain. He was like a king surveying his domain. Down below him, a sea of cattle was being moved by Aboriginal stockmen towards an enormous mobile water-tanker that was already splashing its contents into a line of wooden troughs.

The beasts were thin and fractious, jostling their way noisily towards the water and plunging their snouts straight into it. Some of them seemed to be limping. One straggler could hardly stand.

Ed watched it all with his expression grim.

A rider galloped up the hill towards him and he turned to see who it was. Meg Stenning brought her horse to a halt alongside her father and told him the news.

'We've been invited to a barbecue, Dad.'

'Where?'

'At the Shackletons' on Sunday. To farewell the Hannon widow.'

A tiny smile warmed his features and he nodded. 'So she's going home, is she?'

'Fairly soon.'

'A very wise decision on the lady's part.'

'What else could she do?' Meg sneered. 'She's no bloody use out here. Wouldn't know a steer from a kangaroo.'

'What d'you tell the Shackletons?'

'I said we're busy.'

Ed swung around to gaze in the direction of Larapinta. 'Ring 'em back. Tell 'em we're coming.'

'Are you *serious*, Dad?'

'I'm just about to become the proud owner of Larapinta. Least I can do is to pay my last respects to Tom Hannon.' His smile became a wicked grin. 'Besides, I'm curious to see the kind of woman he married. Aren't you?'

Meg Stenning's eyes were on fire.

— 10 —

Friends and neighbours converged with alacrity on the Shackleton ranch for the barbecue, not only because Auntie Deir always provided excellent food and unlimited drink on such occasions. The chance to meet Kate was too good to miss. News of Tom Hannon's marriage had flashed around the Territory and raised many eyebrows. The fact that his wife was from Los Angeles meant that she was promoted to the status of a glamorous Hollywood star in the minds of some of the locals. Fifty or more of them rolled up to see her.

The barbecue was held in the grounds of the ranch on a hot, humid afternoon. A half-cooked steer turned slowly on a spit over an open fire. With the help of a bevy of women, Auntie Deir organised the food, which continued to be laid out on a mammoth trestle table even though it was already sagging under the strain. Another table was set aside for kegs of beer, bottles of wine and an assortment of soft drinks.

Men and women separated in classic Australian fashion. Keeping their hats on and staying close to the beer, the men swapped stories, moaned about the drought and stole sly glances at Kate.

'Just look at that, mate!'

'I know. I've seen her. Bloody fantastic!'

'Tom Hannon must have been a lucky old devil.'

'Yeah, he had a bit of fun before he rattled the pan.'

'Bet he died with a smile on his face.'

'I wouldn't mind a Sheila like that to warm my bed.'

The women formed another group, complaining about

their husbands, discussing their children, catching up on the latest gossip. They, too, were intrigued to see Kate and to compare her with Tom's first wife. Her figure and complexion were an immediate source of envy.

Children of all ages had been brought along and they were soon creating their own fun, playing games together or darting in and out of the various clusters of people. Accustomed to the suffocating heat, they never seemed to droop or tire.

Everybody appeared to be having a wonderful time and a surface good humour predominated. Underlying it all, however, were conflicting attitudes to the American visitors. At one and the same moment, Kate and the twins were admired, resented, welcomed, rebuffed, flattered and teased. No one was completely at ease with them.

Kate herself sensed it at once. Still deeply affected by Tom's death, she nevertheless made the effort to be open and friendly in a way that she knew her husband would have wanted her to be. After all, she reminded herself, if Tom had lived then these people would have been her friends as well.

Marty and Tina found themselves on the outside looking in. The other children stared at them but were too shy to approach them or involve them in their play. Marty wearied of being the centre of so much attention and he drifted off quietly in the direction of the barn, taking out his Sony Walkman and putting on his headphones with their futuristic aerials. His sister trailed after him.

Trees offered shade and many people congregated beneath them.

Kate stood beside a gnarled trunk with her host, Ralph Shackleton, a forthright man in his late fifties whose shrunken frame was stark evidence of the disease that was eating him up. Perspiration was moistening his brow.

'They reckon you get used to the heat,' he said wearily, 'but Deir and I have lived in the Outback for thirty-five years and it still knocks me about.' He gave a sardonic smile. 'I hope Heaven's cooler.'

'Heaven?' she repeated.

'Hasn't Deir told you? I've got cancer.'

'Oh . . .'

'Don't be embarrassed,' he continued quickly. 'I like it to be out in the open. Saves people whispering behind your back. That would really get me down.'

Kate stayed respectfully silent.

Her attention was diverted by some new arrivals. The striking figure of a smartly dressed old man causing a deferential response all round. His features were so exactly mirrored in the woman at his side that she had to be his daughter.

Kate observed that the newcomers greeted no one. They let people flock to them to offer a welcome.

'Who are they, Ralph?'

'Ed Stenning and his daughter Meg.'

Her interest sharpened and she realised why the old man looked so familiar. Kate had already met a younger version of him.

'There's a son as well, isn't there?'

'Nick. Bit of a loner.'

'He and the old man are always at each other's throats, I'm told. Do you know why?'

'Take a look at Ed and you'll see for yourself. He's got tyrant written all over him. Nick won't be pushed around.'

Kate sipped her drink and became thoughtful. 'Ralph . . .'

'Yep?'

'What about this feud between the Hannons and the Stennings? How long has it been going on?'

'Too long, Kate,' he replied. 'Personally, I think it's bloody silly, the whole thing. A load of nonsense.'

'Why?'

Before he could tell her, they were interrupted by the arrival of a tall, affable man who stood smiling in front of Kate.

Ralph performed the introductions with a wave of his hand.

'Kate – meet Henry Dingwell.'

'Hello,' she said, shaking the newcomer's hand.

'Tom's lawyer,' he explained. 'G'day. Nice to meet you.' He winked at the other man. 'Like I always said, Tom had good taste in cattle and women.'

Ralph chuckled and Kate accepted the compliment with a grin.

Henry Dingwell was something of a surprise. Uncoordinated, untidy in his dress and with an over-casual manner, he was more like a reclaimed sixties hippie than an astute and successful Alice Springs lawyer. Kate warmed to him at once. She could trust him.

Dingwell turned a shrewd eye on Ralph Shackleton. 'Mate, for a dying man, you're looking bloody healthy.'

Kate was shocked by his frankness but Ralph was amused.

'I like to keep 'em all guessing, Henry,' he said.

'You're succeeding.' He turned to Kate. 'I thought if it was convenient, I'd drive down and we can sort out all the legal business.'

The prospect filled her with misgivings but she nodded. 'That'd be fine.'

'Tom was a good man. I'm sorry.'

Auntie Deir now burst upon the scene with a collapsible chair under her arm. She issued a breathless warning to Kate.

'Here come the Stennings. Watch out for Meg.'

'Why her?'

'She can be a real bitch when she tries. I only asked 'em because I thought they'd be a good touch.'

'Yes,' agreed Dingwell. 'The Stennings could afford to send us *all* back to America.'

'Y'don't need to curtsy to 'em, Kate,' joked Auntie Deir. She then opened the chair, plonked it firmly down and gave a command to her husband. 'You can just *sit* before you collapse.'

'Don't fuss, woman.'

'Don't argue!' she countered affectionately.

Ralph lowered himself into the chair as Ed and Meg Stenning came up. Kate was introduced to them and greetings were exchanged all round. The Stennings focused at once on the guest of honour.

Ed's eyes probed her. His manner was gruffly solicitous. 'Sorry about your husband, Mrs Hannon. Must've been a real shock.'

'It was, Mr Stenning.'

'Anyhow, you're doing the right thing – heading back to America. The Outback's no place for a woman.'

She found his steady gaze intimidating without knowing why.

Meg had been assessing the other woman carefully. Kate was wearing her best summer dress, a low-cut cotton garment in pale blue. It had not been very expensive but it was so chic that it made all the other women present look dowdy and provincial. Meg did not like the feeling of being out-gunned.

'Life here is very different from California,' she sneered.

'Have you been to California, Miss Stenning?'

'Sure, but I can't say I was all that impressed.'

'Why not?'

'I found it very superficial.'

'It has an honest vulgarity.'

'I wouldn't know.'

Her patronising tone caught Kate on the quick. She retaliated.

'About the vulgarity? Or the honesty?'

She had issued a challenge and they all heard it. Meg bristled.

A flicker of amusement passed across Ed's countenance. 'Come on, Meg,' he said, taking her arm. 'We mustn't monopolise Mrs Hannon.' He turned to Dingwell. 'Henry – got a minute?'

'Sure,' the lawyer replied.

'Goodbye,' drawled Ed. 'A safe trip home.'

'Thank you,' Kate answered.

'I'm so glad you came,' Meg added frostily.

The group broke up and Ed moved away with Meg and Dingwell.

'Well?' said Auntie Deir. 'What do you think of 'em?'

'Bit much to take, aren't they?' Ralph commented.

'Yes,' Kate agreed. 'They make me feel glad I'm going back home to California . . .'

Ed Stenning took Dingwell aside and handed him a sealed envelope.

'Here's my formal offer f'r Larapinta.'

'Aren't you jumping the gun?' the lawyer suggested.

'There's a cheque inside. A down payment. See the lady gets it.'

'Ed, Kate Hannon hasn't officially told me yet that she's selling.'

'Of course she'll sell,' snapped the old man. 'What else can she do, Henry?'

Dingwell had no chance to reply. Before he could open his mouth, a loud whirring noise in the sky distracted them. There was a general commotion and the children were excited. A helicopter was coming in to land.

Nick Stenning was joining the barbecue.

'Looks like the Prodigal Son has arrived,' remarked Dingwell with irony. 'Just as well we have a fatted calf handy.'

Ed shot him a look of thunder then barked to his daughter, 'Meg! We're leaving.'

'Why the hell should we? He's not going to frighten *me* away.'

Ed's face was granite and his tone peremptory. 'I'll see you at the car, Meg.'

He stalked off through the crowd.

The helicopter skimmed a fence and shot in low, bringing a welcome draught of cold air and causing a few screams of laughter as some of the women's dresses were blown up. After swooping up then corkscrewing in the air, the machine made a dramatic landing nearby to a smattering of applause.

Auntie Deir watched Nick Stenning get out.

'Well!' she exclaimed. 'There's a turn-up for the book!'

Kate Hannon stood beside the barbecue fire and carved meat from the cooked carcass. The heat was intense and the smoke made her cough but she stuck to her task.

A young jackaroo helped himself to some of the meat.

'You're a real good carver.'

'Thanks.'

'I'll be back for more later.'

'There's plenty left.'

The jackaroo sauntered off with his plate piled high.

Kate's eyes were streaming now but she did not step back from the fire. Determined to avoid Nick, she busied herself by slicing more meat from the steer before stacking it on a large metal plate.

Another customer came over to her and she glanced up. Through the billowing smoke, she saw Nick Stenning.

'I didn't expect to meet you here,' she observed coolly.

'Like I said, you never know your luck . . .' His smile faded and his expression became serious. 'I wanted to tell you how sorry I am. About Tom.'

'Thanks,' she replied politely.

'Brave man. I take my hat off to anyone who stands up to my father. And that's what Tom Hannon did.'

She continued to carve away even though her eyes were stinging more than ever. He watched her with interest for a few moments.

'How're you feeling?'

'Like everyone's favourite charity.'

'Does that worry you?'

'When you've supported yourself and two children for the past twelve years . . . it does, yes.'

He looked around and his eyes roved the crowd.

'They mean well.'

'I know that,' she admitted. 'And I don't want to sound

ungrateful. I appreciate what everybody's doing for me.'

'But you have your pride.'

'Yes, Mr Stenning. I do.'

He took the carving knife and the fork from her hands. 'Allow me,' he offered.

'Thank you.'

He started to carve with practised skill.

'So you're running away, are you?' he said.

'What?'

'Turning tail because you haven't got the guts to stay.'

Her temper flared and she almost snarled at him. 'I don't know what the Australian equivalent for "go to hell" is, Mr Stenning – but I wish you would! Excuse me.'

She tried to walk past him but he grabbed her arm just firmly enough to restrain her.

'Tom Hannon loved Larapinta.' He spoke with evident passion. 'It was a great property once. It could be again. This drought can't last for ever.' He put his face close to hers. 'If you go running back to the States like a frightened rabbit, my father will take it over like he's taken over everyone else in his life.'

She struggled to pull away but he held her fast.

'Will you please let me go!' she insisted. 'I don't see that any of this is your damn business, Mr Stenning. I can't even imagine what you're doing here!'

He released her arm. Thrusting a hand into his pocket, he brought out a wad of money and closed her fingers around it before she had time to protest.

'My contribution to the fund. Good luck, Mrs Hannon.'

She glared at him in silent outrage, about to hurl the money straight back in his face. But there was a sudden interruption.

Tina rushed up, breathless and on the brink of hysteria.

'Mom, come quickly! They're killing Marty.'

'Where?'

'Behind the barn.'

Kate raced off with her daughter and the money fluttered to the ground, discarded and forgotten. Nick glanced down at it.

Then his eyes lifted to stare thoughtfully after Kate.

The crowd of children had been joined by a few adults. They formed a circle around the combatants and urged them on, yelling, barracking and cheering. Nobody tried to intervene.

Zoe and Emmie stood apart from the other spectators and watched it all with deadpan expressions. More people came running to swell the crowd and the volume of noise increased.

Marty was rolling on the ground with Johnno, a local boy who was bigger and stronger than him. Caked with sweat and dirt, they kicked and punched as they tried to gain the advantage. The fight had got out of hand now. Both of them wanted to stop but they were unable to, intimidated by the baying spectators, driven on to further efforts.

Kate ran up and pushed her way through the press of bodies.

'Someone stop it!' she cried. 'Stop them! Please! What kind of people are you?'

But her voice went unheard in the general uproar.

Johnno now pinned Marty to the ground and pushed down hard on his face with the heel of his hand, almost suffocating him. Blood was pouring from a cut on Marty's forehead and a dark bruise was forming under the other boy's eye.

The wild roar of the crowd drummed in their ears.

'Smash him, Johnno!'

'Kill the Yankee bastard!'

'Kick his head in!'

'Go on, mate!'

Within seconds it was all over.

Nick Stenning shouldered his way to the combatants and wrenched them apart. He dragged them to their feet and stood between them. Marty and Johnno were now covered in grime and panting heavily.

The crowd fell silent. Some of the adults looked shame-faced.

Nick snapped an order to the two boys. 'Okay – shake hands.'

Marty was the first to respond but his opponent held back.

'Johnno . . .' said Nick, warningly.

The boy accepted Marty's hand and shook it.

'My God!' exclaimed Kate, seeing the state her son was in.

Marty's eyes pleaded with her to play it down. 'I'm okay, Mom . . .'

Some women had now arrived and they began to chastise their children and husbands. Auntie Deir added her disapproval.

'This won't do a bloody thing for Australian-American relations!' She waved them all away with disgust. 'Orright! Show's over . . .'

The men dispersed. Johnno's mother let him know what she felt about it all by giving her son a resounding clip on the ear. Emmie giggled. Zoe, however, was still watching Marty. She now had a glimmer of respect for him.

Nick turned to Kate and tried to soothe her. 'No serious damage.'

'I'll be the judge of that, Mr Stenning!' she retorted.

'At least *someone* in the family is a fighter!'

He turned abruptly and headed back towards the house.

Furious and wounded, Kate wanted to go after him but she checked herself. Instead, she took out a handkerchief and thrust it at Marty.

'Here. Get yourself cleaned up.'

While he was using the handkerchief to stem the flow of blood on his forehead, Marty was handed his Sony Walkman by one of the other boys. He noticed that Johnno was eyeing it with interest.

'You wanna listen?' he offered.

'Yeahhhh!'

Johnno took the Walkman and put the headphones on.

Now that the fight was over, he was as keen to make amends as Marty.

'Like to see my dingo pup?'

Marty beamed. 'Sure!'

The two boys marched off happily together.

Tina watched them go, feeling shut out and betrayed. Tears began to trickle. Needing to be alone, she scurried off in the opposite direction. Kate heaved a sigh. She was at a loss to understand her children sometimes.

Then she remembered Nick Stenning and set off purposefully towards the house. As her anger built, she rehearsed all the things she was going to tell him. His blatant rudeness had caught her on the raw and she intended to hit back hard so that he would never bother her again.

But she did not get the opportunity to say anything.

As she rejoined the barbecue and searched for him, a burst of laughter went up. Nick Stenning was striding towards his helicopter with an attractive young woman in his arms. She was putting up a token resistance but her delighted smile showed that she was more than willing to be borne off by the handsome pilot.

Kate was at once shocked and nonplussed. Nick was hardly being discreet about his intentions. She watched as he bundled the girl into his helicopter then clambered in after her. The couple were soon spiralling up into the sky.

It threw Kate into a state of confusion.

Her fury was tempered by a strange pang of jealousy.

The flat-top truck rolled over the plain and took note of all its humps and hollows. The twins sat in the back with Zoe and Emmie, who were clearly dejected because they could not stay at the Shackleton ranch. Marty was proudly bearing the battle scars from his fight with Johnno. Between his knees was the plastic bucket that had been used to collect the donations towards their air fare.

Tina kept staring at the pile of crisp notes. 'How much do you think there is, Marty?'

'Enough to get Mom and me back to the States.'

'What about me?'

'You'll have to stay here,' he teased. 'I'll explain to Billy.'

His sister gave him a dig with her elbow.

Kate Hannon was driving the truck, her mind in a turmoil as she tried to sort out the mixed emotions she experienced when she met Nick Stenning. Anger still dominated. The accusation that she was running away continued to hurt her deeply.

She had never fled anything in her life.

As they approached the Larapinta homestead, without warning, the truck juddered to a halt and flung its young passengers about.

'Steady on, Mom!' protested Marty.

'What are you trying to do?' wailed Tina.

Zoe realised at once that there was trouble. She leaped to her feet and looked towards the compound. A restless mass of cattle milled around the house water tanks, lowing noisily and trying to dislodge them, kicking up a dust-cloud with their hooves.

Eyes blazing, Zoe swung round to confront Marty. 'Someone left the gate open!'

'I didn't!' he replied.

'Then who did?'

'It was me,' Tina confessed meekly. 'I didn't realise . . . Why have they come?'

'They're after the water,' said Zoe.

'What do we do?' Kate asked.

Zoe led by example. She jumped out of the truck and ran towards the homestead. The others were soon chasing after her.

There was no time to lose. It was an emergency.

— 11 —

Over a hundred cattle were now inside the gates and some of them were pressing against the supports that held the water tanks. Bluey, the dog, was adding to the confusion by circling the herd at frantic speed and barking madly. The cattle were becoming even more restive.

'Drive them back!' called Zoe. 'Before they knock down the tanks.'

'There are so many of them,' said Tina in alarm.

'Yeah,' Marty agreed. 'Look at those horns!'

'Make for the house,' Kate urged.

She skirted the main mass of cattle and got to the house. The children followed her then turned round to face the invaders. It was a daunting sight. Agitated cattle were lurching and stamping everywhere, their eyes rolling and their tongues hanging out as they sensed the presence of water. Bluey was nipping expertly at their heels but the animals were not put to flight.

Kate and the children advanced on the herd, yelling aloud and waving their arms but the cattle ignored them. Intense thirst had brought them to the homestead and they were not going to yield any ground. They continued to surge towards the water tanks.

'It's hopeless!' cried Tina.

'We need horses and whips,' Marty added.

'Keep trying!' Emmie shouted.

'If only the gate hadn't been left open!' Zoe said bitterly.

Kate looked at the moving tide of cattle and came to a swift decision. She pointed to the troughs in the middle of the yard.

'Use the hose and fill them up!'

'That's *our* water!' argued Zoe, outraged by the idea.

'There's enough.'

'One bore can't provide water for five thousand. It's stupid!' Zoe screeched angrily above the clamour, resenting Kate for taking charge.

Kate was in a quandary but she was not going to back down.

'Well, we don't have five thousand here,' she retorted. 'Maybe a hundred. And it's a choice between giving them water or having them stampede through the house.'

'It just won't work!' Zoe screamed.

'We'll see.'

Without waiting for more argument, Kate ran to the hose and fixed it to the nearest tap, screwing it in tight. The hose was thick and heavy. Dragging it behind her, Kate tried to force a way through the mass of cattle, buffeted by their flanks and dodging their horns as they flailed murderously about. The noise was ear-splitting and dust filled her eyes and nose and mouth.

'She'll never do it,' Zoe warned. 'They'll crush her.'

'Isn't there something we can do to help?' yelled Marty.

Kate was struck sideways as a steer suddenly backed into her and she dropped the hose. Zoe sprang into action. Grabbing a stick, she used it to prod the cattle, trying to create a diversion that would ensure Kate's safety. Marty watched the girl and understood. He joined her in pushing and waving back the restless animals.

Tina and Emmie stood beside the tap in a state of fear.

'Mom could get killed out there!'

'She's certainly brave,' Emmie conceded.

'They'll trample her!'

Kate was very alive to the dangers. The hose was now beneath the feet of one of the steers and she had to force it aside so that she could reach down. Another large, sweating body cannoned into her. She lost her balance and pitched to the ground. Flashing hooves were all around her. Large, menacing shapes moved wildly about.

138

The noise was like thunder inside her head. Dust in her throat made her cough and retch. A leg kicked her and she winced in pain. Another leg caught her a glancing blow on the head.

'Get back!' she howled. 'Get off me!'

Struggling to her knees, she held out both arms to ward off her attackers. She was aching all over now and fear had hollowed her stomach but she knew that she had to go on. It was not simply the threat to the house. Her authority was at stake. If she failed in front of the children, she would lose her credibility.

'Give me that hose!' she demanded.

It had been kicked further away from her now and she went after it with new determination, thrusting the steers out of the way with both palms and ignoring a tail that lashed into her face. With a sudden grab, she got hold of the hose again and pulled it on towards the troughs.

Marty and Zoe were doing what they could but the main group of cattle was still bunched around Kate. Tina and Emmie were getting more terrified with every second. If the cattle resorted to panic, they knew Kate would stand no chance at all.

'Be careful, Mom!' shrieked Tina.

'They can get real mean, those cattle,' Emmie warned.

'Oh, no! She's gone down again!'

Kate had tripped over the hose and crashed down hard. Ignoring the fierce pain, she got up again at once as a dozen feet danced perilously close to her. Now almost fully uncoiled, the hose was heavier than ever and it took all her strength to pull it. As one more heaving flank bounced into her, she almost dropped it.

The pressures on her were overwhelming. Covered in sweat and smarting from her injuries, she was being pushed about by solid bodies that closed in on her. The noise, the stench and the chaos were like physical blows. And she was also contending with the hostility of Tom's children.

'I'm not going under,' she vowed. 'I'll get there.'

Winding the hose around her waist, she tied it in a knot so that she could pull it onwards while having both hands free to protect herself. She lurched forward and got within sight of the troughs. It gave her extra impetus.

'She's gonna make it!' shouted Tina. 'Well done, Mom!'

When Kate got within ten yards of the troughs, the hose jerked tight around her waist. Though she untied it and used both hands to heave on it, she could not budge it. Somewhere in the press of bodies, feet were holding the hose down.

'Okay! Let's try again!' she said to herself.

Kate thrust herself back amongst the steers, fighting through the barrage of noise and trying to scatter them without producing a stampede. Through the thickening dust, she saw two front hooves of a scrawny cow firmly standing on the hose. Its horns glinted as she approached and its eyes rolled in apprehension. Kate got round behind it and slapped it hard on the rump. It jumped forward.

The hose was now free and she could go back to the nozzle. It took another bruising journey but she eventually dragged the hose on to the first trough. With what little breath remained, she called out, 'Okay! Switch on!'

Tina turned on the tap and water gushed. As it slurped into the trough, the cattle rushed forward and struggled to get their noses into the water. More and more of them swung away from the house tanks.

By the time that Kate filled another trough, all the animals had trotted over. The attack on the house tanks was abandoned and the threat was past. When they had slaked their thirst, the cattle would be docile enough to be herded back to the plain and locked out of the homestead compound.

Kate's initiative had saved the day.

'Yippee!' shouted Marty.

'Well done, Mom!' yelled Tina.

Dirty, dishevelled and tired, Kate gave a smile of triumph. 'We did it!'

Even Zoe now had a sneaking admiration for her.

Night drew a blanket of darkness over the Larapinta ranch. The children withdrew to their rooms but none of them was really sleepy. Zoe and Emmie lay sprawled on one of the beds, holding a family album under the light of an oil lamp and suffering afresh each time they turned over a page and awoke a new memory.

'This one was taken when Mom was alive,' Zoe noted.

'I know. It was at Auntie Deir's birthday party.'

'That's Dad in the background, talking to Uncle Ralph . . .'

Both of them were affected by the snapshot in which all four of them appeared. Now only two of them were left. Emmie began to sob quietly and Zoe felt a lump in her throat.

A knock on their door made them tense and sit up.

'Who's there?' Zoe asked defensively.

The door opened and Tina wandered in, wearing her nightdress.

'Hi,' she said.

'Hi,' Zoe replied warily.

'What do you want?' asked Emmie.

'I only came to say . . . I'm sorry about your father.' Tina had difficulty in forcing out the words.

Zoe stared blankly at her. Emmie continued to sob.

'Really . . .'

They remained silent but Tina had made contact with them. Her sentiments were genuine. The two sisters realised that.

After a while, the visitor withdrew quietly from the room.

Kate finished cleaning the kitchen and put the last things away. It was time for her to retire to bed herself and to review a day which had given her ample food for thought. Nick Stenning's remarks kept buzzing in her ears. He believed that she was running away.

Taking up the oil lamp, she went over to the back door

to lock it. As her hand settled on the bolt, she looked out through the flywire and was given a bad fright.

Leering in at her through the wire were two faces.

They were ugly, watchful, menacing. Faces that seemed to belong to the dark. Both were split by sly grins. Kate fell back, afraid.

'Gidday,' said the younger of the two men.

'What do you want?' she gasped.

'I'm Bert Simpson,' he drawled in a rough Outback voice. 'This is me Dad. Your old man owed us money.'

'Oh. I'm sorry . . .'

'Y'see, m'Dad's a water-diviner.'

'Ah!' confirmed his father.

'Best in the business. Everyone can tell you about Simmo.'

'Your husband had me under contract,' explained the old man. 'Dousin' f'r weeks.' He produced a grubby docket book and thrust it against the wire. 'See? I got it all written down.'

'Dad always keeps his records up to date, Mrs 'annon.'

'I come to get the account settled.'

Kate felt frightened and vulnerable. The strangers had unnerved her. Seen through the mesh of the flywire, they looked like wild beasts who had come out of the night to spy on her. Their eyes glinted in the lamplight and she was reminded all too clearly of the dingoes whom she had confronted in the kitchen.

She had sensed danger then and did so again now.

'My husband's dead,' she told them.

'Yeah,' Bert said easily. 'Bloody shame.'

'Good man,' added Simmo. 'Always paid his debts.'

'You'll have to talk to his lawyer,' she replied.

'Lawyer?' Simmo did not like the idea.

'I can't help you.'

'Hey,' warned Bert. 'Come on now . . .'

'We want our money!' insisted his father. 'Right now!'

Bert tried the door and was annoyed to find that it was bolted. He shook it hard and it rattled on its hinges. He looked more than strong enough to knock the door down if he chose.

'I don't have the money,' Kate argued.

Simmo pushed his son aside so that he could press his face hard against the wire. His rheumy eyes were gleaming with hatred.

'I want that bloody money! Nobody cons me!'

'Call Henry Dingwell,' she rejoined.

'Pay up – or I come in and get it!'

The threat was no idle one. Kate knew that she would have to deal with the situation firmly. She struggled for outward calm then took a step towards them.

'I keep a rifle here,' she declared. 'If you come here again, I'll use it. Now get out!'

She slammed the inner door and bolted it hurriedly, leaning against it with a pounding heart and hoping that they would leave. Feet trudged away from the house. She sagged with relief.

Kate knew she had not heard the last of them. They would be back.

Nick Stenning lay on the bed with his hands behind his head and reflected on the barbecue the previous day. In his brief stop at the Shackleton ranch, he had made his presence felt. He had scared off his father and sister, stopped a fight and roused Kate Hannon to a pitch of fury. He grinned as he recalled the way she had told him to go to hell. Most men would not have dared to do that.

The girl beside him woke, purred and rolled over to him.

'Hello, darling,' she said drowsily. 'Welcome to the day.'

He was irritated to have his thoughts interrupted.

'Come back under the sheets with me,' she murmured. She ran a hand down his naked body but he caught her wrist.

'Get dressed,' he snapped. 'You're going home.'

Henry Dingwell sat at the head of the table with his papers spread out before him and a glass of beer at hand. Kate and the twins were on one side of him and Zoe and Emmie sat opposite them. They were in the kitchen at the Larapinta house and tension was apparent.

Dingwell did his best to put them all in the picture.

'What it comes down to is that Tom didn't leave much in the way of cash – apart from the two hundred thousand he borrowed from his sister. That money's in a special account in Glenwarra.' He sampled his beer then regarded Kate shrewdly. 'Larapinta's carrying a pretty hefty mortgage. The logical move seems to be to put it up for sale.'

Zoe rose to her feet with a shriek of protest. 'No! This is our home!'

'Sit down, Zoe,' he advised.

'Why should we go to America?' she demanded. 'We don't even *know* Aunt Molly. We want to stay here.'

'That's right,' Emmie agreed. 'At Larapinta.'

'It's just not fair to sell the place over our heads.' Zoe was vehement. 'We have rights, don't we?'

'Of course,' soothed Dingwell. 'And nothing is going to be done in a rush, I promise you. It will all be fully discussed with your stepmother.'

'She's not my mother!' argued Zoe, pointing a finger at Kate. 'I didn't choose her and I don't want her. Why should I be part of her family?' She widened her attack to include the twins. 'They're the ones who should go back to America. They don't belong here and they can't cope. Send them home. Let us stay!'

There was general commotion. Marty and Tina jumped in defensively. Emmie said that she agreed with her sister. Dingwell tried to reason with them all. As the row escalated, he telegraphed to Kate for help with a look of despair.

'Calm down, everybody,' she said firmly. 'Why don't we let Mr Dingwell finish? We can discuss it all later.'

'I've heard enough,' Zoe announced with defiance.

It was a direct challenge to Kate and she took it up.

'You'll sit down again and listen quietly,' she ordered.

'No, I won't,' rejoined the girl. She turned to her sister. 'Come on, Emmie. We're going to our room.'

But Emmie did not move. While she agreed with much of what Zoe had said, she was not at all sure that they should defy the adults. In the final analysis, the two sisters would not make the important decisions. They would have to go along with what Kate decreed. Younger and less assertive than Zoe, she was too frightened to stand up against the others indefinitely. It was time to compromise.

'Come on!' urged Zoe, waiting at the door.

'I'm staying here,' whispered her sister.

Zoe quailed visibly. Suddenly, she was isolated. She was fighting them all on her own. They had driven a wedge between her and Emmie. It did not change her resolve. Mustering what dignity she could, Zoe went out through the door and closed it behind her.

'Wow!' murmured Marty.

Caught on the raw by what she had said about them, he nevertheless admired her for her stance. It took courage to do what Zoe had just done and it deepened his affection for her.

Emmie bit her lip as tears threatened. Kate went swiftly round the table to sit beside her and place a comforting arm around her. The girl responded to the sympathy with a sad smile.

Kate looked over at the lawyer. 'Fire away, Henry.'

'Right,' said Dingwell. 'Now someone's made an offer for the place and it's not real bad, all things considered.'

'Who is it?' she asked.

'Ed Stenning.'

'I thought it might be, somehow.'

'I'm holding his cheque with a formal offer of purchase.'

'Why does he want the place so much?'

'Because he hates it.'

She was startled. 'Doesn't make sense.'

'Ed Stenning hated the whole Hannon family,' he explained. 'Getting hold of Larapinta means that he's wiped them out.'

Kate was baffled. It was all beyond her. 'Look, what *is* this feud everyone keeps talking about?'

'It would take far too long to go into all that.'

'If it's so serious, why didn't Tom mention it to me?'

'Because he didn't want to open that particular can of worms, Kate. No more do I. Just accept it as fact and leave it at that.'

'*Why* does he hate the Hannon family?' she persisted.

Dingwell threw a considerate glance at Emmie, whose face was tight with fear and embarrassment. He leaned over to Kate. 'Let sleeping dogs lie,' he counselled.

Kate shrugged and turned to the task in hand. Almost as soon as she had taken possession of Larapinta, she was being advised to sell it. Such a major step needed to be taken with great care.

'What would you do in my position?' she asked him.

'Really want to know?'

'Yes.'

'Well, to start with,' he quipped, 'I wouldn't have married Tom Hannon. It would have done my image no good at all.'

They all laughed. It helped to ease the tension.

Dingwell remembered something and reached into his briefcase to take out a square object in a large brown envelope. He offered it to Kate.

'This might help you to make up your mind.'

'What is it?'

'We found it in the plane. I thought you should have it. It's Tom's diary.'

She accepted it from him with her emotions in a whirl.

The sun was a fiery ball that balanced on the horizon, casting its golden glow over the arid land. Somewhere in the distance, the familiar howl of a dingo cut through the stillness.

Kate sat alone on the verandah with the diary in her lap. She was so engrossed in it that she did not even notice the flies buzzing around her head or the ranch dog chasing its tail in the yard.

Eventually, she put the diary aside with a soft moan.

'Oh, Tom . . .'

She was utterly devastated, speared by a sense of loss and tortured by the thought of what might have been. The diary was full of hope and love and promise. None of it was left. Instead of coming into a new home with a devoted husband, she was marooned in a wilderness without money and without friends. Her anguish brimmed over into hot tears.

Sunset evanesced into night and she was still in her chair. When she finally dragged herself up and went into the house, she felt that she knew Tom much better than she had before and understood more clearly why she had been drawn to share her life with him. In the light of his cruel death, the diary took on an added poignancy that plucked at her heart without respite.

'Why did you leave me, Tom? I *need* you!'

As she lay in bed, the pain of separation deepened to become a dull, insistent ache that racked her whole body. The diary was a memory that burned through her tired brain.

She could hear Tom Hannon's voice as distinctly as if he were beside her in his rightful place: in the marriage bed.

My sweet Kate . . . I don't know if you'll ever read this. I'm not so good with words so I'll let my heart do the talking. Meeting you is the best thing that's happened to me in a long time. I'm honoured you've agreed to be my wife and grateful that the girls will have the mother they've needed for so long. We'll be a family again. I pray to God that, in time, you'll come to regard Larapinta as your true home.

She reached impulsively across for him but he was gone.

'Tom . . . I can't manage without you,' she whispered.

Then his words returned to echo in her mind.

'. . . come to regard Larapinta as your true home . . .'

Kate could not betray his dearest hopes. She could not deliver the ranch he loved to the man he hated. The diary had scoured her soul but it had prompted her to think everything through.

She had guidance. She knew what to do.

'What's going on?' complained Marty, bleary-eyed.

'It's the middle of the night!' Tina yawned.

'Has something happened?' wondered Zoe, still half-asleep.

The four children trooped into the living room and flopped down. Roused at daybreak, they were at once puzzled and irritated. Why had Kate got them out of their beds so early.

Marty gaped in astonishment and came fully awake. 'Mom – what have you done to yourself?'

Tina approved. 'Hey, you look great!'

Zoe and Emmie hardly recognised the woman who sat opposite them.

For the first time since she came to the ranch, Kate looked like a real countrywoman. She wore jeans, shirt and boots. Without make-up, her face was somehow different. There was a purposive, down-to-earth quality about her now.

The total transformation was more than a change of clothes. It was a commitment.

'I want to tell you that I've made a decision,' she said.

'About what?' asked Marty.

'Under the circumstances, I believe it's what's best for all of us.' She paused, looked at the four young faces then delivered her message. 'We're staying on here – for the time being, anyway. And we're going to keep the place running.'

The children were incredulous. Despair whitewashed Marty and Tina while a flicker of hope revived Zoe and Emmie. They all sat there and gaped while Kate issued a warning.

'I expect you all to make an effort to get along. It'll be less tough on everybody. Remember — we're in this together.'

'It's not fair!' Tina howled.

'We want to go back home!' Marty supported her.

Kate confronted them with controlled calm. '*I* make the rules here,' she announced. 'When you're eighteen, you go where you like, do what you like. But for now, it's my way. I hope that's clearly understood by everyone?'

All four children were shocked into total silence.

The flat-top truck from Larapinta rattled across the cattle grid between the stately gateposts of Cutta Cutta. When it drew up in front of the house, it lurched to a halt and the engine died.

Kate Hannon jumped out with an envelope in her hand. She was in no way overawed by the sight of the imposing homestead and she was not cowed by the prospect of tackling the man who lived there. With her adrenalin flowing, she skipped up to the main door and banged on it hard with her fist.

Meg Stenning came to open it for her and reacted with amazement.

'I've come to see your father,' Kate announced.

'He's busy.'

'I think he'll see me.'

'Ring and make an appointment.'

'It's about the sale of Larapinta.'

Meg's hostility waned slightly and she nodded. 'You'd better come on in.'

Kate was led along a wide passageway lined with antique furniture. The carpet had a luxurious feel to it and expensive prints adorned the walls.

Meg knocked on the door of the study then took her in.

Ed Stenning was seated behind the desk in a huge, leather-backed chair with gold studding around its

149

edges He looked up from his papers and blinked in surprise.

'Sorry if I'm disturbing you,' said Kate briskly.

Playing the gentleman, he rose from his seat and smiled. 'Depends on why you're here, Mrs Hannon.'

'I'm returning your cheque.'

She held it out to him but he did not take it. His smile was replaced by a flint-eyed mask of enmity. 'What did you say?' he growled quietly.

'Larapinta isn't for sale,' she explained.

He shot his daughter a look then glowered at Kate. 'Why not?'

'Because I've decided to stay.'

'This doesn't make sense.' Reluctantly, he took the envelope from her and fingered it.

'I intend to keep Larapinta running.'

He laughed harshly. 'All by yourself?'

'Any way I can,' she retorted.

He placed the cheque on his desk with slow deliberation.

'I can wait, Mrs Hannon. In a month or two, you'll be down on your knees, begging me to buy.' Menace thickened his voice. 'And this delay's going to cost you. Plenty.'

Kate confronted them both with iron determination. 'We're going to find water. It's got to be there somewhere. We'll drill until we have all the water we need.'

'You don't have the money to drill,' Meg taunted.

'I'll get it.'

'Not from any banker round here,' Ed warned.

'Have you got *them* in your pocket as well, Mr Stenning?'

His rage burst out and he thumped the desk with his fist.

'You're out of your mind!' he snarled. 'What do you know about running a ranch and raising cattle? You've only been in the country five minutes. Tom Hannon was born and bred here and even he couldn't make a go of it

at Larapinta. How can you succeed where he failed?'
Disgust filled his words. 'You know *nothing*!'

'I can learn.'

'While you're learning, your steers are dying,' Meg
smirked.

'We'll make out somehow.'

'It's suicide,' Meg rejoined.

'Excuse me.' Kate spun round and headed quickly for
the door.

'Mrs Hannon . . .!'

Ed's rasping cry made her pause and turn back.

'You haven't got a hope in hell!'

Kate accepted the challenge without hesitation. 'We'll
see, Mr Stenning. We'll see . . .'

She was out through the door in an instant.

Auntie Deir gave her husband his medicine then tucked
him into his chair so that he could have his nap. It pained
her to see him wasting away in front of her but she had
promised herself that she would look after him to the end.
Ralph and she had been together for a very long time
and she did not want it all to end in the impersonal
surroundings of a hospital.

She heard the sound of a truck approaching and went
out to investigate. It was Kate. She was at once pleased
and astonished. The woman who stepped down from the
cab was not the one she had met before.

'Come along into the kitchen,' she invited.

'Thanks . . .' Kate reached back into the truck for something then carried it into the house. As soon as they
reached the kitchen, she upended the plastic bucket and
emptied the money on to the table.

'Well, strike me hooray!' exclaimed Auntie Deir.

'We're going to stay!'

'That's bloody marvellous news!'

'I'm going to give it a go, Auntie Deir.'

'We'll help you all we can.'

'It's what Tom would have wanted.'

'I know. And I was hoping you'd come round to the idea. What changed your mind?'

'He did.'

'Tom?'

'Yes,' Kate said simply. 'I can't let him down.'

— 12 —

Marty leaned over the stable door as he watched Zoe tack up her horse. For the chance to be alone with her, he was quite happy to put up with the pungent smell and the buzzing swarm of flies. It was not only her attractive face that appealed to him. There was a quiet strength about her that impressed him enormously.

Zoe clearly loved horses and knew how to handle them. Talking to her mount all the time, she lifted the heavy saddle and swung it expertly on to the animal's back.

'Fancy some company on your ride?' Marty did his best to sound casual.

'No, thanks.'

'Oh.' He was crestfallen. 'Why not?'

'Because you don't know much about horses.'

'I know how to stay on, Zoe.'

'But you're not an experienced rider,' she said reasonably. 'If you came out with me, I'd spend all my time worrying about you. Wouldn't be able to enjoy myself properly. I mean, what would happen if a snake frightened your horse and it reared?'

'Yeah,' he admitted. 'Maybe it is better if I give it a miss. Hate to spoil it for you.'

Zoe tightened the girth then let out the stirrups. She patted the horse's neck and checked the bridle once more before leading the animal out into the yard. Marty followed her and admired the easy way that she mounted. But he was still troubled by her attitude towards him.

'You don't like us very much, do you?' he asked.

'Not when you look down on Emmie and me.'

'I don't look down on you!' he denied vehemently.

'Well, it's more Tina than you,' she conceded. 'But you're the same underneath, Marty. I suppose it's to do with being American. You always think you're so much better than other people.'

'I'm not better at riding,' he pointed out.

Zoe smiled for the first time and her sadness lifted for a few moments. It soon returned as she considered the future.

'You hate Larapinta, don't you?'

'No, of course not,' he said unconvincingly. 'It's just . . . not my scene, that's all.'

'We love it here. It's our home.'

'Then why aren't you more cheerful? Mom has decided to stay. Isn't that what you want?'

'Not really.'

'You'd rather *leave* Larapinta?'

'I'd rather we stayed and you left.'

She dug her heels into the horse's flank and it trotted away.

Marty was left to nurse his wounded pride.

Everything suddenly looked different. Now that she had made her decision, Kate Hannon found the landscape altogether more beautiful. As she drove the flat-top truck back to the Larapinta homestead, she looked around the range and was filled with a kind of elation. She was not blind to the problems. It would be a tremendous struggle. But her whole life had been that and it had turned her into a fighter. For Tom's sake, she was going to keep the ranch in the Hannon family.

It was the best way she could repay him for his love.

The homestead surfaced in front of her and her spirits soared. It was an outpost in the wilderness but it did have a rough magic to it. She began to realise why her husband adored Larapinta.

Her happiness turned to anger in a flash.

She braked to a halt and created a flurry of dust. Up

ahead of her, parked not far from the homestead, was a helicopter. She knew at once who the pilot would be.

She drove on again at full speed and stopped in front of the verandah, leaping out of the vehicle and racing into the kitchen. She stopped dead as she entered. All over the floor were boxes and sacks and large canisters.

Nick Stenning stood in the middle of it all.

'Auntie Deir called,' he explained. 'She thought you'd be needing a few groceries. I brought plenty. We buy in bulk out here.' He gave her a friendly grin. 'And congratulations! I hear you're staying.'

Kate subdued her feelings of hostility and remained polite. 'Let's hope it was the right decision,' she said.

'I think this must be the first time a Stenning's set foot on Larapinta without having his head blown off.' His eyes twinkled. 'One way or another.'

'Thank you for bringing all this.'

'My pleasure.' He nodded to the window. 'What happened to your garden? Been trampled flat.'

'Cattle got in. Searching for water.'

'Someone didn't close the gate, obviously.'

'It won't happen again.'

'Not now you've taken over,' he said encouragingly.

She ignored the heavy-handed compliment and looked around. 'Where are the children?'

'Outside. None of them seems too pleased.'

'I know.'

'Your kids want to go back to America. To the soft life.'

Kate held back a reply. There was something about him that both needled her and yet attracted her. It was very perplexing.

Nick continued to store the provisions in the larder, heaving a sack of flour off the ground with no discernible effort. She helped him and they worked in silence. Suddenly, she paused.

'Can I ask you something?'

'Sure.'

'Tom's stockmen. How do I go about finding them?'

'Gone back to their tribe.'

'Is it far?'

'Too far for you to drive in that old truck.'

'Oh. I'll have to get there somehow.'

'Well, I can fly you there tomorrow, if you like,' he offered. 'Providing you can see your way clear to let me have a bed for the night.'

His blue eyes seemed to pierce through her and she battled to hold on to her equanimity. There was an element of challenge in his gaze. Kate met it.

'Okay,' she said. 'It's a deal.'

The decision to remain at Larapinta had increased rather than eased the tensions between the two sets of children. Each tended to withdraw into their own private worlds. Over dinner that evening, the twins sat opposite Zoe and Emmie without saying a word. In their own ways, each of the children felt trapped and helpless.

Conscious of their resentment, Kate kept up a light patter and tried to draw them into conversation but she failed every time. She was on the horns of a dilemma. Whether she chose to leave or stay, she would alienate some of the children. There was no compromise solution. It was daunting.

Nick watched it all with interest. He admired Kate for the way that she coped with what was obviously a fraught situation and he noted the firm resolve that lay beneath her pleasant manner with the four teenagers. There was another strike in her favour – Nick liked her cooking.

When the meal was over, there were chores to be done then the children sloped off. Tina moped in the living room. Marty sat out on the porch and toyed with his guitar. Zoe and Emmie went to their bedroom to talk things over.

'I wish she wouldn't,' complained the older girl.

'Wouldn't what, Zoe?'

'Try so hard.'

'It's not her fault.'

'She's not our mother, Emmie. Why pretend she is?'

'At least we can stay at Larapinta.'

'For how long?' asked Zoe realistically.

'What do you mean?'

'Kate doesn't know the first thing about the Outback.'

'She saved the water tanks from the cattle,' Emmie recalled. 'That shows she's got some idea.'

'Maybe. But how can she run a ranch like this? It was hard work for Dad and he grew up here. Kate is bound to make a mess of it.'

'What then?'

'We'll be forced to sell up.'

Emma paled. 'America?'

'Probably.'

'Can't we live with Auntie Deir?'

'She's not really kin,' Zoe reminded her. 'Besides, she has enough on her plate looking after Uncle Ralphie. No, Em. Looks like we'll be packed off to California. There's no one here.'

'I miss Dad . . .' The younger girl summed up both their feelings.

They sat side by side on the edge of the bed and held hands for comfort. Notwithstanding their stepmother, they felt that they only had each other in the whole world. It was vital to cling together.

There was a tap at the door and Kate let herself in.

'Hello. Sorry to butt in . . .'

Under the stern gaze of the two sisters, she crossed to the table and put a small black book down on it.

'Henry Dingwell gave me this,' she explained. 'It's your father's diary. I thought you might like to read it.'

Devoid of response, Zoe and Emmie stayed where they were.

'I'll see you in the morning. Good night . . .'

Kate left them to it and stole quietly away.

*

The clean sharpness of the night air was a welcome contrast to the blistering heat of the day. Nocturnal sounds occasionally fractured the silence. Overhead was a canopy of stars. The sense of isolation was powerful but not intimidating.

Kate sat on the step of the verandah and looked up at the sky. Filling her lungs with the cool air, she felt strangely roused. The Outback was a severe trial but it had its own blessings.

A sturdy figure ambled out of the front door with a bedroll under his arm and made for the bunkhouse across the yard. Kate's call stopped him in mid-stride.

'Nick!'

'Yeah?'

'I . . . haven't thanked you properly.'

'That's okay.'

'It was good of you to bring the groceries.'

'Nice to know there's something I can get right.'

He came back to the verandah, dropped his bedroll then settled down beside her. Kate stiffened momentarily but he was relaxed and comfortable. A new awareness of each other stirred.

'There's an awful lot to learn, isn't there?' she said.

'Helluva lot. You'll be the talk of the Territory by the end of the week. One woman, four kids, no money – and only one bore left.'

'It might rain.'

'You never know your luck,' he murmured.

'I happen to believe it's important to take risks.'

'What happens if you lose?'

'I can't afford to lose.'

She gazed up at the sky again and studied the intricate, glittering patterns of the stars. They were like diamonds set in black velvet. The sight was so restful and inspiring.

Nick watched her with conflict in his heart. He was torn between loyalty to his father and affection for this woman who had once climbed up a hill to seek him out.

As he looked at her in profile, his feelings for her surged up and made him give some advice.

'You've got to drill for water,' he insisted, his concern for her showing clearly. 'You won't survive with just that one bore. It could dry up.'

'I know.'

'What are you going to do about it?'

Kate hesitated to confide in him. He was a Stenning and she was a Hannon. Sworn enemies. Then something brushed aside her doubts and she heard herself discussing her plans quite openly.

'I was thinking of asking Henry Dingwell if he'd release some of the money Tom borrowed from his sister.'

'You do that,' he urged. 'As soon as you can.'

'Do you think there's water on Larapinta?'

'Bound to be. All you have to do is to find it.'

'Tom is supposed to have employed this man . . . a water-diviner . . .'

'That'd be Simmo. Bloody old rogue. Don't trust him, Kate.'

'I won't . . .'

Her face was now only inches from his and she could feel his breath. Though shocked when he first arrived, she had come to feel very grateful to him. He supported her decision to stay on and it was reassuring to have some approval. At the same time, however, Kate was all too aware of the scale of her task. It was monumental.

'What do you really think?' she wondered.

'About what?'

'All this. Woman like me trying to be a rancher.'

'I think you've got kangaroos in your top paddock.'

'Kangaroos?' she repeated, puzzled.

'Aussie expression. Same as "ants in your attic".'

'I'm still none the wiser, Nick.'

'Means you're a little bit mad, Kate.'

She laughed. 'Is that good or bad?'

'It's necessary. Only the mad take on the impossible.'

'I'll remember that.'

He rose to his feet and picked up the bedding. 'Don't forget now,' he reminded her. 'Drill for that water.'

'I will.'

They stood facing each other, neither willing to break away.

'Thanks for putting me up,' he said.

'You're welcome.'

'Makes a change.'

They both smiled. Their mutual antagonism seemed dead now.

'Nick,' she wondered, 'why are you doing this?'

'I want to see you get it right.'

'Are you sure it isn't just to spite your father?'

'That's part of it, maybe. But it's not the main reason.'

'Then what is?'

A new look came into his eyes, softening them even as it brightened their colour. A feeling of intimacy suddenly existed between them. They both felt caught unawares by it.

'I'm doing it for you, Kate.'

Her cheeks were on fire and her heart was pumping audibly.

What's happening to me? she thought. Why am I attracted to this man? Is he flirting with me so soon after Tom's death? What kind of a woman does he imagine I am?

She tried to pull her eyes away but she was hypnotised. Against all reason, she felt drawn to him, wanting to touch him, needing him to take her in his arms, desiring him in a way that shocked her.

A footstep rang out on the verandah and they both turned.

Tina was watching them. She looked rather embarrassed and moved her fingers in a brief farewell before going into the house. The girl's interruption had been timely. It had broken the spell.

'G'night, Kate,' he said quietly.

'Good night,' she whispered.

He marched off to the bunkhouse some fifty yards away. A light came on inside.

Kate was transfixed, caught up in a vortex of whirling emotions and unable to wrest her gaze from the window. Everything about Nick Stenning had offended her to the core when they had first met yet now she was trembling because he had spoke one simple sentence to her.

'I'm doing it for you, Kate.'

Why? What had she done to provoke his interest?

As she tried to understand the strength of the feelings that he had triggered off, guilt clawed at her. She was still Tom Hannon's wife even though he was dead. It was indecent even to think about another man so soon. Tom had the right to be mourned.

Yet Nick Stenning continued to haunt her mind.

Kate scolded herself bitterly. Only a whore would welcome a man's attention in her situation. It was disgusting. She was a widow with four children to look after and she had to accept her responsibilities. There was no room for an emotional involvement. It was wrong and highly inconvenient and totally impossible. She had enough problems to face without complicating matters. Kate needed all her energy and concentration simply to get through each day. Life at Larapinta was quite overwhelming.

Why am I still looking at his window? she wondered. What would Tom think of me? And the children?

Kate paced restlessly up and down the verandah as she wrestled with her feelings. Then something brought her to a sharp halt.

The barbecue at the Shackleton Ranch. An attractive girl being carried off to his helicopter.

Is that how he sees *me*? Someone who can just be taken off for his pleasure? A woman on her own with no defences? An obvious target? An easy lay?

Kate was insulted to the depth of her being. He was revolting. She would not let him anywhere near her. It was unthinkable.

She glared at his window but the light had now gone out.

A gentle breeze turned the sails of the windmill very slowly in the moonlight. The approach of a vehicle brought an ugly jumble of sound into the stillness along with a pair of raking headlights. A battered old truck coughed and wheezed its way to the Larapinta bore site then jolted to a stop. The door opened and a swaying, sighing, crooked figure got down from the cab.

It was Simmo, the water-diviner.

He had been drinking something other than water and it had left him vengeful. Clearing his throat, he spat into the sand then sized up the windmill. He rid himself of a malicious cackle.

Simmo took some dynamite from the back of his truck. Cradling the sticks in his arms, he moved unsteadily across to the pump housing and packed some of the dynamite beneath it, teasing out the fuse wire for a couple of yards or more.

He now addressed himself to the windmill itself. With some more sticks of dynamite in his pocket, he began to ascend the steel ladder that ran vertically up the side of the superstructure. When he had hauled himself halfway up, he swung a leg out to wrap it around a stanchion so that he could steady himself. Then he placed the dynamite against a cross-member and taped it into position.

His arms and legs were aching from the effort by now and his head was muzzy. Fumbling for a match, he lit it and set fire to the dangling fuse. When he uncoiled his leg and pulled it back to the ladder, however, he lost his balance and slipped. The descent was much quicker than he had planned.

Simmo hit the ground with such a thud that he was dazed. When he gathered his wits about him again, he saw the fuse wire high above him, eaten away by the flame. It had only inches to go to the dynamite. He was threatened by his own sabotage.

'Agh! Oh, Gawd . . .!'

When he tried to move, there was a shooting pain in his leg and he realised that it was broken. He tried to drag himself to safety along the ground, crawling along in agony like a wounded insect, glancing over his shoulder at the hissing fuse.

He made a last frantic bid to get free but it was too late.

The dynamite exploded in a shattering blossom of fire.

Nick Stenning was undressing when he heard the blast. He guessed what it was at once. Pulling on his clothes again, he dashed out of the bunkhouse and went straight to the shed where the truck was kept. He had the engine revving in seconds and moved away at speed.

'Nick – wait!'

Kate came running out of the house and flagged him down. He braked hard, stopped long enough for her to dive in, then accelerated away with a roar of urgency.

'What was it?' she asked, querulous with fear.

'Sounded like the bore site.'

'Oh, no!'

'Hold tight. This could be rough.'

Nick went hell for leather, coaxing every ounce of speed out of the truck and leaving the ground at times when they hit a hard bump. Kate clung on grimly, her body tensed against the next jarring impact and her eyes anxiously staring through the windscreen.

When she saw the flames, her stomach turned over. A bonfire was lighting up the sky for miles around and illuminating a scene of utter devastation.

The windmill was now a twisted mass of wood and metal, half its superstructure blown away and the remainder tilting crazily. Everything had been destroyed – turkey's nests, bore drains, pipes, pumping gear.

Larapinta's sole water supply was now a pile of rubble.

'Who could have done it!' she wailed.

'There's your answer, Kate.'

'Where?'

He brought the truck to a halt on the edge of the site and they leaped out. Simmo lay sprawled grotesquely on the ground as the last of the windmill towered above him, threatening to collapse any moment. Nick reacted like lightning. Thinking that the old man might still be alive, he jumped bravely in amongst the wreckage and started to pull the debris off Simmo's body.

It was Kate who screamed the warning.

'*Nick* – look out!'

As he swung round, the windmill came crashing down on him with vicious force and knocked him senseless, pinning him to the ground near the dead body of the old man.

'NICK!!!!' Kate's cry of anguish was a shock of realisation of her deep feelings for him. It was the scream of a lover separated from a mate.

She scrambled wildly towards him but tripped over a spar of timber and fell headlong to the ground. Her face ended up only inches from that of Simmo and she made a gruesome acquaintance with the contorted ugliness of death.

Gasping in horror, she dragged herself up and stepped over the prone figure to get to Nick. Her heart stopped when she saw the blood oozing from gashes on his head and body. Fire was licking its way towards him.

'Hold on, my darling! I'll get you out!'

She threw herself on the tangled mesh that held him down then jumped back in pain. The metal was far too hot to touch and much too heavy for her to shift on her own.

Panic throttled her. If he stayed there, he would burn alive.

'I don't believe it,' she croaked, holding her head in her hands. 'Am I going to lose *him* as well? I've lost everything else since I came here – can't I hang on to him?'

She looked around for some means of prising the sections of windmill off him. Seeing a long steel pole, she rushed to pick it up then tried to use it as a lever under the metal. It was hopeless. Though she raised the windmill a small amount, she could not pull him from his prison.

There *had* to be another way.

'Oh, God! Please help me!'

Then her eye fell on Simmo's truck. It had a winch in the back.

Kate groped her way towards it in a reckless dash, scraping her arm on some jagged metal as she passed and ignoring the trickle of blood that started. Nick was the only person who mattered. She was terror-stricken at the thought that he might die.

Leaping into the cab, she gunned the engine, drove the vehicle in a rattling half-circle then backed it up towards the mound of rubble. She clambered into the back of the truck in a flash and quickly unwound the cable on the winch.

Flames were now only a yard from his head when she got back to him. She tried to stamp them out but they singed her shoes and would not be denied. There was a large iron hook at the end of the cable and she slipped it under the tangled metal that pressed him down. Taking great care not to injure him in the process, she slowly winched the thick stanchions off his body.

'I'll help you, Nick. I'll bring you out.'

The anger she felt towards him when she glared at the bunkhouse had now vanished, to be replaced by a truer emotion. She loved him and she felt the surging power of that love.

'Almost there, my darling. I'm coming.'

Kate was only just in time. When she was able to leap in and drag him out, the flames were almost upon him. She got him to the truck, made a cursory examination of his wounds and tore part of her shirt away to bind the deepest gash.

It was slow, laborious work to lift him into the back of the truck and her sweat mingled with his blood as she struggled. At last it was done and he lay prostrate in the Larapinta vehicle.

She kissed him softly.

The drive back was a nightmare. Kate was afraid to go too fast in case she aggravated his wounds and terrified to go too slow in case he bled to death. Every time the wheels hit a bump or sank into a hollow, she winced on Nick's behalf. The Larapinta truck was anything but the ideal ambulance.

Her nerves were frayed to breaking-point by the time her headlights picked out the homestead. As she brought the truck to a halt, the four children came bounding over to her in their night things. They were horrified to see the condition she was in.

'What was that explosion, Mom?'

'The bore has been blown up,' she said briskly. 'I'll tell you more later. Right now I need help to carry Nick inside. He's hurt bad.'

The five of them managed to get him into the building without too much difficulty and laid him on one of the bunks.

'Marty, run to the kitchen and get the first-aid box,' Kate ordered.

'Sure!' He was off like a flash.

'Zoe, the police will need to be informed.'

'That means George Bowman,' she said. 'I'll ring him.'

When Zoe had gone, Tina and Emmie stood hypnotised by the sight of blood still pouring from Nick. An ugly bruise was disfiguring the side of his face and his breathing was forced.

'Okay, you two. Fetch me some warm water – fast!'

They scampered off to obey Kate's order.

Ten minutes later, the worst of it was over. Kate was alone with the patient, tending his wounds with care and devotion, willing him to revive. In order to bind the gashes on his body, she had to cut away his shirt and expose his bronzed, muscular torso. As she bathed and bandaged a last jagged cut on his arm, she looked down at him with a mixture of sorrow and love.

Then the miracle happened. He opened his eyes.

'Where am I?' he croaked.

'You're safe now.'

'That windmill . . .'

'You had an accident. I drove you back here.'

As consciousness returned, he looked down at his wounds in total disbelief. When he tried to sit up, the pain was crippling.

'Lie quite still,' she advised. 'You were lucky. There's nothing broken. But you took a bashing and you've lost a fair amount of blood. What you need is a good night's sleep.'

Nick saw her torn shirt stained with his blood and started to work out that Kate must have rescued him from the debris and brought him back to apply first aid.

She had saved his life. He extended a hand and opened it wide. When he felt her hand touch his palm he closed his fingers in gratitude and squeezed gently.

Their eyes met and their true feelings showed through. Out of the crisis had come a new and deeper understanding.

Nick's injuries had taxed him badly and he soon drifted off to sleep, his hand falling limp and releasing hers. Kate finished dressing the last wound then put him to bed, removing his boots and trousers with care before covering him with a blanket. When it was all done, she bent over and kissed him tenderly on the forehead.

Then she straightened up and remembered something else.

The bore site had been destroyed.

Concern for Nick had wiped it from her mind but it now returned like a red-hot needle that lanced through her brain. Without water, her cattle would die. An act of sabotage had struck a killer blow at Larapinta. Kate shook all over as she saw the implications.

There was no other well on her land and drilling for new sources had not even begun. Five thousand head of cattle were in desperate need of water and none was available. It was a calamity.

Nick Stenning may have been saved but the lifeblood of Larapinta had been drained away. Kate was facing disaster.

The accumulated strains of a long night took possession of her and she shuddered. Tears of despair ran down her cheeks as she sobbed convulsively. She believed that she had come to the end of the line.

— 13 —

A sense of death pervaded the mulga. The desert plain was dry, forlorn and barren. Stricken trees pointed their rotting branches at the blue sky. Skeletons of cattle lay bleached white. The early morning sun gave the dust its blood-red tint.

Creatures moving about in the wilderness were like visitors to some gigantic cemetery. Death and decay were all around them.

A big red kangaroo and its mate, the blue flier, rested in a dense stand of mulga, licking their wrists in order to lower the blood temperature and keep cool. The harsh, mechanical sound of a Jeep made them stiffen with alarm then bound off together across the plain.

George Bowman sat behind the driving wheel of the Jeep and squinted in the glare. A tall, wiry, angular character in his forties, he was the local constable, a hard man upholding the law in a hard country.

A kangaroo suddenly careered across the dirt road directly in front of him and he braked to avoid a collision, sending up a screaming cloud of thick red dust.

As the Jeep set off again, a flock of cockatoos passed overhead, filling the sky with noise and colour. Bowman spared them a jaded glance then wiped the sweat from his face with a bony hand.

When he arrived at the Larapinta homestead, Kate Hannon was waiting for him on the verandah. He whistled to himself in frank admiration. He had already heard about her but he was not prepared for the shapely blonde who greeted him.

They shook hands and strolled towards the bunkhouse.

'Larapinta certainly gets its share of trouble,' he observed.

'I know,' she said ruefully.

'What happened exactly?'

'We heard this terrible bang last night and drove out to the bore as fast as we could. It's been blown to pieces. There was this old man – Mr Simpson – lying on the ground.'

'Simmo? That water-diviner?'

'Yes,' she said. 'Nick thought he might still be alive and tried to pull him clear of the debris. Then the windmill collapsed on both of them. I managed to get Nick into the truck and brought him straight back here.'

'How bad is he?'

'You'll see for yourself.'

'What about Simmo?'

'Still at the bore. He was dead.'

'Poor old galoot,' said Bowman with a sigh. 'He was a good diviner in his day – as good as most of the blacks, and that's sayin' somethin'. Simmo could find water in the Sahara.' He grimaced. 'Pity he didn't try drinkin' it for a change.'

They went into the bunkhouse and found Nick lying on one of the bunks. He had put his jeans back on now but his chest was still uncovered and swathed in bandages.

'G'day, George . . .' He stirred painfully.

'Hi, Nick.' They shook hands and the policeman ran a shrewd eye over him. 'Blimey, mate, you look as if you just went ten rounds with a grizzly bear.'

'It was twenty, actually.'

'Close call?'

'Very close. Kate here saved my life. Had to winch half the damn windmill off me.'

Bowman was impressed. 'That was quick thinking.'

'Simmo dynamited the bore,' Nick continued. 'Got killed when it went up. Serves him right, if you ask me.'

'But why did he do it?' asked the policeman. 'Not like Simmo.'

'There might be an explanation,' Kate suggested. 'He was here the other day, Constable Bowman.'

'George,' he corrected.

'Simmo turned up with his son one evening. They startled me.'

'What did they want?' Nick asked.

'Money. They claimed that Tom owed them for some work they'd been doing for him. Demanded it there and then. When I said I couldn't pay, they threatened me.'

'I wish I'd been there!' muttered Nick.

Kate was baffled. 'It still doesn't seem reason enough to do something as crazy as this.'

'No,' agreed Bowman. 'Unless someone put him up to it.'

Family loyalty made Nick sit up and stare levelly at the policeman.

'Any idea who, George?' He was almost challenging Bowman to name Ed Stenning.

Seeing Nick's expression, the constable backed off.

'Not at this moment.' He became brisk. 'I'll be needing a full statement from both of you. No hurry. It can wait a day or two.'

'Have you had breakfast yet, George?' asked Kate.

'Yeah. Thanks, Mrs Hannon.'

'Kate,' she told him. 'You're welcome to second helpings.'

'Another time.'

Nick was still bitter about the sabotage.

'What a lousy, bloody thing to do! Larapinta's only bore.'

Bowman concurred. 'Destroying a bore's about the worst crime you can commit in the Outback in the middle of a drought. Poetic justice, Simmo copping it like that.' He nodded a farewell to them. 'I'll be in touch.'

'Hang on, George,' called Nick. 'I think I might hitch a ride back to town with you.'

'In your condition?' Kate argued, solicitously.

'I'll be fine.'

'You need to take it easy.'

'I've got things to do in Glenwarra,' he explained. 'Okay if I leave the chopper here?'

'Of course.' She was still worried. 'Will you see a doctor.'

'Sure.'

'We'll pick up Simmo's body on the way,' Bowman decided.

'What's left of it,' Nick added.

When he reached for his shirt, he felt a sharp stab of pain.

'Let me help,' volunteered Kate, moving forward.

He accepted the offer and flashed a wry smile. 'You could always take up nursing if things don't work out.'

'They'll work out,' she promised. 'They've got to.'

As soon as Nick was fully dressed, he hobbled out to the Jeep with Constable Bowman. Kate stood outside the bunkhouse and watched them until they were no more than a spiral of dust on the horizon.

Deep in thought, she started to walk across the yard towards the house. As she went past the barn, something brought her forcibly out of her reverie. It was the sound of an animal in pain. Kate went quickly to the door and entered the shadowed interior. The noise guided her to the far end of the barn, where she saw its cause.

A cow was in the act of giving birth.

Marty knelt in the straw, entranced by it all. 'Look, Mom!' he whispered, excitedly. 'It's fantastic!'

Touched by his wonder and intrigued herself, she crouched down beside him to watch. The head and front legs of the calf were now hanging out but the rest of the body seemed reluctant to emerge. Lowing in distress, the cow looked around balefully and tossed its head. She shifted about in the thick straw but her calf still did not move.

'It's stuck,' said Kate.

'What do we do?' Marty asked in alarm.

'I don't know but we can't just leave it like that.'

'Can I ring a vet or something?'

'Out here? He'd probably have to come fifty miles by plane. We don't have that time to play with, Marty.' Another consideration weighed. 'And we don't have the money for a vet.'

'So what do we do?'

The cow was making even more noise now as it stamped about and the calf was rolling its eyes in fear, taking its first frightened look at a new world yet still trapped in the one it was trying to leave. It opened its jaws to give a soundless cry.

Kate stood up and moved forward decisively. 'We'll have to help it. Grab hold of it.'

'But we might break its legs.'

'Not if we're careful,' she said. 'Besides, they're pretty sturdy little fellas. This one needs a hand, that's all.'

They each took a grip on a moist front leg and pulled with gentle firmness. At first there was no response then the calf began to slip slowly towards them. Disturbed, confused and evidently in pain, the cow continued to shift about and moo loudly. Kate and Marty applied more pressure and the body of the calf came into view. For no apparent reason, it then stopped again, held fast.

'Pull harder!' Kate called.

'I don't want to hurt it.'

'Take both legs!'

While Marty gripped the other leg, Kate got her arm around the neck of the animal and nodded a signal. They both gave a concerted pull. Nothing happened.

'Harder still!' Kate urged.

'I'm doing all I can, Mom!'

'Just once more, Marty – heave!'

They put an extra effort into it and the result was immediate. In a sudden explosion of afterbirth, the calf came shooting out of the womb and fell on to the straw, knocking both of them to the ground. Kate and Marty rolled over, then looked back at the helpless creature as it lay there beside them. The mother swung round, came to sniff its calf then started to lick it with great tenderness.

'We did it!' said Marty in delight.

'Yeah!' said Kate, panting for breath.

'See? He's fine. A bouncing baby!'

Kate was amused. 'First a nurse; now a midwife.'

'Isn't he cute, Mom?'

'Very.'

Marty reached over to stroke the calf, running his hand over the soft, damp body with a kind of reverence. Kate was moved. Her son had been through a significant experience in his young life and she had been there to share it with him. He was patently thrilled by it all.

It was the first really good thing that had happened to him since he had come to Larapinta, the first time when the smell and the feel of the Outback had not put him off. Helping to deliver the calf had been more than an achievement for Marty.

'I wanna keep him here, Mom!'

'Okay. Got a name for him?'

'Buddy!' He made an instant decision. 'After Buddy in the band.'

The boy studied the animal for a moment, looked up at the cow with intense interest, then he turned to his mother with quiet awkwardness.

'Mom . . . Can I ask you a question?'

'Sure, honey.'

'Was it like that when . . . when . . .'

'More or less, Marty. Though they didn't have to grab you by the legs to yank you out.' He gave an embarrassed giggle. 'But it was more or less the same process. Except that it was a bit more tricky.'

'Why?'

'There were *two* of you.'

He laughed and started to stroke the calf once more.

'Come on now,' Kate insisted. 'Time for school.'

'Aw, no!' he groaned. 'It's such a dumb way to learn lessons!'

'Go get yourself cleaned up,' she ordered. 'Then it's school for you, young man.'

Still moaning, he followed her to the door, pausing to steal one more look at the calf lying happily in the straw as its mother licked it all over.

'See ya later, Buddy . . .'

The spare room had been set up as a schoolroom with chairs and tables arranged in a semi-circle around a radio transmitter. A few posters brightened the walls. Sunshine flooded in through the window.

Emmie Hannon sat alone with her chin cupped in her hands and her expression vacant. She did not hear Tina come into the room behind her.

'Are you okay?' the American girl asked.

'Yes,' Emmie murmured.

'You sure don't look it.'

'Why should you care?'

Tina suppressed the retort that rose to mind. She could see how miserable the other girl was and tried to be sympathetic. Marty and she were in a dreadful situation but it was far worse for the Hannon sisters. Both parents dead, they had been cut adrift completely.

'I *do* care, Emmie,' she said, sitting beside her. 'Wanna talk about it?'

'You wouldn't understand.'

'Why not?'

'All you think about is yourself.'

'Sometimes, maybe,' she conceded. 'Not now.'

Emmie regarded her with suspicious eyes. Tina responded by putting a hand on her arm. The Australian girl relaxed slightly and gave a tiny smile. The chasm between them seemed to close over for a moment.

'It's the bore,' Emmie mumbled. 'Blown up.'

'Mom says the man who did it was killed himself. It was a wicked thing to do. I don't feel at all sorry for him.'

175

'Can't you see what it means, Tina?'

'Sure. We'll have to ration our water for a while.'

'Cattle will die,' Emmie explained simply. 'We don't have another bore. The herd won't survive. Without cattle, there'll be no money coming in. Larapinta will have to be sold.'

Tina had not followed it through before. Now that she did, her self-interest quickened. The saboteur might actually have done her a favour. If Larapinta went under, they would go back to Los Angeles.

But even as she felt hope warming her, she did not forget that for Emmie and Zoe it would mean yet more tragedy: eviction from their own home, exile from their own country. As she stared into the sad face of Emmie Hannon, she had an insight into her anguish.

The moment between them did not last long. Marty and Zoe came rushing into the room.

'Haven't you switched on yet?' Zoe asked.

'It's not time,' Tina countered.

'Ten seconds to go,' Marty announced, checking his watch. 'One, two, three, four . . .'

Tina sniffed. 'Marty Adamson, have you stepped in something?'

Despite themselves, the two sisters giggled.

Marty ignored them as he completed his countdown.

'Ten!'

He switched on the radio and the bright, friendly voice of a young Australian woman twanged over the air waves.

'Morning, boys and girls. This is School of the Air. Dotty Phillips here, talking to all the cattle stations within a four-hundred-mile-radius of Alice Springs. Bringing you all together into one big schoolroom.' She cued in her listeners. 'How is everyone today?'

'Good morning, Miss Phillips,' droned the four children.

'Before we start today's lesson, we'll call the roll,' resumed the teacher. 'Beginning with the "As" . . .'

'What's that smell, Marty?' hissed his sister.

'I've been in the barn.'

176

'Boy, you stink!'

'Are you listening out there?' asked the teacher. 'In that case, I'll—'

'Miss Phillips,' interrupted a boy's voice filtered by static, 'y'know last week I was tellin' you about our pig, Mary? Well, she had six piglets on Tuesday night and we've given them all names. They're called —'

'That's wonderful, Shane,' she returned, cutting him off. 'Why don't you tell us all about it when I reach the "Ws"?'

'Okay, Miss Phillips,' he accepted.

Kate slipped into the room and watched the four children.

'Now,' said the teacher. 'Starting with the "As" . . . We'll begin as usual by calling Marty and Tina Adamson from Larapinta Station.'

Stubbornly silent, the twins glared at the radio.

'Marty,' continued Miss Phillips, 'if you can hear me, would you please say "Yes" when I call your name . . . Over . . .'

The boy refused to speak and the teacher became impatient.

'Come on. We don't have all day . . . I'm calling our two new Australians – Marty and Tina Adamson from the USA.'

Kate stepped in close to Marty and he weakened. Flicking the switch in front of him, he spoke dully into the microphone.

'Hi.'

'That's fine. Hello Marty. And Tina . . .?'

The girl turned to her mother on the verge of tears.

'I'm an American,' she argued. 'I'll always be an American!'

'So will I!' added Marty.

'Rightio,' said Miss Phillips, 'we're off to a flying start . . .'

The teacher went on through the roll on a call-and-response basis and various young voices came over the air. Kate could see that she would have to intercede. The School of the Air was just one more bone of contention with the children. The twins found it slightly absurd and the Hannon sisters, who had been sent away to boarding school, saw it as a mark of the way they had come down in the world.

Kate met their objections head-on. She asserted her parental authority with a blend of calmness and reason.

'We're a long way from town and we don't have any money,' she stressed. 'The four of you will have to cope the best you can. Anyway, you're not alone. Children all over the Outback go to school this way.' She sensed mutiny. 'I'll say it again. How much you get out of this is up to you. I can't be here all the time to supervise your lessons and I can't make you study. If you wish, you can sit here and stare at the walls for six hours every day. It's your choice.'

Kate went out but her words hung in the air. The children were sobered by her directness and began to listen to the radio. Tina, however, was still distracted by something. Her nostrils twitched.

'You reek, Marty, do you know that?'

'Shut up!' he hissed.

'All I can say is – thank God Miss Phillips can't smell you!'

The four of them shared a rare laugh then opened their books as the lesson began. They made an effort to concentrate this time.

California had spoiled her, Kate realised now. Even though she lived in a modest apartment, she had come to take so many things for granted. High technology in the home made life so much easier and less tiring. Where Kate had simply pressed a button in Los Angeles, she now found herself doing a job the hard way. The absence of a shower and the temperamental generator were additional hazards.

Her problems did not end there. The worst she had ever

had to contend with in her apartment was a spider in the bathtub and a lone cockroach in the kitchen sink. Insects and vermin swarmed all over Larapinta. Even the birds could cause trouble.

'Urgh!'

Balancing on the ladder that ran up to the domestic water tank, Kate used a broom-handle to fish out an obstruction. It was a dead bird, petrified and glistening. She dropped it on to the ground and flies converged on it at once.

Disgusted by what she had found in the water supply, she came back down the ladder to the ground. A noise directed her attention to the plain, where she saw a shiny Land Rover approaching at speed. It was soon close enough for her to identify Meg Stenning and her father in the front seats. The daughter was driving.

When the Land Rover pulled up, they got out.

'Good morning . . .' Kate gave them both a muted greeting.

'It's not a social visit,' Ed asserted gruffly.

'I didn't think it would be.'

'We heard you had some trouble.'

'News travels fast.'

'Simmo always had a grudge against your husband.'

'He isn't the only one, is he?' she challenged.

Ed scowled. 'Any man who blasts a well doesn't deserve to live. It was criminal.'

'Mr Stenning, why don't you come to the point?'

Her bluntness startled him. He was not used to being spoken to like that, least of all by a woman. Kate Hannon was getting above herself. The sooner he dispatched her back to California, the better.

Legs apart and hands on hips, he put it to her straight. 'Larapinta's dying, Mrs Hannon. Your herd's half-starved. Your valley's a dust bowl. And you just lost your only source of water.'

'It's not for sale,' she affirmed.

'Now, you listen to me,' he insisted, taking a pace

forward. 'For four generations, Stennings've worked this land. We turned a desert into one of the biggest cattle ranches in Australia. It took blood, sweat and tears. But we got there.'

'Spare me the family scrapbook,' Kate said acidly. 'Hannons have been at Larapinta for four generations as well. They held it together somehow. So will I.'

'What the hell do you know about running a cattle station?' he demanded angrily.

'I know that it's difficult. Especially when you're pestered by one of your neighbours.'

Ed Stenning fumed in silence for a few moments then moved in closer to her.

'I'm a man used to getting his own way.' His voice had taken on a chilling menace.

'You'll be disappointed this time.'

'Nobody stands up against me and survives.'

'What about your son?'

It was like a whiplash across his cheek and he winced.

Meg took over. She had noticed the helicopter parked on the landing strip and gave a loud sneer.

'If you imagine that my brother will help you, you're wasting your time. He'll let you down as he's let down everybody who's depended on him. Nick's got no backbone.'

'That's not true!' Kate retorted hotly.

'We know him for what he is,' Ed warned with measured contempt. 'A fool unto himself. So don't you try to use my own son against me. Because it won't work.'

'Is that all you have to say, Mr Stenning?' Kate wrestled with her anger and tried to sound calm.

'For the moment.' He smirked. 'We'll talk again soon.'

'There's nothing for us to talk about.'

'Yes, there is. The purchase price. It goes down a bit each day you hang on here. Sell out while it's worth it.'

'Only a Stenning could make this ranch pay,' Meg emphasised.

Ed grinned. 'We'll be back.'

All the tension, bitterness and pain of the past twelve hours had built up inside Kate like a rising flood. She resented being bullied, most of all by a man who might be implicated in the destruction of her well. His threats were too much to take. The dam burst and her fury gushed out.

'No, you will *not* be back!' she yelled. 'Who the hell do you think you are – coming here like a pair of vultures! We may be up against it at the moment but we'll fight through somehow. One thing is certain: as long as I'm at Larapinta this is Hannon land and Stennings are not welcome. So get off my property and *stay* off it!'

Ed went puce and looked as if he was about to explode. Instead, he swung on his heel and led the way back to the Land Rover. It soon roared away in a shower of red dust.

Kate was trembling all over but she felt that she had just won a minor victory.

— 14 —

Zoe Hannon was the first to spot the plane as it approached.

'Mail's in!' she called.

Tina came darting into the room and joined her at the window.

'Where?'

'Up there. See?'

'Wow!'

'They'll make the drop any second.'

'Come on, then!'

The two of them rushed eagerly on to the verandah. Emmie soon came out too and danced on her toes in excitement. Stripped to the waist, Marty left his work in the barn and came out to watch. His calf tottered out behind him.

The light aircraft was flying at low altitude. When it got close to the homestead, it swooped right down and dropped a padlocked mailbag near the landing strip. The pilot gave them a cheery wave then the plane gained height as it set off to its next delivery.

'Let's go!' shouted Emmie.

The three girls charged off towards the bag with happy cries. Zoe won the race but she let the others help her to carry the mail back to the house. Kate was waiting for them on the verandah with Marty. She had the key in her hand.

'Bring it inside,' she suggested.

They hurried into the living room and gathered round her.

As she undid the padlock, Kate felt her own excitement surge. Living in such isolation meant that their rare contact with the outside world took on an extra significance. She thrust in a hand and pulled out a thick bundle of letters held together by string.

'Any for me?' Tina's impatience made her jump up and down.

'I'll see, honey.'

'Mom, please – hurry!'

'I'm glad *I'm* not in love,' Marty teased.

'Shut up!' yelled his sister.

'Makes people act crazy.'

'Who'd want to fall in love with you, anyway!' she argued.

'Now, calm down,' ordered Kate.

She undid the string and flicked through the letters. The children watched with their nerves on edge, praying that there would be something for each of them.

Kate pulled out an airmail letter and held it up.

'Bingo!'

'Oh, I knew it!' exclaimed Tina, snatching the letter and hugging it to her chest. 'I knew Billy would write. Oh, God . . . thank you, thank you, thank you.'

'"Oh my beating heart . . .!"' Marty sniggered and did a comic mime of his sister.

'Be quiet,' Zoe snapped, taking Tina's side for once.

'It was only a joke . . .'

Marty was given a letter of his own and he sloped off to read it outside. Having torn open her missive, Tina scuttled off to the verandah to enjoy it in privacy.

Kate found some letters for Zoe and Emmie.

'Great!' said Emmie. 'From Adelaide. Our old school.'

'Mine's from Sarah,' Zoe noted with pleasure.

They, too, went off to open their mail outside.

Left alone, Kate searched through the mail for the letter she was hoping to get from Molly in San Diego. It was not there. Tom's sister had still not answered the questions Kate had put when she finally managed to phone her about the plane crash. It was a severe disappointment. Financially and otherwise, Molly was a vital factor in her future at Larapinta.

There was another unpleasant shock for Kate.

Some letters, catalogues and a magazine were addressed to Tom Hannon, sent in ignorance of his death and causing his widow to feel new pangs of remorse. Kate put it all aside and went out to the verandah with the back copy of the *Los Angeles Times* that Judy had sent her with a scribbled note. She settled down on the step and began to read it. A tide of nostalgia washed over her.

Marty then came slowly across and plonked himself down beside her. He was carrying the opened letter and it contained bad news.

'The guys got a new guitarist.'

'Oh, Marty. I'm so sorry.'

'Couldn't they have waited just a little?' he complained.

Kate shrugged. 'That's showbiz for you.'

'Yuh.'

He sat there slipping into depression. The band had been the central feature of his life in California. His link with it had been severed completely now. Even if he went back, it would be too late.

As the two of them sat there, Tina came shambling over to them, tears waterfalling down her face and despair written all over her.

'I wish I was dead!' she groaned.

'Oh, God . . .' Kate was on her feet at once.

'It's so *cruel*!'

'Honey, what happened?'

'Billy says it's over. He's met someone else!'

She threw herself into her mother's arms and sobbed her heart out. Kate rocked her gently to and fro, making soothing noises, patting her consolingly on the back and sharing in her tragedy.

Marty had lost his band and Tina had been robbed of her boyfriend. Both of them felt a keen sense of rejection.

Something which had given them each a confidence, focus and identity had now been taken away.

Kate knew that it was her fault. In terms of their emotional lives, the move to Australia had been disastrous for her children. What could Larapinta offer to make up for it all?

Tina wept on and Marty was plunged in sorrow. Guilt and sadness weighed down on Kate like a heavy rock. At that moment, she found herself wishing that they had all stayed in Los Angeles.

Set in the wilderness, the Aboriginal camp comprised a group of humpies, the bark huts that served as primitive housing. The place was mean, austere and squalid, yet it had a kind of excitement to it, the sense of a people living on the rim of civilisation, inhabiting what was truly the last frontier.

The women were sitting around an open fire to do the cooking. Children played in the mulga. Some old men clustered in the shade of the trees, smoking and talking among themselves, dignified tribal elders unconsciously forming a classic tableau.

Kate stopped the truck and turned to Zoe.

'You okay?' The girl nodded. 'You haven't spoken since Larapinta.'

'Nothing to say.'

'Thanks for coming with me, anyway,' said Kate. 'I couldn't have found the camp without you.' She looked across to the men. 'Your father talked about Gillie. He said they were "tribal brothers". Is that right, Zoe.'

'They grew up together.'

'Then you must have known Gillie all your life.'

'Yes.'

Kate pursed her lips. During the long journey from Larapinta, she had been unable to break through to the girl. Her silence could be put down to her grief but there was also an element of revenge in it. Kate sensed that Zoe was getting back at her.

'Let's find Gillie, then, shall we?' she suggested.

'He's over there.'

They got out of the cab and strolled through the camp. The children smiled shyly at the visitors and the women looked up with polite curiosity. Kate and Zoe stopped near the trees and two of the Aboriginals stepped out to meet them.

'Hello, Gillie,' said Zoe.

'Gidday.'

'Hi, Jamie,' she called.

'Hi.'

Gillie was a prematurely aged black man with a natural kindness in his features. Jamie was younger and more watchful. Both were short, wiry and wearing nothing more than old trousers.

'This is Kate,' the girl said.

'Hello,' they greeted her pleasantly.

Gillie and Jamie appraised Kate with great caution.

'She wants both of you to come home to Larapinta.'

The two Aboriginals were plainly startled.

'You're not sellin' to Boss Stennin'?' asked Gillie.

'No,' Kate replied firmly. 'But we can't run it on our own.'

Uncertainty creased the black faces. The Aboriginals obviously had grave doubts about returning to Larapinta, especially since it was now run by an American woman. Used to dealing with the no-nonsense style of Tom Hannon, they eyed Kate with frank suspicion.

At the critical moment, Zoe spoke up.

'We need you, Gillie – both of you.'

'Yes, we do,' Kate agreed. 'Very much.'

'We'll come,' Jamie said. He extended his hand to Kate.

While they waited for the men to get ready, the visitors went back to the truck and got into the cab. Kate was not only thrilled that the two Aboriginals were going to work for her. She was at once surprised and heartened by the way that Zoe had behaved. It was the girl's intervention that had done the trick. In pressing the men to come back to Larapinta, Zoe had been committing herself to the whole enterprise. For the very first time, she had openly supported Kate.

'Thanks, Zoe.'

'They wouldn't have come otherwise.'

'I could see that.'

'Gillie belongs on Larapinta. I wanted him back.'

The Aboriginals were ready. After issuing their farewells, they each wheeled an old motorcycle across to the truck. Gillie and Jamie had now put on shirts and boots. Their meagre belongings were stuffed into bundles strapped on to their pillions. Slung around Gillie's shoulders was a rifle. They kick-started their machines and sounded their horns. Kate drove off and they stayed beside her.

The return journey was very different. Instead of sitting next to a sullen and impassive girl, Kate was now in the presence of a giggling teenager. Gillie and Jamie were the cause of the fun. They put on a motorcycle display that had both Kate and Zoe laughing aloud.

Shooting out in front of the truck, they zigzagged crazily, drew elaborate patterns in the dust and took part in impromptu races with each other. At one point, they seemed to be on a collision course and Zoe hid her eyes, but the Aboriginals changed direction at the last possible moment and celebrated their feat with a symphony of horn-sounding and yelling.

'It'll be lively with those two around,' Kate observed.

'They know how to enjoy themselves.'

'Maybe they'll teach us the secret . . .'

The girl registered the remark with a little nod.

Just as it was reaching its climax, the daredevil riding display came to an end. The two Aboriginals swung off towards a patch of scrub where a couple of emaciated steers were stumbling along. Kate drove after them.

The men brought their machines to a halt and dismounted. Gillie took hold of his rifle and loaded it. To Kate's horror, he then levelled the weapon at one of the animals and fired. It collapsed in a heap on the ground. Ejecting the cartridge, he took aim at the second steer, which was making a pathetic attempt to escape. The bullet sent it crashing down beside its companion.

Kate halted the truck, her eyes now moist.

Sensing her distress, Gillie called across to her. 'Gotta do it, missus. They was dyin', anyway. Puttin' 'em out of their misery's the on'y way.'

He was right and his action had been humane, but it still left her badly shaken. Kate wondered just how many more upsets the Outback held in store for her.

Though Henry Dingwell's main office was in Alice Springs, his firm also had an office in Glenwarra and he operated from there on a regular basis. Nick Stenning was pleased to find him in when he called. Dingwell gave him a warm welcome then offered him a seat.

'What can I do for you, Nick?'

'Just come to bat the breeze with you.'

'I know you better than that,' said the lawyer. 'I'm sure you have a good reason for coming here.'

'If I remember what it was, I'll let you know.'

Nick had now recovered from the injuries he received at the bore site though his face still carried the memory of the gash and the bruising. He was in no rush to declare his business. They engaged in smalltalk until the telephone rang.

'Excuse me,' said Dingwell, picking up the receiver. 'Hello . . .'

'Henry?' He knew the voice instantly. 'Kate Hannon here.'

'G'day, Kate . . . How is it down there?'

At the mention of her name, Nick sat up and listened.

'Hot,' she replied. 'Very hot. Twenty steers died yesterday. We shot another twelve this morning.'

'That's bad,' he commented, knowing what was coming.

'I need part of that money, Henry.'

'Tricky.'

'Tom borrowed two hundred thousand from Molly,' she argued. 'Legally, it must be mine now.'

'Oh, it is. Legally.'

'So what's the problem?'

'The money is frozen.'

'Then unfreeze it,' she insisted. 'I need to drill. My husband borrowed the money for just this purpose.'

Dingwell inhaled deeply and scratched his head. Then he flicked open his desk diary and checked something.

'When can you get over here, Kate?'

'Tomorrow, probably. Why?'

'You'll have to sign some papers.'

'No problem,' she replied, assuming that the money was now more or less hers. 'If I left early in the morning, I could make it between twelve and one. If the truck doesn't fall apart, that is.'

'I'll shout you lunch,' he offered.

'I'd like that.'

'Bye, Kate . . .'

'See you tomorrow . . .'

Dingwell put the receiver down and turned to Nick.

'She is one persistent lady, that Kate Hannon.'

'Only way to deal with you lawyers. Otherwise, you'd just wait on your asses and nothing'd get done.' He grinned familiarly. 'What was all that about money problems?'

'It was confidential.'

'Oh, come on now,' mocked Nick. 'I had a front-row seat. Couldn't help overhearing your conversation.'

'*What* conversation?'

Nick gave up. 'Have it your way, Henry.'

'I will . . . Now, then. Remembered why you called in to see me?'

'Sure. Wondered if you felt like a beer.'

'I always feel like a beer,' confessed the lawyer, getting up from behind his desk. 'Lead me to it.'

Nick got to the door first and opened it for his friend.

'By the way,' he said casually, 'where're you taking her for lunch tomorrow?'

The Vineyard was an extremely popular restaurant with an open-sided, vine-covered pergola. It was some distance from Glenwarra but the quality of the food and the courtesy of the service made the drive more than worthwhile. It was crowded as usual at lunch time.

Kate Hannon sat with Henry Dingwell at a table near the door. She felt like a prisoner who has just been released after being kept in isolation. It was a return to civilisation for her. Instead of her jeans and shirt, she was actually wearing a dress and make-up again. Her femininity blossomed.

Dingwell was rather bemused. There was something almost playful about her, as if she were determined to kick her heels a little while she was away from her responsibilities at Larapinta. He watched her tucking into a barbecued steak with relish.

'You've changed,' he observed.

'Have I?'

'You're more relaxed. And more certain. It suits you.'

Kate took her cue to raise the subject which had brought her out from Larapinta. She laid aside her knife and fork then leaned across to him.

'I'm certain about one thing, Henry. Needing that money to drill for water. Give me your pen.'

'Why?'

'I want to sign those papers before anything happens to change my mind.' She snapped her fingers. 'Come on.'

'A typical pushy Yank!' he noted with a laugh.

'If we want something, we go out and get it.'

'You might at least wait till the coffee.'

'I could be drunk by then,' she pointed out.

'I certainly hope to be.'

They smiled, then she used a finger to splash him with some wine from her glass. He ducked away and wiped his shirt with his serviette.

Kate stopped playing. 'Well? Where are the papers?'

'I did warn you it wasn't going to be easy,' he reminded her.

'You haven't brought them?' She sounded cheated.

'Yes, but there's a snag. We need Molly's signature as well.'

'Oh, no! So what happens now?'

'These things take time, Kate.'

'I don't *have* time,' she emphasised. 'Cattle are dropping every day through lack of water. This is an emergency.'

'If we move fast, maybe we can get it sewn up in a few weeks.'

She was aghast. 'Weeks! I need to drill immediately.'

'Then you'll have to forget your sister-in-law's cash.'

'You have some other source?' she asked hopefully.

'I'll try a couple of banks,' he decided.

'Try them *all*.'

'Leave it to me.'

Kate was very disappointed by the setback but she was determined not to let it spoil her lunch. She had been cooking for five people three times a day at Larapinta. To be waited on herself in a good restaurant was an absolute treat for her and she wanted to luxuriate in it. There was also the thrill of being in a crowd again. She had not realised how much she missed it.

She gazed around at all the happy faces and munching mouths. Then she froze. At a table in one corner were the two people she had least expected to see, especially together.

Nick Stenning and his sister.

Kate was stunned and stared at them with rising apprehension.

Was it part of a family conspiracy against the Hannons?

The waiter filled their glasses then sidled away from the table. Meg took a sip of her wine then looked cynically at her brother.

'What do you want, Nick?' she pressed. 'I'm sure you didn't just want to ask after my health. Or Dad's, for that matter.'

'How is he?'

'As if you cared!'

'I care enough to want some straight answers to some straight questions,' he said seriously, and leaned forward. 'Did the old man have anything to do with the dynamiting of Kate Hannon's bore?'

'No!' She denied it vehemently.

'Is that the truth, Meg?'

'Of course it is.'

'Despite the fact he hates my guts, I wouldn't like to see the old bastard go to gaol. And it's where he'd end up if he was involved. Malicious damage to property's a criminal offence.'

'He had nothing to do with it,' Meg stressed. 'I told you.'

'Any idea who did?'

'No, I don't.'

'It's worked out so convenient for Dad,' he pointed out. 'He wants Larapinta and we both know why.'

'Yes,' she snapped. 'And I bet you couldn't wait to tell her about that water on her property!'

A strange expression wiped his face and he became sad.

'No, I haven't mentioned it,' he admitted. 'And I may spend the rest of my life regretting it.'

Meg was knocked cold by the revelation. With divided loyalties at issue, her brother had actually favoured his own family. She regarded him in mild disbelief then made a sudden move to rise.

Nick grabbed her wrist and held her there.

'Swear to me!' he insisted. 'Swear to me that neither of you had anything to do with that bore!'

They were attracting a lot of attention now and a tall, well-built man was leaving the bar to make his way swiftly towards them.

'You're bloody concerned about the Hannons all of a

192

sudden,' Meg replied with deep scorn. Then she nodded in Kate's direction. 'Or is it just *her*?'

'Swear!' he ordered, tightening his grip.

'My word of honour!' she returned. 'Satisfied?'

He released her wrist as the man from the bar came up.

'Everything okay, Meg?' he asked, glaring at Nick.

'Sure, Phil. Just a family spat.'

'If he's been annoying you . . .'

Nick met the threat with a flint-eyed stare.

'We're leaving, Phil,' Meg announced.

'I still don't know why we came,' he said.

Meg finished the last of her wine and then stood up.

'I know you'll forgive me for dashing off, Nick,' she said with forced sweetness. 'I'm meeting Dad at the showground.' Her tone changed. 'He's the last of a breed. A giant. What a pity you're nothing like him!'

She took Phil's arm and the two of them made a rapid exit from the restaurant, leaving a ripple of speculation in their wake. Nick sat there for a moment before draining his glass in one long gulp.

He got up, sauntered towards the door and stopped beside Kate and Dingwell, tipping a non-existent hat to them.

'G'day.'

'Nicholas, dear boy!' said Dingwell effusively. 'Fancy seeing you here!'

'Fancy seeing you, Henry!'

Kate watched as the two men shook hands and seemed to be sharing a private joke. Conflicting emotions whirled inside her. Desperate to trust Nick, she feared betrayal. Wanting to love him, she was afraid of rejection.

He turned to her with an enigmatic smile. 'How are you, Kate?'

'Fine, thanks. You?'

'On the mend. My nurse did a great job on me.'

'Good.'

'Off to Alice Springs?' asked Dingwell.

'Yes, Henry. What about you?'

'Love to but can't, mate. Too busy.'

'I wouldn't miss a trip to Alice today for anything,' confided Nick. 'Should be a great occasion.'

'Why?' asked Kate. 'What's happening in Alice Springs? Is it something special?'

Nick favoured her with his full dazzling grin.

'Come along and find out.'

— 15 —

Sitting alone in the MacDonnell Range, the town of Alice Springs is at the heart of Australia's great red centre. The small community is the hub of a whole continent. It evolved from a rough and dusty village into a modern township but it still retains much of its old Territorial character.

Rich in Outback history and steeped in Aboriginal culture, it is a permanent reminder that life for the early settlers was impossibly hard and punishing.

Alice Springs is idiosyncratic. No other place in Australia holds a regatta in a dried-up river bed, featuring bottomless boats powered by human legs. The River Todd only ever flows after excessive rain so it is always available for the annual flotilla to take part in what is called Henley-on-Todd.

Then there is the famous Camel Cup.

'I never realised it would be like this.'

'That's why I brought you, Kate.'

'It's fabulous!'

'Wait till the fun really starts.'

'Where did all these people *come* from?'

'Hundreds of miles away in some cases,' he explained. 'Thousands, even. We get visitors from overseas some years. The Camel Cup is that kind of occasion. Brings 'em all running.'

They were in the middle of the saddling yard at the showground but it could just as easily have been an Arabian marketplace. Camels stood everywhere, fitted with gaudy saddles and decked out in all kinds of mock-

Arabian harness. The jockeys were even more outrageously dressed. They looked colourful and bizarre in their burnouses and they wore crash helmets beneath their exotic headdresses.

Some of them had applied thick make-up to turn Australian faces into grotesque caricatures of desert tribesmen. Hooked noses, black beards and villainous red scars were the favourite touches. One man, dressed as a Bedouin chief, had even given his camel false eyelashes.

It was the most novel event in the Australian racing calendar and Kate Hannon responded to the carnival atmosphere. Crowds were dense and excited, betting was brisk and the race track announcer poured out a stream of information over the public address system. The camels added their own distinctive flavour to it all.

Nick and Kate halted in front of an Aboriginal camel-man who gave them a toothless grin. He was evidently pleased to see Nick.

'Digger, this is Mrs Hannon . . .'

'Hello,' said Kate.

She collected an even broader grin by way of reply, then the old black man turned to Nick and sounded concerned. 'Where you bin? I thought you wasn't comin'.'

'Can you imagine me not turning up today, Digger?'

'No, not you.' The toothless grin was reinstated and the Aboriginal chuckled.

'I've got a very special stake in this Camel Cup, remember.'

Kate wondered what he meant. Before she could ask him, he led her over to a brightly bedecked camel that was squatting contentedly on the ground and eyeing the world with languorous interest.

'This is Farouz,' said Nick.

'Hi . . . He's uh . . . very handsome.'

'*He* happens to be a she.'

'Oh!'

The camel snorted in disgust and went on chewing the cud.

'It's okay, Farouz,' soothed Nick, patting the animal's neck. 'It wasn't meant as an insult.'

Kate was curious. 'Camels don't come from Australia, surely?'

'No, no,' he explained. 'They were brought over in the early 1880s. It was an easy means of transport around the Outback. They carried stuff to the goldfields in West Australia. There's thousands of camels here now. We even export them to Saudi Arabia.'

'Really?' She was amused by the idea.

'Farouz not for export,' said Digger, beaming.

'Is she yours?' Kate asked him.

The Aboriginal had a fit of giggles and turned away.

'Farouz is mine,' Nick admitted. 'Bought her seven months ago. I've been in training ever since.'

'For what?'

'I'm riding her.'

She was astounded. 'In a *race*? But isn't it dangerous?'

'Very. That's the attraction. Thrills and spills.'

'Be careful,' she warned involuntarily.

'I've learned how to stay on, don't worry . . . Gonna bet on me?'

Kate looked around. 'Bet?'

'You won't find any betting ring,' he said knowledgeably. 'It's all done on a one-to-one basis. You shout your odds for Nick Stenning and you'll have no shortage of takers, I promise you. There are some people here who bet in big numbers as well. Thousand dollars a race is nothing to 'em.'

'Well, it is to me,' she countered.

'That mean you won't be backing me?'

'Not with money, maybe,' she confessed. 'But I'll cheer you every inch of the way.'

'It's a deal.'

All that he did was to touch her shoulder lightly but it sent an electric charge through her. What was it about this man that intrigued her? Why could he exert such power over her?

A couple of hours earlier, Kate had been sitting in the Vineyard in a lather of anxiety because she thought that Nick was ganging up against her with his sister. Now she was calmly wandering around the showground at Alice Springs with him.

What the hell am I doing here? she wondered.

One glance at Nick Stenning in profile gave her the answer.

Several thousands of spectators had flocked to the flat open area that surrounded the dirt oval on which the races were run. There was no grandstand and thus no class division. Everybody was on the same level. It made for immense good humour and an absence of friction.

Dress varied enormously – everything from burnouses to shorts was worn, with a few ingenious compromises between the two. The din was infectious. People talked, laughed, argued, speculated, laid bets, ate, drank and threw themselves into the spirit of the occasion. The Camel Cup was no place for the half-hearted.

Ed Stenning sat beneath the shade of a large multi-coloured umbrella with a group of friends. His ancient Rolls-Royce was parked nearby and its boot had yielded up a well-stocked picnic basket. On the ground beside him was the statutory esky, the portable cooler in which his beer supply was kept.

Meg was in the group yet set apart from it by her appearance. While many of the other women wore their best finery, she had stuck to jeans and a shirt. Seated beside her with a proprietary air was Phil, the station foreman at Cutta Cutta, swigging his beer with relish and enjoying the sensation of being one of the family.

Phil was perfectly happy with her choice of apparel and her refusal to wear make-up. To his way of thinking, she did not need the devices that other women relied on to make themselves more attractive; she had qualities that placed her far above the rest.

'Who's going to win the big race, Ed?' someone asked.

'*My* camel is.'

'You sound pretty certain about that,' said Phil.

'When I buy anything, I buy the best,' retorted his employer, reaching to take the race programme from the table. 'My jockey has been in training for ages. No way we can lose.' He found the page with the checklist of competitors. 'There's nobody here who can stay with my camel. I intend to take that cup back to Cutta Cutta and put it on the mantelpiece in my study. In fact . . .'

He stopped abruptly as he saw the name at the bottom of the list. His cheeks reddened and his mouth tightened. He put the programme down. Phil picked it up and turned to the relevant page. He saw the name and read it out.

'Nick Stenning.'

'Trust him!' Meg sneered.

'I'll show him!' Ed growled.

'Old bull versus young bull,' Phil noted wryly.

'That's not funny,' snapped the older man, quelling him with a stare. His confidence returned. 'I don't give a damn *who* is in the race. We'll still win. Place your bets now.'

He munched a sandwich and chatted affably with his friends.

Phil took the opportunity to have a quiet word with Meg.

'He's brought that woman.'

'What?'

'Your brother. He's here with Hannon's widow.'

She was stung. 'Are you sure, Phil?'

'Saw them over by the marquee,' he reported. 'Being real sociable with each other.'

'What's he's playing at?' she hissed. 'Why her – of all people?'

'Your old man'll be none too pleased. Stenning and a Hannon together. Don't look right.'

'That woman's been nothing but trouble since she came,' said Meg vengefully. 'What's she doing here, anyway? She doesn't belong in the Outback. It'll murder her.

God knows why Tom Hannon married her in the first place!'

'She's a fine-looking woman,' Phil conceded.

'Tom needed more than that.'

Her tone was crisp and dismissive but a wistful thought flitted through her mind.

'You still haven't told me how it got its name.'

'Alice Springs?'

'Yes. Who was Alice?'

'A giant kangaroo.'

'Kangaroo?'

'Yeah. They kept catching her and locking her up behind this high fence but it was no good. Every time, Alice springs straight out.'

'Stop teasing!' she said, punching him playfully.

'You really want to know?'

'Yes. And no more terrible jokes, Nick Stenning.'

'Alice Springs used to be called Stuart,' he told her. 'It was an ideal base to strike out from in the pioneering days so it became pretty important. That's why they built an overland telegraph station here in 1871. Right next to the spring.'

'So who was Alice?'

'Wife of the South Australia Postmaster General.' He grinned. 'Just as well she wasn't called Bessie or Aggie or something.'

They were standing on the edge of the track as they waited for the first race to start. Kate was fascinated by the whole experience and delighted that she had come. After the time spent at Larapinta, she felt liberated. Nick was good company and he was turning out to be surprisingly considerate.

He watched her flicking a hand in front of her face. 'Flies bothering you?'

'A bit.'

'Borrow my hat,' he offered, taking it off.

'What about you?'

'I'm used to flies.' He set the hat on her head and adjusted it with care. 'There you are, Kate. Perfect fit.'

'Thanks.'

It was a crumpled old hat but its broad brim protected her from the sun and the flies. Also, it made her feel more Australian. Kate liked that.

The first race now got under way and they turned to watch it. Camels were whooshed to the starting line by their jockeys and made to squat down in a row. The jockeys climbed on to their mounts, the starter's pistol fired and pandemonium ensued. As the camels jerked to their feet and tilted their riders, the crowd erupted. Partisan roars came from every side and there was a concerted cheer as the first hapless victim hit the dust.

Hooves flying and necks thrust out, the camels tore around the track and kicked up a red cloud in their wake. The joke Arabs urged their mounts on and had the spectators shrieking with laughter at their antics. Another rider was thrown to the ground and he picked himself up immediately, lifted his burnous up like a skirt to reveal a pair of hairy legs, then set off in pursuit of the pack with yells of comic desperation.

Kate could not remember when she had last had so much fun. She was completely caught up in the excitement of it all, shouting, pointing, shaking with mirth. Her problems and tensions were forgotten for once as she surrendered to the occasion and allowed herself the luxury of release.

As a third jockey took a tumble, she turned to Nick. 'I hope that doesn't happen to you.'

'What if it does?' he teased. 'I've got my nurse standing by!'

He put his arm around her shoulders to move her forward to a better vantage point. Another current surged through her then gave way to a feeling of deep contentment. Nick had proved something to her that she would not have believed possible.

She could be truly happy again.

The saddling yard was the same mixture of confusion and anticipation as riders got ready for the next race, psyching themselves up, talking to their camels, downing a last glass of beer to steady their nerves. Ralph Shackleton and his wife moved slowly through the crowd then noticed Kate with surprised delight. They exchanged pleasantries.

'Ralphie insisted on us comin',' said Auntie Deir. 'I didn't think it was a good idea and I still don't.'

'Shush!' he ordered.

'The doctor said you should be in bed.'

'Well, I'm not going to bed,' he rejoined, gazing fondly around. 'I want to be among people. While I'm still alive, I want to be where there's a bit of life.'

'See what I have to put up with?' his wife complained.

Kate smiled at the good-natured banter. There was a wealth of affection beneath it all. Only a sound marriage could survive in the Outback and theirs had been particularly happy. Kate felt a pang of remorse when she remembered that it would soon be over.

'Where'd you get that hat from?' Auntie Deir gave the hat an admiring glance and flicked it.

'Nick Stenning loaned it to me.'

'Oh?'

'I came with him.'

The older woman was mildly astonished but she underplayed her reaction and pretended to shrug it off.

'Why not? Good for you to let your hair down.'

'Did you know he's riding a camel in the Cup?' said Ralph.

'Yes,' replied Kate. 'Farouz.'

She pointed to the animal, which was now having a pair of long false eyelashes fitted to her by Digger. Farouz bore the indignity with a world-weary disdain.

'Did Nick mention that his old man's got a camel racing as well?' asked Auntie Deir.

'No, he didn't,' Kate admitted, rather taken aback.

'Father versus son. That'll make the crowd sit up and take notice. Not every day a Stenning competes with a Stenning.'

Kate saw the implications at once. She wondered why Nick had not told her about his father's stake in the Camel Cup. It put a very different complexion on the whole race.

'G'day, Mrs Hannon!'

'Oh . . . g'day.'

The greeting came from the young jackeroo she had served at the Shackleton barbecue. Pleased to be recognised, she waved back as he tipped his hat to her. The jackeroo called out a greeting to Auntie Deir and Ralph before he was swallowed up in the crowd.

Then Nick emerged from the dressing shed.

'My God!' murmured Kate to herself. 'Is that *him*?'

He was dressed like Valentino in *The Sheik*. The effect was oddly romantic, all the more so because he seemed so at ease and unselfconscious in his strange attire. He struck a chord in Kate and she watched open-mouthed.

Auntie Deir decided on a tactful withdrawal. 'I need a beer . . .'

'I need two,' Ralph declared.

They slipped away before Kate had even noticed. She composed herself and started to walk towards Nick, but someone got to him first. An attractive young woman in a white summer dress rushed up to him and threw herself into his arms.

'Nicky!' she yelled. 'You look gorgeous!'

She kissed him enthusiastically and he backed away slightly in embarrassment. The girl stroked the material of his burnous.

'If you want to take me back to your tent after the race,' she offered, 'I'm ready, willing and available.'

'Another time, Sal,' he said, prising himself away.

'It could be just like that night after the barbecue.'

He dismissed her with a friendly pat and crossed over to Kate.

'Must be the outfit,' he said with a boyish grin.

'You look very dashing.' Her manner was now subtly cooler and he was aware of it.

'Yeah, not bad is it?' he continued. 'I was afraid I'd look a bit of a galah. But it's turned out okay.'

'I hope Farouz agrees.'

'Me, too. She can be a bit contrary sometimes.'

A noise diverted his attention and he looked across the enclosure to see his father and Meg arguing vociferously. Phil stood in the background and Ed's jockey was on hand as well. The row escalated and many heads began to turn.

'What's going on?' asked Kate.

'Dunno.'

He watched in alarm as his father started to roll up his trousers before snatching the cap from his jockey's head. Nick was quietly appalled. He might hate his father but he still had some concern for his safety. It was time to interfere.

'Back in a minute, Kate.' Nick pushed his way through the crowd and confronted his father.

'Are you crazy? You'll kill yourself!'

'None of your business!' Ed snarled.

'It's dangerous out there, Dad.'

'Don't you lecture me, boy,' he retaliated. 'I was riding camels before you could cock a leg over a rocking horse.'

'Stop him, Meg,' urged Nick, appealing to his sister.

'I'm not sure that I want to now,' she said, bridling. 'It's probably high time someone put you in your place.'

'What's he trying to prove?'

'Dad doesn't need to prove himself to anyone. He's riding Napoleon and I'll bet on him against you any day!'

Nick spun around and went to rejoin Kate. His sister followed him.

'I hope you break your bloody neck!' she shouted.

Kate was shocked and Nick turned to her with a tight smile.

'As you can see, we're a very close family.'

There was a hush of expectation when the race for the

he swung Farouz out and called for a supreme effort. His mount responded at once and began to gain rapidly on Napoleon.

A tidal wave of sound swept the two riders along.

'You're there, Ed!'

'Take him, Nick!'

'Now!'

'*Come on!*'

Farouz found an extra spurt over the last twenty yards and just managed to get her nose in front of the line. Nick Stenning was the winner. Elation made him punch the air with a fist. He had beaten his father in the most public way and the satisfaction was immense. A race in Alice Springs between two camels had enabled him to pay off a lot of old scores.

Ed Stenning, by contrast, was shattered in defeat. Ashen-faced, out of breath, covered in dust and slumped sideways, he could barely stay on his mount. He had put everything into the race and it had not been enough. His pride was severely wounded.

Nick continued on his lap of honour, basking in the ovation. Exhilaration made him forget his tired limbs and burning lungs. He searched for Kate's face in the crowd, found it briefly, saw her smiling and was happy.

While one Stenning was receiving acclaim, another was being helped off his camel by his anxious daughter. Meg assisted her father to a chair then ministered to him with a drink and a towel. He had lost but he had not disgraced himself, she reminded him, trying to revive his spirits as well as his exhausted body.

But the hour belonged to her brother. When he reached the presentation area, he dismounted and walked across to the winner's circle. Officials stood on a dais and the Camel Cup itself, a large, gleaming piece of silverware, waited on a table.

During the brief speech by the president of the organising committee, Nick's gaze never left his trophy. It was a symbol of his achievement, a tangible reminder of a hard-fought victory over his father and a reward for years of stoic endurance.

'And so the Camel Cup goes to . . . Nick Stenning!'

Kate Hannon led the cheers that avalanched down on him. She shared in his delirium as someone ran up to him with a magnum of champagne, popped its cork spectacularly, then poured its frothing contents into the cup. She could not have been more delighted for him.

Then someone intervened.

Lifted over the barrier by friends, Sal, the girl in the white dress, ran to join in the celebrations by planting a kiss on Nick's lips. The cup jerked and spilled champagne all over both of them. It set the crowd into a fresh round of cheers.

Kate, however, did not take part this time. As she looked at Nick with his arm familiarly around the girl, jealousy and pain swelled up inside her. She turned round and burrowed her way through the mass.

Unaware of her departure, Nick continued to luxuriate in his moment of joy, beaming at the world and covered in vintage champagne. Suddenly, Ed Stenning was there. He came to the barrier not ten yards from where his son was standing.

Their eyes locked for a moment. Then Ed gave a crooked smile and lifted his hand in a token salute, showing a dignity in defeat that took his son by surprise.

Nick was rooted to the spot, shocked by the tears that sprang to his eyes, oblivious to everything now except the old man who was his father.

Ed merged into the crowd and disappeared from sight.

— 16 —

It had been an exceptional day. As the crowds began to
drift away from the showground at the end of another
Camel Cup, there was a general feeling of contentment.
Drunk, sober, asleep or awake, everyone had had a magnificent time and carried away memories that would sustain them for a year until they could return. They trudged
happily towards the main gate over ground littered with
rubbish and sparkling with beer cans, yet it was hallowed
in its own way.

Some headed for the pubs, others made for their tents
and caravans, others again started the long journey home
by road or air. Rising to such a dramatic climax, the
Camel Cup had been an outstanding success.

Alice Springs had done it yet again.

Kate Hannon did not agree. Alone of the throng con-
verging on the main exit, she felt jaded and hurt. It was
her own fault for letting Nick Stenning get so close to
her. In lifting her guard, she had made herself highly
vulnerable. He had let her down as his sister had predicted
and it was galling.

As she wandered along in the crowd, she tried to come
to terms with her seesawing emotions. When she first met
Nick, she had disliked and resented him. That attitude
had been hardened at the barbecue, only to be revised
when he turned up at Larapinta with the groceries. The
explosion at the bore site had pushed them into a more
intimate situation and Kate had not drawn back.

When she saw him over lunch with Meg, however, all
her resentment and suspicion had resurfaced again. Nick

had extinguished it with the invitation to the Camel Cup, leading her on to think that she was special in his life and that he really wanted her there. The girl in the white dress had shown him up for what he was.

Valentino said it all. The costume bared the inner man.

A hand fell on her shoulder and turned her round.

'Where d'you think you're going?' Nick asked. He was wearing his own clothes now. Valentino had gone.

'I looked for you to say goodbye,' she replied tartly. 'But you had your arms full again.'

'Not by choice.'

There was an awkward pause as they sized each other up.

'I'm flying back with the Shackletons,' she announced.

'I just spoke to them. Told them *I'd* take you.'

'What right did you have to do that?'

'I brought you,' he said. 'My responsibility to get you back.'

'There's no need.'

The second pause was longer but less awkward.

'I have a place in town.'

'So?'

'I hoped you might let me cook you dinner.'

'Thanks all the same but I have to get back.'

'Why?'

'Because I have four children expecting me at Lara-pinta.'

'Ring them,' he advised. 'Tell them you're staying in Alice for the night. They can cope. How old are they? Fourteen? Blimey, when I was that age, I was spending nights alone out in the bush with nothing but a dog and a bloody harmonica for company.' He could see that she was still hesitating. 'If you're worried about 'em, get one of the Abos to sleep in the house with them. Tell them to ask Gillie.' He grinned. 'Then you'd have peace of mind.'

Kate was not enjoying peace of mind at that moment. Everything was happening much too fast for her liking.

Her feelings were into their seesaw routine once more. She had an urge to stay and a compulsion to leave.

Do I love him or hate him? she wondered. What's happening to me?

'Well?' he pressed.

'Where would I stay?'

'Plenty of motels in town. I recommend the Koala.'

'And you?'

'Told you. Got my own shack.'

More reluctance. 'I still think I should go back.'

'You will, Kate. First thing in the morning.'

'I'm not sure about that . . .'

'You don't need to be sure. I'm sure enough for both of us.' He gave her his slow grin. 'Hey, I won that race. Don't I get any congratulations?'

'Of course,' she said with a smile. 'Well done!'

'And don't I get thanks?'

'For what?'

'My hat.'

Kate, realising with a start that she was still wearing it, snatched it off in confusion and handed it to him. Nick was very amused by the performance and promptly set the hat back on her head.

'Bring it with you,' he suggested. 'I'll show you where I hang it.'

It was settled as easily as that.

Nick took her to the Koala to book in, then they went to his 'shack' for the dinner he had promised her.

The tiny house nestled behind a newsagent's shop in the main street. It opened on to a small paved courtyard that was shielded by bougainvillaea from prying eyes. The place was impeccably clean, furnished with antiques and quite unlike anything Kate had ever seen before in Australia. The one-bedroom dwelling seemed to have more affinity with the Far East.

While Nick busied himself in the galley kitchen, she marvelled at his original oil paintings and water colours, his extensive collection of classical records and his array of books. His capacity to surprise her was endless. She had never suspected him of any interest in the arts.

'What's the verdict?' he asked.

'Better than that hill near Glenwarra.'

'That's only my summer residence.'

She noticed a striking photograph of a young woman. The antique frame had been set up on a mahogany table so that it could catch the light from the window.

'Who's this?' she wondered.

'My mother.'

'Oh.'

'She died a long time ago. That's how I like to remember her.'

Nick went through the double doors into the courtyard and laid the table. It was getting dark now and he lit candles before ushering Kate to her seat. When he disappeared back into the kitchen, she was bathed in the romantic glow of the candles and inhaled the fragrance of the night-scented flowers all around. It was a world away from Larapinta and the hardship that it represented for her.

He brought the meal out on a tray and served it with a flourish. Then he watched her carefully while she sampled it, eager for her comment.

'Delicious!'

'Be honest. I can take criticism.'

'Absolutely delicious!'

'In that case, I may try some myself.'

He poured them a glass of Australian champagne apiece then toasted her in silence. She clinked his glass with her own and drank deep. The champagne tickled her throat.

'Glad you came to Alice?' he said.

'Very.'

'What did you think of the Camel Cup?'

'Ripper!'

Even as the word came out, she wished that she could take it back. It was Tom Hannon's word and belonged with her memories of him. She felt a stab of guilt at having used it so thoughtlessly.

Nick had genuine talent as a cook. Each course was better than the last and she had soon run out of superlatives. The wine, the candles and the setting did their work and they lapsed into a gentle, reflective mood, at ease with each other, drawn together.

'It's not what I expected,' she confessed.

'Is that good or bad?'

'Good. I loved all those paintings.'

'My mother taught me to appreciate art,' he confided. 'In fact, she taught me just about everything I know that's worth knowing. This place is a bit of a shrine to her, really.'

She sensed the deep bitterness behind his remarks and shifted her mood to match his. Leaning across the table, she put her question with unashamed bluntness.

'Nick, what's the problem between you and your father?'

He stared into the flame of the candle for a long time.

'Was it to do with your mother?' she prompted.

'Yes,' he admitted quietly. 'She came from Melbourne, originally. Knew all there was to know about music, art and so on. As for books, she never stopped reading. My mother was anything but the typical Outback wife.'

'Where did your father meet her?'

'In Melbourne. He was there on business.' His tone was almost wistful. 'He loved her at first and he was so different from any man she'd ever known. A sort of attraction of opposites.' He clenched his hands together. 'Then it all changed. I never really knew what happened. I just came home one day and found her – drunk, bruised and battered about . . .'

Kate was stunned. 'Your father?'

'He'd almost killed her.'

"*Why?*"

'Because that's the kind of man he is,' he said ruefully. 'Her drinking got worse after that. She died an alcoholic.'

'How old was she then?'

213

'Thirty-two.'

Kate was appalled by the wastage of a young life.

'In case you're wondering,' explained Nick sardonically, 'it's the reason I never married.'

'The question had occurred to me,' she confessed.

'It's tough on a woman, expecting her to live with your anger day in and day out.'

'It's tough on you as well, Nick.'

'I feel it inside me all the time. This . . . rage. I only have to be with Dad for two seconds and it starts to burn a hole in me. I've tried to fight it, Kate, but it's always there.'

She felt his pain and shared his anguish. Love for his mother and hatred for his father had torn him in two and left him with a psychic wound that refused to heal.

'Perhaps it's a question of letting go,' she advised. 'It's something we all have to do eventually. I have this black fury inside me as well. About Tom. *Why* did he have to die? That's what my mind is screaming. It was so unfair!'

'Yeah.'

'But he *is* gone and I do have to carry on somehow. I have to learn to cope with that anger – as you must do as well.' She gave a nostalgic sigh. 'Part of me will always love Tom. And be grateful.'

There was a short, eloquent silence. Each of them had confided things that they never imagined they could talk about, exposing a raw nerve to the other's view. It helped.

Nick ran a hand through his hair and shook his head sadly.

'When they were presenting me with the Cup today, I looked up and saw my father standing there in the crowd. He smiled at me. I can't remember the last time I saw my old man smile.'

'When did he last see you smile?'

Nick stared across at her, his gaze questioning and demanding.

'It's late,' she decided. 'I have to be up early.'

'Running away again?'

'It was a lovely evening.'

'Then why does it have to end now?'

'I have to get back to the motel.'

'Please stay, Kate . . .'

His plea was like a hand stroking her heart but she fought it off, averting her eyes and grabbing her purse from the table.

'I can't. I'm sorry, Nick.'

'Why not?' he whispered.

Her emotions were twisting into knots and she knew that she had to get away at once before she became involved in a situation that was far too dangerous and complex for her to handle.

'Why not?' he repeated.

'I still have some letting go to do,' she said, rising quickly to her feet. 'Thanks for today. It was wonderful.'

She vanished into the shadows before he could even speak.

Nick heaved a sigh and slapped the edge of the table in irritation. Then he gazed into his glass of wine and ran a finger ruminatively around the rim as he tried to understand what it was about Kate Hannon that attracted him to her so powerfully. No woman had ever had such an effect on him before and it was chastening.

Had he at last found the woman that he needed?

Another face appeared in the wine and scrambled his thoughts. It was his mother. Drunk, bruised and battered. He snatched up the glass and threw its contents into the bushes.

He got up from the table and went swiftly into the house. Pausing to study her photograph, he felt the old wound begin to fester once more. He broke away and went straight to the bathroom. Stripping off, he stepped under a cold shower and let the icy sting of the water bring him to his senses.

When his mind had been cleansed, he tempered cold tang with some hot water then reached for some shampoo, pouring it liberally on to his head before working it in with his fingers.

He did not hear the door to the bathroom open behind him.

'I wanted to come back,' Kate said simply.

Head covered in white froth, he turned to look at her.

This time it was her eyes that did the questioning and demanding.

Dropping her purse on the floor, she stepped fully-clothed into the shower cubicle with him. The warm water drenched her instantly, flattening her hair against her head and making her dress cling tight to her body to reveal the full splendour of her contours.

When she tried to hug him, he eased her away and instead placed his lips against hers with delicate softness. It was their only point of contact as they circled slowly under the water as if performing some kind of ritual dance.

Kate was quivering with pleasure. To be so close to him without being able to touch him made her throb with anticipation. Nick was exuding animal passion but he denied himself a real embrace. They put everything into the kiss. Their love, their loneliness, their need, their suffering, their hope. It seemed to go on for ever.

Then he began to undress her, peeling off her clothes with such gentleness that she felt as if she were discarding an unwanted layer of skin. And all the time she luxuriated in the warm water as it cascaded over them.

When she was fully naked, he moved her back slightly so that she was on the very edge of the spray. Then he reached for the soap. Lathering his hands with rich suds, he ran them over her shoulders and up her neck then down to her breasts, caressing them until the nipples were proud and tingling.

With fresh lather, he worked his way down to her hips and thighs and calves, even lifting her feet to soap them individually. Then he turned her around and coated her back in lather, bringing it down to cover the rounded sweep of her buttocks and continuing down her legs.

Kate took the soap. It was his turn.

Using both hands, she massaged the lather into his shoulders, his arms and his chest, enjoying the feel of the taut, strong body under her fingers. Then she soaped her palms more thoroughly before reaching down between his legs to take hold of him.

Nick pulled her close so that they slithered deliciously against each other then he kissed her with a fierce ardour that took her breath away. They slid, stroked, rocked and squeezed before spinning back under the water so that it could sluice them off again. The sensation was quite wickedly erotic.

Kate opened to him in every way.

He lifted her up and carried her to the bedroom, laying her down on the coverlet. With one jolting thrust, he surged straight into her, filling her more completely than any man had ever done before and setting off a whole range of tiny ecstasies. Kate put her hands on his buttocks and pressed down hard. He pumped away with mounting vigour, kissing and caressing at the same time and committing himself wholeheartedly to her.

Kate responded to his rhythm at once and abandoned herself totally to the savage delight that was coursing right through her.

Her orgasm came with such dynamic force that she felt as if she were being split in two and sank her teeth into his flesh to muffle the sound of the long groan of pleasure that burst from her. It went on and on, reaching every part of her body, deepening and intensifying, sending her into convulsions of indescribable joy.

Nick rode her until it had run its full course, guiding her on to new sensations and prolonging her euphoria with subtle skills. Only when she flopped back on the bed did he slow down and stop. He pushed the wet hair back from her forehead and kissed away the frowns.

'How was it?' he whispered.

'Out of this world!'

'Good.'

'What about you?'

'I loved it.'

'You must come as well,' she insisted.

'Oh, I will, Kate. But not as fast as that. I like to take my time.' He nuzzled against her cheek. 'Besides, you can come more often than I can. You were ready then and I didn't want to keep you waiting. As for me . . . we've got all night.'

'Yes.'

Kate gave a little gasp of disappointment as he pulled out of her. He lay down beside her and cradled her in his arms, licking some of the droplets from her face.

'What made you change your mind?' he asked.

'I don't know. When I reached the motel, I just . . . wanted to come back to you. I needed you.'

'Me – or it?'

She smiled. 'Both.'

He put his lips to hers in a long, lazy, searching kiss then he knelt up so that he could look at her properly for the first time. Desire melted into reverence.

'You're beautiful,' he murmured.

'So are you.'

'We're beautiful together.'

He bent over to lick her foot, taking each moist toe separately into his mouth to suck it with patient softness. Working his way slowly up her leg, he left a trail of delicate kisses that made her glow with contentment. He moved on up her body until he came to her breasts.

Kate closed her eyes and purred her satisfaction. She was soon aroused again, wanting him once more, eager to give him pleasure as well.

Nick went into her with a slow, deliberate thrust that took him deeper even than before. His full weight was now on her and his hands fondled her breasts. Kate was on air. She felt aroused, enraptured, wholly possessed. She felt loved.

His movements were at first almost imperceptible, minute twitches and shifts and changes of angle. They be-more definite and Kate was soon on fire again, writhing under him with accelerating delight and urging him to pump harder and faster.

He took her to the brink and then stopped, adding a delectable agony to it all, making her beg for consummation. When she had come down from her peak, he started again, working up slowly until he had brought her to the verge once more then pausing at the critical moment to leave her hanging in blissful suspense.

'Don't stop!' she implored.

'I love you, Kate.'

'I love you!'

The third time there was no holding back. Squeezing her breasts in time to his thrusts, he plunged in and out of her with gathering power until he sparked off a climax that was one long moan of sheer exaltation. And as her orgasm began to fade, it was replaced by his own, a gushing torrent that made him cry out aloud.

When it was all over, they lay in each other's arms in a state of languid satisfaction. They were lovers. Nothing else mattered at that point in time. They had helped each other to break through a vital barrier. Both of them had at last let go.

He leaned over to give her a kiss of gratitude then tried to get up from the bed. She wrapped her legs around him and held him tight.

'Stay here, Nick.'

'I was only going to switch the shower off.'

Kate listened. The water was still running. It was an omen.

'Leave it,' she said. 'I want to hear it.'

Rounding up a thousand head of cattle was a whole new experience for Marty and Tina. It might have been less arduous if they'd seen more of what was going on. But their eyes and their mouths were soon filled with dust kicked up by the flashing hooves.

'My butt hurts like crazy!' Marty confided.

'And mine,' said his sister. 'I sure wish we could ride like Zoe and Emmie. They're terrific.'

'Yes. Especially Zoe.'

The natural ease with which the two girls rode was an inspiration to the twins and made them persevere. Dressed in country-style clothing for the first time, they were trotting around the edge of the herd, concentrating on the difficult task of staying on top and in control of their horses.

'It looks so different in the movies,' Tina complained.

'I know. I always thought it'd be fun to be a cowboy.'

'Not any more.'

She pulled her mount to a dead stop then took out her camera as Zoe galloped into view. Tina followed her with the lens and then took the action photograph when her subject was chasing a few mavericks back to the main herd.

Ably supported by Bluey, who was barking at the heels of the cattle, Zoe and Emmie tore across the range at impressive speed, turning their horses at will and displaying a fearless attitude. Gillie and Jamie were controlling the drive with their motorbikes, haring around the outside of the herd as they guided them along.

Tina took several photographs of the two Aboriginals.

'Those guys ought to be stunt riders,' she opined.

'They are!' said Marty. 'Just look at 'em go, will you?'

They hurtled across the plain, creating a slipstream of red dust.

Their machines rasped, hooves galloped and the cattle protested noisily, then a different sound contributed to the din. Out of the sky came Nick's helicopter, descending at speed with its rotor blades whirring frenetically.

'Mom's back!' cried Tina, pointing up.

'Yeah.'

'Oh boy, I must get a shot of the chopper.'

Before she could focus her camera, however, the helicopter went into a sudden dive and swooped down to within feet of the ground, sending the cattle pounding away in the opposite direction.

'What the hell is he playing at!' Marty shouted.

'I think he did it on purpose,' his sister decided.

'But he frightened the herd.'

'No, he didn't. He drove them where they're supposed to go.'

Nick brought the helicopter down again and was quite obviously helping the round-up. Quite used to mustering cattle in that way, he manoeuvred his machine with a daredevil skill that had even the two Aboriginals cheering. The twins goggled.

'See, Marty? Told you.'

'What a pilot!'

'I hope Mom's wearing her safety belt.'

'She'll have to, the way he's throwing that machine around.'

The herd was now moving at speed towards a distant gorge but there was one renegade. A calf broke away on its own and tried to gallop off into the scrub. Marty saw it and spurred his horse on to intercept the animal, turning it back so that it had to rejoin the herd. He was thrilled with his success, all the more so because Tina managed to get a photograph of his moment of glory.

Zoe brought her horse cantering over and reined it in.

'Well done, Marty!' she congratulated him. 'You're learning fast.'

'Oh, it was nothing . . .'

But it was. It altered his whole perspective on the Outback.

He actually began to enjoy himself.

The gorge was narrow and steep, with red-faced cliffs towering into the night sky. Stars shone in profusion overhead. Cattle were lowing in the distance. A warm breeze was blowing.

The camp-fire burned brightly on the yellow sand. Kate, Nick and the children lay nearby on their swags, exhausted but pleased with the day's work. Sitting apart from them were the two Aboriginals. Gillie was carving something out of a piece of wood and Jamie was playing a tribal song on his harmonica.

As the music drifted plaintively through the still air, Nick was pointing out the various constellations to Kate and the children.

'That one there is the Great Bear,' he explained.

'Which one is Ursa Major?' asked Tina.

'Same one. It's another name for it.' His finger picked out a group of stars. 'The seven brightest ones in that constellation are called the Plough. See the shape?'

'Yeah,' said Marty. 'Uh, what about that one, Nick?'

'Orion. The hunter.'

'How about the Southern Cross?' asked Kate.

'There it is.' Emmie nudged Marty and pointed upwards.

'Where?'

'See the two very bright stars in a line?' Nick resumed. 'They're the pointers. Now look where they're pointing. *That's* the Southern Cross.'

'Oh, yeah,' Marty confirmed. 'I see it now.'

'Me, too,' added Tina, enthralled. 'Wow! They're so

gorgeous, those stars. I never really noticed them before. All you see at night in LA is neon.'

Kate studied the sky with fascination then lowered her gaze to take in the gorge and the mulga plain beyond that was dimly lit by a melancholy moon.

'It seems so different all of a sudden,' she whispered.

'Depends on the way you look at it,' Nick argued. 'This land has been the home of the Aboriginal people for forty thousand years. It's part of Dreamtime. It has a magic all of its own.'

'Tom said that,' she recalled fondly.

'It can be your enemy or your friend.'

Kate's smile had real optimism in it for a change. She felt instinctively that everything would somehow work out for them. The future at Larapinta was bright with promise.

The music finished and merged into the darkness.

'Thank you, Jamie,' she said. 'That was lovely.'

The Aboriginal beamed as if he had just been given a large tip.

Further down the gorge, the cattle were still lowing. The sound made Kate more reflective and she admitted to some doubts.

'Nick, I can't help feeling guilty about selling off Tom's steers.'

'Tom would have done it himself.'

'Would he?'

'It's the only practical thing to do. You have to be realistic. The money you get could be enough to see you through until the drought breaks.' He gave a rueful shrug. '*If* it breaks.'

'You never know your luck.'

Nick chuckled and threw her a meaningful glance.

Marty got up from the ground with his guitar and went to sit on the other side of the fire with Gillie and Jamie. The others watched as he began to strum his instrument. Softly and unexpectedly, he sang 'Waltzing Matilda' in a voice that was sweet and sure. The song took on a poignant quality as it drifted along the gorge.

In the flickering firelight, shadows danced on his face. Marty sang on with firm purpose, making an offering to his mother, to his new family and to Tom Hannon's beloved land. Everyone was profoundly moved by it all.

It was his commitment to the future.

Nick's hand reached out in the gloom towards Kate and she squeezed it affectionately. Marty noticed the contact and smiled. Emmie now decided to join in. Shyly producing her recorder from her handbag, she moved to sit beside Marty then played along with him, signalling her readiness to accept her new family and to share in whatever lay ahead of them.

The whole gorge was now filled with melodious sound.

It still echoed when night's warm embrace closed around them.

The giant tanker had filled more troughs at Cutta Cutta and hundreds of thirsty cattle were thrusting their snouts into the water. Not far away, a group of calves was being branded. Phil was supervising the operation but Ed Stenning was determined not to be left out. Sleeves rolled up, he held the branding iron as each new calf was held down for him to put his mark on it. Ed liked to show his men exactly how things should be done.

The sound of a horse made him look up and frown. Meg was galloping hell for leather towards them on her roan. Ed poked the iron back into the fire before snatching off his gloves and thrusting them at one of the other men.

'Take over,' he ordered abruptly.

Watched by Phil, he strode across to Meg as she brought the horse to a dusty halt and dismounted. Her face was tense and sweat was pouring freely from it.

'It must be important,' he guessed.

'It is, Dad. Wunjuk's on his way to Larapinta.'

He winced. 'Wunjuk!'

'I'll bet Nick's behind it,' she said with contempt. 'Wunjuk's the best water-diviner in the territory. What if he finds that underground lake?'

'Tom Hannon never found it. Neither did Simmo.'

'Wunjuk is something special,' she conceded. 'Besides, Nick has probably told them by now about the lake. When they know it's there, all they have to do is track it down.'

'We'll have to take that risk, Meg.'

'I say it's too big a risk.'

'Leave it alone!' he snapped peremptorily. 'You'll do as you're told!'

'We've got to fight back at them.'

'*I* make the decisions round here, Meg.'

'Nick beat you at Alice Springs,' she reminded cruelly. 'Are you going to let him beat you again?'

'That's enough!' he roared.

Blood rushed to his face and the veins on his forehead stood out like strands of barbed wire. Ed Stenning was a fearsome sight when enraged and Meg backed down at once. She knew that his word was final.

Phil had observed it all with concern. He now came over to see if he could be of any assistance to Meg. Before the foreman could even open his mouth, however, Ed subdued him with a snarled command.

'Keep out of this, Phil.'

'I only want to —'

'This is family.'

Meg flashed Phil a look that contained gratitude and warning. 'It's okay,' she said. 'I can handle this.'

'Fine, Meg,' he muttered. 'I'll ... see you later.' He nodded and walked slowly back to the others.

Ed continued to glare with disapproval at his daughter as if daring her to challenge him again.

Meg felt this was one instance when her father was in the wrong, though she knew he would never admit it. But she had his temper and it now flared inside her. Smarting at his rebuff, she grabbed the pommel of her saddle, inserted a toe into the stirrup and hauled herself up on to the horse. Without another word, she spurred the animal back across the plain.

Behind Ed, the ranch-hands were all watching with interest.

'What are *you* looking at?' yelled Ed, turning round.

His voice was a branding iron in itself.

Wunjuk was a wizened Aboriginal of indeterminate age with nothing between him and total nakedness but a pair of dark blue cotton trousers that had been bleached by the sun and worn desperately thin by time. As he sat in the cab of the flat-top truck between Nick and Kate, the old man scanned the surroundings with intense interest. Every so often he would mumble a few words in his native tongue to Nick.

Kate was praying that the diviner could save them. When they set out from Larapinta, her hopes had been high and her spirits up. The further they went, however, the more her doubts began to spread. Wunjuk had to succeed, she kept telling herself, or the ranch would die on its feet. Larapinta's whole future was now in the hands of a frail old Aboriginal with tattered trousers.

After they had driven several miles in the morning heat, Wunjuk suddenly pointed a finger and grunted to the driver. Nick swung the truck off the track and bounced it across the hard, uneven ground. It scrunched to a halt near a patch of mulga.

Wunjuk got out immediately and walked in a line holding two bent wires in front of him.

Kate was sceptical. 'Is that really going to work, Nick?'

'Has done for thousands of years.'

'But it's so . . . primitive.'

'That's why it's so reliable. Abos have survived in the Outback since the dawn of time. And it's only because they know how to hunt food and track down water. Give Wunjuk time.'

'Why isn't he divining on the site of the old wells?'

'He says the sub-artesian table's almost finished. He's searching for a fresh source.'

'How long will it take?'

'A few days – if the water's there.'

'If!' she exclaimed. 'It's *got* to be there, Nick!'

'It will be.'

'You're not sure, are you?'

'Kate . . .' He looked into a face that was crumpled by agitation and he longed to take her in his arms and comfort her by telling her that there was a lake somewhere beneath Larapinta territory. But something held him back. Something deeper and more complex even than his love for her. Something that he could neither understand nor combat.

Nick was restrained by a perverse loyalty to his father, by a vestigial sense of duty to a man he loathed. He eagerly wanted Kate to find water on her own account but he could not divulge the contents of the survey commissioned by Ed Stenning.

The inner conflict was tearing him apart.

Kate pleaded with him for a measure of reassurance. '*Is* there water there, Nick?'

He could not meet her gaze. Instead, he glanced across at the old Aboriginal with his two absurd pieces of wire.

'Wunjuk knows what he's doing.'

Tina lay alone on the bed in her room and sifted through the private treasures that she kept in an old cigar box. Tears flowed once more as she read Billy's last letter to her. The pain of his betrayal had not dulled as the weeks passed. When she was with the others, Tina could cope by losing herself in work or play. When she was left on her own, the memories returned to plague her like a swarm of mosquitoes. They could bite.

There was a knock on the door and a quiet voice said, 'Can I come in?'

Tina sat up and quickly put everything back into the cigar box before wiping her eyes with the back of her hands.

'Who is it?' she asked.

The door opened and Zoe came in with a smile of sympathy. 'You want to talk?'

Tina shook her head and put the cigar box on the bedside table.

Zoe strolled across to her and ignored her first response. 'I find it helps sometimes if you talk,' she reasoned. 'Emmie and I talk all the time. If you keep it inside you, it just goes sort of sour and you're no good to yourself or to anyone then.' She leaned against the bed. 'What was Billy like?'

'He was nothing special,' said Tina dismissively.

'How old was he?'

'Eighteen. Just.'

'That's not a boy,' commented Zoe, impressed. 'That's a young man.'

'He was pretty grown-up,' conceded the other.

'Was he tall? Fair or dark? Fat or thin?'

There was a moment of indecision as Tina scrutinised her visitor. She had talked to Kate about her boyfriend but a mother could never really appreciate what she was going through. Only a girl of her own age could really know what she must feel like. Beth would have understood. If she was back in Los Angeles, Tina knew that she would have told her best friend everything and got support in return.

But Beth was not here. Zoe was, keen to help. Tina yielded to the need to confide in someone.

'Billy was tall,' she said. 'Nearly six foot. Dark brown hair. And he was thin – not skinny, mind. He had great muscles. Used to work out with weights. But he was slim.'

'Good-looking?'

'Real handsome. The other girls used to go crazy because I'd snapped him up. They were so jealous, Zoe. You wouldn't believe what I had to put up with, honest.'

'Was Billy at the same school?'

'Yeah – then he left.'

'Did he live near?'

'No, we were downtown and he had his own apartment in Venice.'

'His own place?' Zoe was taken aback.

228

'Sure. It was only small but it was all his.'

'Do you mean that you and Billy could go there . . . alone?'

'We were in love,' said Tina simply.

Zoe stared at her for a few moments and then decided to trade her own secrets. She sensed that Tina would be very discreet.

'I've never really had a boyfriend,' she admitted.

'No, Emmie told me about your boarding school. All girls.'

'And there are not too many boys out here.'

'So I notice!' Tina moaned.

The two of them laughed involuntarily at their plight.

'There was the boy I met at a party in Glenwarra once,' Zoe went on. 'He took me outside in the dark and kissed me. Twice.'

'Then what?'

'Nothing. I never saw him again. Can't even remember his name.'

'Boys are slobs, Zoe. Most of them stink, you know that?'

'Marty doesn't stink,' Zoe retorted defensively.

'Well, no. He's different. He's my brother.'

'Marty's okay. He can certainly play that guitar.'

'I know,' sighed Tina. 'I had to listen to him practise for five years!'

They laughed again and it drew them unconsciously together. Tina pondered a major decision then reached for her cigar box. Setting it on her knee, she lifted the lid and reached inside.

'Like to see a photo of him?'

'Billy? I'd love to.'

'This is one I took myself on Santa Monica beach.'

She handed over the photograph, which showed Billy in a pair of black swimming trunks, posing in front of the Pacific Ocean and breathing in deeply to inflate his chest.

'Wow!' Zoe examined the photograph with great interest.

'That's him . . . *was* him.'

'He's really nice looking, Tina.'

'Yeah.' It all came back to her. 'I hate him.'

'So do I,' decided her new friend.

The bond between them was strengthened even more.

Kate Hannon sat in front of the roll-top desk and leafed through a pile of correspondence. Apart from letters to friends in California, she also had to deal with several bills. To raise the cash to pay them, she was having to sell off a sizeable proportion of her herd. She was still in two minds about it, there was no other money available.

As she flipped through the bills, she heard a faint rustling sound close by as if the curtains had just been disturbed by a gust of wind. She tossed a glance over her shoulder but saw nothing and addressed herself to her work again. Kate heard a second rustle. She knew exactly where it came from this time because something brushed against her ankle.

She looked down and instantly froze with horror.

A large brown snake was resting against her foot. It had evidently been coiled up under the desk and was now coming out to look around. Still rubbing against her, it moved a few more inches forward.

Kate was horrified. She could neither move nor cry out for fear of provoking the snake into attack. She was trapped. Literally, a sitting target. Her blood congealed.

Tom had warned her about snakes and she knew that many of them were poisonous. What alarmed her most was that it had got into the house without being noticed. After her encounter in the kitchen with the two dingoes, she thought she had got past the worst. But the snake was a far more deadly and frightening creature. She had no defence against it.

Blind panic made her mind spin. She was afraid for herself, of course, but her main concern was for the children – her own and Tom Hannon's. If anything should happen to her, they would have no one to look after them. It brought home to her very strongly the awful vulnerability of the single-parent family.

They need me, she thought. I can't leave them on their own. Don't let me die! Please, God. Not this way. Not now.

The snake slid across her foot then paused to conduct a search of the room. It felt like a ton weight on her and she was in agonies of apprehension in case her foot twitched accidentally. All she could do was remain absolutely still and hope that it would go away.

But the snake did not move again. Like her problems at Larapinta, it was not going to disappear of its own accord, she realised. It had to be dealt with in some way otherwise it would kill her.

Hysteria gripped her and her mind filled with screams. *Please save me! Somebody – help me!*

But nobody came and the snake remained where it was, lifting its head slightly and letting its tongue dart in and out. She tried to exert some control over herself and work out exactly what would happen if she did get bitten. There was no hospital in Glenwarra. She would have to fly the two hundred miles to Alice Springs to get the snake serum – if indeed it existed – and she was convinced that she would be dead long before she arrived.

It was such a gruesome way to go. To know in advance and to suffer the slow torture of the wait. To see her assassin and to watch it bide its time. To fear for her children and to be able to do nothing at all for them.

Kate Hannon was on the rack and the pain was murderous.

'If you want to learn about boomerangs, Gillie will teach you.' Nick's voice. Approaching from outside. Hope at last.

'How do you get it to come back to you?' Marty asked.

'Wishful thinking.' He laughed. 'No, I'm kidding. It's all in the wrist . . .'

The two of them walked in through the door and waved to Kate. They saw her face, pleading with them. Then they saw the snake.

'Hell!' Nick murmured.

'Mom!' Marty whispered.

Nick gestured Marty to stay completely still, then crept slowly to the wall to take down the rifle that was hanging on two wooden pegs. As he checked to see if it was loaded, the snake began to move again, working round to Kate's other leg. Suddenly, it reared its head to strike and she could bear to look no more. She closed her eyes tight and braced herself for the agony of the bite.

Bang!

The shot hurled the snake across the room and it landed near the window in a lifeless heap. Nick put the smoking gun under his arm and looked over at the creature.

'A king brown,' he observed. 'You were lucky. They're venomous.'

Kate felt her self-control crumble and she got up to fling herself into his arms for safety.

'Oh, Nick . . . Nick!'

'It's okay, it's okay,' he soothed. 'It's all over.'

Marty regarded him with wonder and admiration.

Ed Stenning and his daughter sat at opposite ends of the magnificent antique dining table that formed the centre-piece of the room. They were sharing their evening meal at Cutta Cutta and Ed insisted on all the formalities. Traditional cooking had been served by the staff and the two of them went through the bizarre ritual of eating dinner as if at a banquet.

Meg pushed her plate aside and reached for the map of Larapinta that lay beside her. The results of the water survey were clearly marked, indicating a large under-ground lake.

'Do you think this survey could be wrong, Dad?' she asked.

'The geologist studied that terrain for months – when Tom Hannon wasn't looking. If he says there's a lake down there, you'd better believe it.'

'Oh, I do,' she returned with an ironic smile.

'What's the joke?'

'It's on you, I'm afraid. I was just thinking how much you had to pay to have that survey done without anyone knowing.' A mocking note intruded. 'Now some smelly old Abo might get the same result for a few dollars.'

She glanced down at the map covetously and became serious. 'We want Larapinta, don't we? Then we should go out and make sure that we get it. Mrs Hannon'll never sell once she hits that lake.'

'There's no guarantee she *will* hit it. Even with Wunjuk.'

'If she does find water, it's goodbye to our chances. So, are you just going to let that bitch *keep* Larapinta?'

'It's hers by right, Meg.'

'What right!' demanded his daughter contemptuously. 'She knew Tom Hannon for two weeks, that's all. What sort of basis for marriage is that? She wasn't the sort of woman he needed out here and she's got no right to stay on.' She grabbed the map and waved it at him. 'That land is *ours*, Dad. We have to *do* something!'

'You'll do nothing,' he decreed.

'You're going soft,' she accused. 'This isn't the Ed Stenning that everyone knows. You always taught me to have the guts to go out and take what I wanted.'

'Don't you talk to me about guts!' he exploded, rising to his feet in fury. 'I built a whole empire on guts. It's what my name stands for in this territory and don't you ever forget it!'

Meg changed her tack and came over to stand in front of him. 'Larapinta is there for the taking,' she coaxed. 'Take it. That woman doesn't *deserve* it!'

'Kate Hannon doesn't worry me,' he said airily. 'Sooner or later, she'll come crashing down. She can't run a ranch on her own.'

'What if Nick is there helping her?'

It was like a knife between his ribs and he gasped.

Almost a week passed and Wunjuk had still not located any water. Kate's hopes began to fade and the future took on a bleaker aspect. The pessimism spread to the children. They became more watchful and subdued. They knew only too well the implications of Wunjuk's failure.

'Marty! Breakfast, honey!' Kate flung open the door of the barn as she called him. Sunlight flooded into the dim interior. She went on in.

'Marty, you can play with that calf later . . .'

Her words trailed away as she saw her son's face. He was kneeling in the straw beside the prostrate body of the calf he had helped to bring into the world. Tragedy turned him into a helpless little boy once more.

'Buddy's dead,' he murmured. 'His mom just didn't have enough milk.'

'Oh, Marty!'

'I came in and found him like this.'

He stroked the dead calf for a moment then got up to fling himself into his mother's arms, crying bitterly at the injustice of it all. During its brief life, he had doted on the animal. Now it was one more victim of the killer drought.

'It's not *fair*, Mom!'

'I know, honey,' she soothed. 'I know.'

Kate shared his agony and rocked him gently to and fro. When his tears finally stopped, she walked with him back to the house. Marty did not feel like anything to eat now and went off to his room to be on his own. Everything seemed suddenly to press down on her, and Kate trudged back into the kitchen with leaden gait.

The other children had still not answered her call but she had no strength to repeat it. What she needed was a cup of black coffee to revive her. She reached for the kettle and held it under the tap. When she turned it on, however, all she got was a strange gurgling noise and a trickle of muddy water that dried up within seconds.

The tank was empty. It was the last straw.

'No!' she howled, throwing the kettle to the floor.

Kate pounded the tap with her fists in an outburst of frustration, then she collapsed into a chair with a groan of utter despair.

'Oh, God . . . how much longer can we go on!'

— 18 —

A small group of cattle rested in the shade of the tree that stood in the middle of the yard at the Larapinta homestead. They were relaxed and unsuspecting, chewing slowly and flicking their tails to keep the flies at bay. None of the animals saw Gillie climbing among the branches above them with his rifle slung across his back.

Music floated out from the schoolroom. Children from forty cattle stations scattered over a wide area were linked by radio in an impromptu orchestra. Marty was playing his guitar while Emmie was blowing her recorder, their instruments swelling the sound that came from dozens of others.

The old Aboriginal worked himself into a comfortable position then reached for his gun. Choosing a steer that had plenty of meat on its frame, he took aim and fired. The shot smashed into the animal's brain and sent it crashing to the ground. Startled by the noise, the other cattle lowed in distress and trotted quickly away.

Kate appeared on the verandah and the four children stared out of the schoolroom window. Though the steer was dead, it continued to twitch for some time, its eyes looking sightlessly upwards.

'Why did he shoot it?' Marty asked in alarm.

'For meat,' said Zoe. 'Dad always had a steer hanging out in the meat shed.'

Marty said nothing but he was patently upset. He watched as Gillie and Jamie wound ropes around the fallen steer then used the truck to drag it across the yard. A trail of red blood stained the hard ground.

The Aboriginals drove round the corner of the barn and went out of sight.

'Let's get back to the music,' suggested Emmie.

'I've had enough,' Marty decided.

He put his guitar aside and went quickly out of the room.

'What's wrong with him?' asked Zoe.

'It's Buddy,' Tina explained. 'When that calf of his died, it really got to him.'

Zoe was sympathetic. 'Shall I go after him?'

'No. He'd just like to be alone for a bit.'

While the children rejoined Dotty Phillips for their music lesson, Gillie and Jamie got on with their work. After hauling the dead steer into the meat shed, they hosed it thoroughly all over then hacked off its head and its legs. The carcass was then hung from a huge hook suspended from the main beam. With long, sharp knives, they began to skin the steer.

They chatted happily as they worked, going through a familiar routine in a brisk and objective way. When it was all over, they left the carcass dangling from its hook and hosed down the floor. Then they went out of the shed.

Marty came up and pressed his nose against the flywire inside the building. He swallowed hard when he saw the carcass turning slowly on its hook. A great rush of nausea attacked him and he went outside to vomit in the dust.

It was Tina who wrapped comforting arms around him this time.

The telephone call sent Kate Hannon haring into Glenwarra as fast as she could drive. She stopped outside Henry Dingwell's office, leaped out of the cab and rushed through the door. Before the secretary could stop her, Kate had gone straight in to see the lawyer.

'Henry, you're a genius!' she announced.

'Am I?' he said, rising in surprise from behind his desk.

'You're wonderful! I could kiss you.'

'Don't let me stop you.'

237

'Is it true what you said over the phone? You've actually fixed up a loan?'

'Of course,' he replied airily. 'I usually get there in the end. That's the Dingwell motto. Never give up.' He gestured her to a seat then picked up some papers from his desk. 'Here we are.'

'So who's lending me the money?'

'Don't bother about that, Kate. Just sign on the dotted line.'

'But I need to know which bank it is,' she argued.

'It's a private loan,' he told her. 'All perfectly legal and above-board. See for yourself.'

Dingwell handed her the papers. While she glanced through them, he came round to stand behind her and point out a key clause in the contract. Her eyebrows shot up.

'Why is there so little interest?'

'You have an anonymous benefactor.'

'Who?' she demanded. 'I can't enter into an agreement with someone unless I know who it is. What's all the secrecy?'

Dingwell perched himself on the edge of the desk and composed his features into a rueful half-smile.

'Kate, I had one helluva job trying to raise that loan. Most places wouldn't even listen to me. All the banks turned me down.' His tone was reflective.

'Why?' she said in mild alarm.

'Because Larapinta is a bad risk. It was in trouble when Tom was alive and he'd raised cattle all his life. The banks were uneasy about lending money to someone who was . . .'

'Say it, Henry – a greenhorn.'

'Someone who was less experienced,' he added tactfully. 'Also, they aren't at all convinced that you have water under your land.'

'So why is my benefactor ready to stick his neck out? It all seems a little weird.'

'Kate,' he asserted, 'let me lay it on the line. This offer

238

is not only the best one you'll get. It's the *only* one. Now, then – do you want the money or not?'

She brushed her doubts aside and reached for a pen from the desk.

'Where do I sign?'

Meg Stenning sat in the passenger seat of the Land Rover while Phil drove her along the main street in Glenwarra. She had been morose and preoccupied on the journey from Cutta Cutta and his patience was wearing slightly thin. She seemed to be miles away.

'Hey!' he snapped. 'Remember me?'

'What?' She came out of her reverie. 'Oh, sorry, Phil. My mind was on something else.'

'It always is these days.'

'Don't be angry with me,' she said, putting a hand on his arm and sounding a gentler note for once. 'I'll make it up to you.'

'I'll hold you to that,' he replied, glancing across at her before turning back to look through the windscreen. 'Shit!'

Phil braked hard as he saw Kate Hannon, arms full of parcels, step out directly in front of him. The vehicle squealed to an emergency stop only inches from her, causing her to drop the parcels and raise her hands protectively.

When he jumped out to accost her, there was more concern than anger in his manner and he could see that she was shaken.

'What the hell were you doing?'

'I'm sorry,' she mumbled. 'I looked the wrong way. I keep forgetting that you drive on the other side of the road here.'

He bent down to retrieve the parcels from the ground as Meg alighted from the vehicle.

'I'm sure Mrs Hannon isn't hurt, Phil.' Her tone was deliberately frosty.

'No . . . I'm fine,' Kate agreed, jolted by seeing her.

Phil handed over the parcels along with a polite smile. 'That's the lot.'

'Thank you.'

'Let's go,' Meg said abruptly.

As they turned away, Kate acted on impulse.

'Wait!' As Meg swung round, she addressed her. 'I'd like a word with you. Alone.'

Meg considered it for a moment then nodded to Phil, who got back into the Land Rover.

'Well? What is it?' Meg asked impatiently.

Kate took a deep breath and tried to sound conciliatory.

'Meg,' she said, 'I know there's been a lot of ill-feeling between the Stennings and the Hannons in the past. But I'd like to change all that.'

'Kiss and make up? That what you're suggesting?'

'Something like that.'

'Yes,' retorted Meg with asperity, 'that would just suit you. Being on good terms with your lover's family.'

'It isn't like that!' Kate denied, wounded to the quick.

'Then what is it like?'

'I'm making a genuine effort to be friends. Nick doesn't come into this.'

'No?' Meg remained cynical. 'Pull the other leg.'

Kate had to struggle to hold down her rising temper. 'You hate your brother, don't you?'

'Nick isn't worth hating,' Meg replied with blistering scorn. 'But thanks for the olive branch. I'll tell Dad. It'll give him a good laugh.'

Meg got back into the Land Rover and left her standing there.

'What was all that about?' Phil wondered.

'Drive on.'

'She looks stunned,' he noted, easing the vehicle on down the road. 'What did you tell her?'

'The truth. Stennings and Hannons don't mix.'

'Nick obviously doesn't feel that way.'

'He's not a real Stenning any more!' she snarled.

'He's not out of the same drawer as you and your Dad,

that's for sure.' Phil glanced in his wing mirror and saw a forlorn Kate still looking after them. 'Mrs Hannon had a narrow escape. I almost hit her.'

'If I'd been driving,' confessed Meg, 'I *would* have hit her.'

He was shocked. 'On purpose?'

'I don't like people who step in my way!'

There was a chilling sincerity in her words.

Drilling began at the new bore site and they all watched anxiously. Gillie and Jamie held their breath. Marty crossed his fingers. Nick and Kate were in a state of great tension. The three workmen who operated the equipment were concerned as well. This was effectively Larapinta's last chance of survival.

With a loud, rumbling noise, the bore drilled its way down through the parched soil until it had reached its maximum depth. The switch was thrown into reverse and the bore worked its way back to the surface. They leaned forward to see the result then groaned. The earth stayed completely dry. The drilling had been a failure.

'Go deeper,' Kate urged.

'I'm sorry, that's as far as it can go,' Nick explained.

'Are you *sure* this is the spot where Wunjuk said to dig?'

'Quite sure, Kate.'

'I thought you said he was reliable.'

'Nobody has a hundred per cent success.'

Kate looked around at the others. They were all eyeing her with sympathy and awaiting her decision. Though she was crestfallen, she did her best to maintain her composure.

'We'd better pack up . . .'

As the workmen began to dismantle their equipment, she walked off to a little rise from which she could survey the plain. It was a nostalgic moment because she knew that Larapinta would now no longer be hers. It would have to be sold. Without water, she was finished.

'We did our best, Tom,' she murmured. 'Sorry.'

All her brave plans and bold ambitions were now dashed. All the efforts she had put into the ranch had been wasted. The pain of defeat gnawed at her and she clutched her side.

Then came a moment of absolute magic.

'Mom!' yelled Marty in excitement. 'Look!'

The dry earth near the drilling rig seemed to shake a little, then a small amount of water appeared. It oozed then bubbled then shot out of the ground with tremendous force, gushing straight into the air before mushrooming out like a giant fountain.

'Kate!' shouted Nick. 'You just struck water!'

Everybody danced about with joy and let it pour over them.

'Ripper!'

'You beaut!'

'Bloody fantastic!'

'We're saved!'

Kate threw herself into Nick's arms, crying and laughing at the same time. As they stood there beneath the friendly torrent, she felt as if she were standing beneath the shower with him at his house.

The night in Alice Springs had indeed been an omen.

Celebrations continued well into the night at the homestead with food and drink and endless songs. They had discovered the underground lake and their problems were largely over. The first toast was drunk, appropriately, with water.

Kate raised her glass and gazed with pride at her family.

'To us,' she said. 'All of us. And – the future!'

'The future!' they repeated in unison.

The success had bound them all together into one happy unit.

When it was time to go to bed, the children retired to their rooms and Nick sauntered off alone to the bunkhouse. Kate waited until everyone else in the house was sound asleep then she let herself out through the kitchen door and ran stealthily across the yard. There was a tiny glow in the window of the bunkhouse.

She let herself in and found Nick stretched out on one of the bunks with a light blanket over him. An oil lamp burned nearby and it caught his hair in such a way that he seemed almost to have a halo.

Kate slipped off her dressing gown and got under the blanket beside him. She nestled familiarly against his naked body and tasted his lips in a first, long, loving, exploratory kiss.

'Nick . . .'

'Yes?'

'Thank you.'

'For what?'

'Making it all possible.'

'The water? That was Wunjuk's doing.'

'I was thinking of the cost of that drilling.' She caressed his face with delicate fingers. 'Thank you for lending us the money.'

There was a long pause. A smile of admission spread.

'How did you know it was me, Kate?'

'Who else?' She became serious. 'I'll repay every cent . . .'

'Sssshhhh!'

He kissed her gently and they loved the night away.

Meg Stenning had no love to help her through the dark. Consumed by hatred, she lay on her bed as Phil slid into her with a grunt of triumph then started to pump away. His strong hands were under her buttocks and he squeezed them hard each time he pushed into her. He was an ardent lover but he lacked any finesse. There was something almost crudely mechanical about the way that he was thrusting in and out with developing momentum. His head was buried in her neck and his mouth worked hungrily on her flesh.

She submitted to it all with distant interest and minimal

pleasure, staring at the ceiling and running her hands up and down his back. Her mind was on Larapinta and the water that had just been found there. When she thought of Kate Hannon, her anger smouldered. When she recalled that her own brother had helped, vengeance stirred in her heart.

Phil was now bucking furiously and grunting noisily. When his full groan began, she dug her fingernails into him and emitted a high-pitched cry that merged with his own release. Meg writhed beneath him until his orgasm had spent itself then she gave him one last hug before lying there motionless.

As soon as he got his breath back, he lifted himself up on his elbows and stared at her with a hurt expression.

'You were only pretending!'

'Phil . . .'

He used both hands to lift her head closer to him.

'Next time,' he warned, 'do it for real.'

Zoe stood in the middle of the yard and held the lunge as the horse trotted in a wide circle. Marty was in the saddle, rising in the stirrups at her command and finding the whole exercise much more comfortable than his previous attempts on horseback. Zoe was a good teacher and he obeyed her every instruction.

'Right,' she said. 'Now try it on your own.'

'Okay.'

She came over to remove the lunge and the cavesson from the horse, then gave it a firm slap on the rump.

'Go on, Pegasus!'

At a rising trot, horse and rider circled the yard a few times then Marty reined his mount in. He was thrilled with his progress.

'I think I'm getting the hang of it.'

'Emmie will take you out for a proper ride,' she said.

'What about you?' he asked in obvious disappointment.

'I'm too busy here.'

'Thanks, anyway. You've been a terrific help, Zoe.'

'Good.'

They smiled at each other in a moment of unguarded affection. Both of them had come a long way since those early days of sullen detachment and bloody-mindedness. Marty admired her tremendously for her quiet competence at a whole range of difficult things and Zoe, for her part, had been impressed by his willingness to adapt to an entirely different lifestyle.

'It's getting better, isn't it, Marty?' she asked.

'What is?'

'Larapinta.'

'Since we found water, it's the centre of the universe!'

'I want you to like it,' she confided. 'It's our home.'

'I do like it now, Zoe. It's growing on me.'

'Does that mean you'd be glad to stay?'

Lingering reservations made him shrug and delay his answer. 'Let's just say that I'm not so desperate to get away.'

'What about Tina?'

'Oh . . . Tina likes it a lot here,' he said without conviction.

'But she'd still rather go back to California.'

'I wouldn't say that.'

'I'm not blind,' Zoe retorted. 'She was as excited as the rest of us when we hit water but she's not really happy at Larapinta. Deep down, she prefers Los Angeles. Even without Billy.'

'Maybe,' he conceded.

Emmie came trotting up from the stables on her pony.

'Ready to go, Marty?'

'Sure.'

'Remember what I taught you now,' said Zoe, grinning up at him.

'I haven't forgotten a word of it,' he promised.

Emmie swung her pony around and headed for the main gate. Marty used his crop to give Pegasus a light tap on the rump then he moved away at a rising trot. Zoe waved them off and her eyes stayed on her pupil. Without realising it, Marty was one of the reasons that she herself had come to enjoy being at Larapinta again.

The riders went out across the plain for a couple of miles, allowing their horses to trot, canter and gallop at intervals. They reached a part of the range where dunes rose up in a repeating sequence to break up the flatness of the prospect.

'Come on, Em. I'll race you to that big sandhill.' Marty's confidence had swelled considerably now.

'How much start would you like?' she teased.

'I'm riding Pegasus,' he boasted. 'He can fly!'

He gave an exultant shout and spurred the horse into a gallop, but Emmie was not to be left behind. Her pony bounded across the range in a flurry of hooves and soon overhauled the bigger but more cumbersome Pegasus. Marty's inexperience told and the girl was well ahead of him when she reached the sandhill, cresting it with a final spurt and disappearing from view.

When he got to the dune himself, he went around its base to the other side – but there was no sign of Emmie. He tugged on the reins and brought Pegasus to a halt. The horse was breathing heavily now and its flanks were streaked with running sweat.

Marty could see a thousand hiding places and had no idea which one Emmie had chosen. He cupped his hands to form a megaphone.

'Where are you!'

His voice reverberated in the stillness but got no answer.

'Emmie!'

He decided to give up the search and make his way home, as the girl was obviously playing some sort of game with him. When she saw him turning tail, he was sure she would come out of her hiding place.

'Come on, Pegasus!' he urged, digging his knees in.

But the horse stayed resolutely in the same position.

'Come on, boy! Off we go!'

Even a taste of the crop did not dislodge Pegasus. He stood there obstinately and ignored all Marty's exhortations. In the end, Marty dismounted and led him by the bridle. The two of them made their way round the sandhill and back across the mulga plain.

It was a long, hard slog in punishing heat and he was soon in a bath of perspiration himself. Strange images rose all around him as the shimmering heat waves distorted everything. A lizard cocked an eye at him from its perch aloft a dead tree, then dropped to the ground when he approached, and darted for its bolt-hole. A plains turkey came out of nowhere to strut past with its comical walk.

Marty pressed on until his legs were aching, then he paused for a rest. Emmie was still nowhere to be seen. He patted the horse and talked to it soothingly in the way that he had seen Zoe do. Then he remounted and gave the signal to move off. Pegasus began to trot slowly across the plain.

'Good boy!' said Marty in delight. 'Good horse.'

Then his voice was drowned out by the sound of a huge explosion not far away. Pegasus reared and took off at a frightened gallop. It was all Marty could do to cling on.

'Hey! Whoa, boy! Stop, will you! Help!' he shouted, but the horse thundered across the red soil in the direction of a low hillock. Smoke was rising behind it in an ominous column. Marty hung on as tightly as he could when the horse galloped up the incline and over the summit before scrambling to a halt when it reached the plain once more.

Its hooves sent up a cloud of dust. When it cleared, Marty saw a scene of utter devastation. The new bore site had been blown up. The ground had caved in, the equipment was a tangled mass of metal and everything was covered in smoking debris.

Marty's stomach lurched when he saw something else.

Ed Stenning was standing on the edge of the site.

In his hand was a stick of dynamite.

'Kate, don't do this! For Pete's sake, think again!'

'I have no choice, Henry.'

'It'd be a terrible mistake,' he counselled.

'Just whose lawyer, are you?' she challenged. 'Mine or Ed Stenning's?'

'You know the answer to that,' he rejoined with hurt dignity. 'But it's my job to advise you. And the simple fact is that you don't have sufficient proof.'

Kate pointed to her son, who was sitting between them in the cab of the Larapinta truck as it tore through Glenwarra.

'Marty saw him,' she argued. 'Ed still had dynamite in his hand. What more do you want – a written confession and colour photographs?'

'Kate, please,' he urged. 'Calm down.'

'I *am* calm.'

'It'll be Marty's word against Ed's. The charge won't stick.'

'Then *make* it stick!'

She brought the truck to a juddering halt outside the police station and switched the engine off. Her own motor continued to run, however, and it was clearly in overdrive. Dingwell fought to keep his own self-control in an emotional situation.

'It never does to be too hasty,' he reasoned.

'Henry,' she said in quivering despair, 'it's all gone. That explosion destroyed the whole of Larapinta. I have to do *something*!'

'Slow down,' he suggested. 'That's all I ask. Slow down.'

Kate gripped the steering wheel tight to stop her hands from trembling and stared grimly through the windscreen.

'You're fighting way above your division here, Kate,' he reminded her. 'Ed Stenning's a real heavyweight. He can afford an army of best lawyers in the state. They'll punch hell out of you and Marty.'

Dingwell paused to consider the options. He knew that they might all live to regret a decision taken in the heat of the moment. Once a police prosecution was set in motion, all kinds of difficulties would arise. It would be far better to avoid a court case if at all possible. He selected a compromise solution.

'Let's confront him, Kate.'

'Ed Stenning?'

'Yes. We'll fire a shot across his bows. Threaten him with a court case that'll blow this state apart. It's worth a try. He might come clean and own up. That would save us all a lot of pain.' He put a hand on her arm. 'Think you're up to it?'

'I certainly am, Henry!' Rancour invaded her voice. 'And there was I, going to offer Cutta Cutta half our water. There was plenty for us both until he dynamited the bore.'

'We can only *presume* that he dynamited it,' he corrected.

'I saw him,' Marty said simply. 'Not twenty yards away.'

'It's the first point I'll raise with Ed,' Dingwell promised.

'No, Henry,' Kate decided. 'I'm going alone.'

'Is that wise?'

Iron determination pushed her words through gritted teeth.

'It's the way it's going to be. This is personal.'

Ed Stenning stumbled to the drinks cabinet in his study and flung open the doors. He was dusty, dishevelled and shaking all over. He poured himself a generous glass of whiskey and lifted it to his lips. Before he could drink it, however, Nick stormed into the room.

'What are you doing here?' asked the old man in surprise.

His son was fuming, barely holding out his temper. 'Did you dynamite Kate Hannon's bore this morning?'

'No!'

'You're a *liar*!'

'You know better than that!' Ed retaliated, raising his voice to match Nick's. 'Have I ever lied to you? About anything?'

'Kate's boy – Marty – he said that he saw you.'

'He did.'

'So what's your excuse?' Nick taunted. 'Did you happen to be passing and pick up the dynamite out of interest?'

'I heard the explosion,' Ed explained. 'I rode over there to see what was going on. That's all. I *swear*!'

His son's response was immediate and bitter. 'Swear on what? My mother's grave?'

There was a tense pause as Ed regarded him with deep anger.

'It always comes back to that, doesn't it?' He swallowed his drink in one urgent gulp and wiped his mouth.

'I didn't want to believe it,' Nick said quietly. 'That you'd go so far. I didn't want to believe that you'd stoop so low.'

'Shut up!'

'The irony is that you've hurt Cutta Cutta as well as Larapinta. Kate wasn't going to keep all that water to herself. She offered to share it with you. Asked me to come over here and work out some kind of deal.' Acrimony gave his voice more edge. 'Instead of which – *this*! The dirtiest trick of all. I never thought you were *that* bad.'

Ed Stenning suddenly looked very old and grey. He poured himself a second drink and downed it at once before facing his son again.

'You finished?'

'Not quite,' Nick returned. 'Kate's gone to the police.

250

You won't buy your way out of this. I hope they send you to prison. You can rot there for all I care!'

Ed recoiled as if from a blow, then he tried to collect himself. When he felt ready to speak again, his voice was calm and very sad.

'If that's the way it's to be,' he said, 'then I'll have to face it. But as we're talking truth, let's drag it all out.'

'What do you mean?'

'Let's talk about your mother. It's long overdue.'

'No.' Nick turned to leave but his father's voice detained him.

'I didn't lie about blowing up that bore. But I lied to you about your mother.' Nick turned to confront him. Ed's voice sagged. 'I'm getting old, son. Too old to live with your hate any longer.'

He moved across to his desk and took a large framed photograph from a drawer. It was a picture of him and his wife on their wedding day. He set it up on the desk so that Nick could see it, then he gazed down sorrowfully at the smiling face of Olivia Stenning.

'I loved her,' he began softly. 'She was everything I wasn't. She had class. I thought some of it might rub off on me if I married her. We were happy for the first few years. Very happy. But after you and Meg were born, she changed.' He turned the photograph over and laid it flat. 'Your mother started to drink, Nick. It hurt like hell to watch her. I tried everything. Gave her whatever she asked for but it wasn't enough.' He winced as the memories became more painful. 'She left home more than once. I always tried to come up with a good excuse for you and Meg, to explain why she wasn't here. Then I heard she was seeing other men. I flew to Adelaide to bring her back.' He looked across pleadingly at his son. 'I still loved her, you see. But she had no time for me. She didn't give a damn any more – about me, about her children . . .'

Nick's face had drained of colour. He stood absolutely still as the terrible revelation unfolded and his own fond image of his mother was shattered into a thousand pieces.

His father was telling the truth now. He could see it. Tears were moistening the old man's eyes. His shoulders stooped, his head was on his chest, he was oppressed by the weight of the secret he had kept to himself all these years.

'I begged her to come home,' continued Ed. 'And she did. Then I got home early one afternoon – we'd been mustering – and I found her on the floor covered in blood. She'd been "entertaining" a man. Tom Hannon's father. He'd beaten her up then made a run for it and left her there . . . Do you know what happened next, Nick?'

His son nodded. 'I came into the room. I saw her lying there like a broken doll.'

'I remember your boy's face when you looked at me, thinking I'd done it to her. What was I gonna tell you?' He set the photograph back up again and looked at his wife. 'There's still not a day goes by when I don't think of her. Love dies hard. Like hate. And there's still not a day goes by when I don't think of Hannon and what he did to her.'

Father and son stared at each other across a chasm of silence. Ed was exhausted by the effort of dredging the truth out of himself and Nick was shattered with remorse.

The silence was broken by a commotion in the hall.

'Hey, lady!' Phil's voice protested. 'You can't go in there.'

'Try and stop me!'

Kate Hannon surged into the room and stopped dead in front of the two men. Astonished to see Nick there, she was even more amazed by the mournful expressions on their faces. But it did not deflect her from her purpose. She marched over to the old man.

'Mr Stenning,' she asserted, 'I want to speak to you.'

'He didn't do it, Kate,' Nick said quietly.

'Marty saw him. Standing there with a stick of dynamite in his hand. How in God's name can you defend him?'

'He's my father,' replied Nick. 'And he's telling the truth.'

Kate backed away as if he had just slapped her face.

'You're his son, okay,' she railed. 'You're a Stenning through and through. How could I think that you were different?' She moved to the door then paused to throw another remark at him. 'And don't worry about the money you loaned me for the drilling. You'll get it back!'

She went charging out into the corridor and Nick followed.

'Kate! Come back!'

Ed Stenning was surprised but not resentful at the news that his son had financed the drilling. For some reason, all his rage had left him. The bitter misunderstanding which had kept him and his son apart for so many wasted years had now been cleared up.

Picking up the photograph once more, he put it to his lips to give his wife a gentle kiss of forgiveness then he crossed to the fireplace and set the frame on the mantelpiece.

There was no need to hide her away in the drawer any more.

Burning rubber along the dirt road, the Larapinta truck scorched on at breakneck speed. Kate drove with a recklessness born of fury, anxious to put as much distance as possible between her and the man who had so signally betrayed her.

'I hate him!' she said. 'I loathe him!'

The one person she had found to love and trust had now turned on her. It was devastating. She could not believe that the man who had got so close to her that night in Alice Springs could do such a thing. He had loved her. Confided in her. Committed himself to her. Yet now he had deserted her when she needed him most.

When it came to a real crisis, he had taken his father's side and tried to protect a guilty man. It all came back to the same thing: the old blood feud between the Hannons and the Stennings.

What *was* the cause of it?

Why should Kate imagine that *she* could alter it?

Well, let him run back to Cutta Cutta. It won't stop me taking his father to court, she vowed. I'll fight all the Stennings if I have to. I'll show them that I've got the true Hannon spirit.

Whatever happens, I'll see this through to the end.

Fury was intermingled with self-blame. As she looked back over her friendship with Nick, she wished she had not been so open; had not allowed him to take her in, made herself so vulnerable. It was because of their intimacy that she felt so desolate now.

Her mind was revolving as fast as the wheels of the truck.

I should never have trusted him. He's a man and men always let me down sooner or later. My first husband ran out on me. The second died on me before our marriage even started. Now this man has stabbed me in the back. Whenever I get involved with someone, it ends in disaster and I'm the one in tears.

'I hate you, Nick Stenning!' she shouted to the air. 'I hate all men!'

She was suddenly aware of a loud whirring noise approaching from above. Nick's helicopter was trailing her. It soon swooped right down in front of her and tried to make her stop, but she swung out of its way and accelerated.

'Go away!' she screamed. 'I don't want to see you!'

The helicopter dived again and flew right alongside her so that he could lean out and shout across.

'Pull over, Kate! I have to talk!'

'I never want to speak to you again!'

He moved in closer but she took evasive action, driving the truck off the road and across uneven terrain to rejoin the track where it looped round ahead. The dust and discomfort went unnoticed. She was simply intent on avoiding him.

He was a Stenning. That said it all. They thought they

could get away with anything – even dynamiting a well. She was determined to resist them.

Nothing would make her stop for him.

Nick pursued her all the way back to Larapinta but he could not make her slow down. The truck was fuelled by high-octane rage. It sped on through the sunset and roared in through the main gate at the homestead before skidding to a dusty halt in front of the verandah.

The helicopter dipped right down and hovered a few yards away from the vehicle. Kate jumped out and levelled a rifle at Nick's chest.

'Get off my land!' Her voice was the snarl of a wounded animal at bay.

The bar at the Stenning Arms was packed with stockmen that evening. Noise was at its customary deafening level and beer was flowing freely. Stories were being swapped on all sides and laughter was raucous. A pall of cigarette smoke hung over it all.

Bert Simpson cringed over his beer in a corner and tried to talk to anyone who would listen. He waved an arm wildly.

'You all better drink up,' he urged. 'Be the last you can afford for a long time.'

'Listen to him!' mocked someone.

'Shut up, Bert,' advised another voice. 'You're a born whinger.'

'Just like your dad.'

Bert smashed his glass on the floor with sudden anger. It gave him all the attention he wanted. He glared round at the taut faces.

'You leave my father out of this!' he warned. 'I got some news for you all. I just come from the lock-up. That Hannon bitch is pressing charges against Ed Stenning for blowing up her bore!'

Everyone was listening now. They crowded round him to hear what he said because they had a personal stake in it.

'Yes,' continued Bert. 'There's not a man in this bar who doesn't feed his kids on a Stenning pay packet. If *he* goes, then you can kiss your bloody jobs goodbye. And all because of her. That madwoman's already killed my father. She'll wreck this whole town before she's through.'

His words excited an immediate response and wild threats were made against Kate. The rabble-rouser quelled them with raised palms and egged them on to action.

'Don't just moan about it!' yelled Bert. 'She's over at the police station right now. What are you going to do about it? Are you men or bloody mice?'

They brushed him aside and surged through the front door.

Having given her statement to the police, Kate was just about to leave the building with Henry Dingwell. She was satisfied that legal action had now been set in train though he remained very sceptical about their chances of success.

'What happens next?' she asked.

'That's the last of it for a while,' he explained. 'They won't need you now until the committal hearing.'

'I see.'

'You can always drop the charge, you know. That would be my advice.'

'Save your breath.'

They had reached the exit now. He made one last plea.

'Think it over – that's all I ask. Okay?'

'Good night, Henry.'

'Kate . . . About Nick . . .'

'I don't want to talk about it,' she said firmly.

He sighed. 'Good night.'

They came out of the police station and went off in opposite directions. Kate strolled down the road towards the car park with her mind pulsing. The events of the day had left her destroyed.

'Here she comes!'

'Bitch!'

'Damn Yank!'

'Who the hell does she think she is!'

Kate saw the phalanx of men up ahead of her and jerked with fear. There were twenty or more of them, dark, menacing figures muttering among themselves. As they began to move forward, she quickened her pace and turned into the car park, reaching her vehicle only seconds before they caught up with her.

Locking herself in, she stared out at them and tried to hide the terror that was now stirring inside her.

'What do you want? Go away!'

The men surrounded the truck with silent menace and pressed against it. She felt it rock slightly and her blood curdled. With a shaking hand, she switched on the ignition and the engine came to life. When she flicked on her headlights, some of the hard, accusing faces were caught in their glare.

Kate released the handbrake and moved slowly forward, resolved not to show her panic. She realised who they were and why they had come. They were Ed Stenning's men, trying to intimidate her into backing down.

Her grit asserted itself. 'Out of my way,' she murmured. 'You won't stop me.'

Increasing her speed slightly, she pushed the men aside and drove into the road itself, but her problems were not over. An even bigger group now awaited her, forming a wall of solid flesh directly in her path. The grim, impassive faces told their own story. Kate Hannon was the common enemy. The whole town was against her.

Her first impulse was to sound her horn and accelerate right at them so that she forced them to scatter, but she mastered the urge. She had to counter their menace with her own quiet resolution. She had to prove to them that they could not influence her in any way.

Kate drove on slowly until she reached the wall, then it seemed to fold around her so that she was completely enclosed. Her vehicle was still moving but it was being pushed and shaken by dozens of hands now and fists were banging on the doors.

'You don't scare me!' she kept saying to reassure herself.

The truck rolled on and the ordeal continued. Faces thrust themselves at her through the windscreen. Ugly gestures were made at her. Kicks were hurled at her vehicle.

Frozen stiff and staring straight ahead, she drove steadily on until she at last broke clear of them. Though she desperately wanted to change gear and race away, she felt it would look like a retreat and so she maintained the same slow pace to the end of the road.

Only when she had turned the corner and wiped the hideous scene from her rear-view mirror did she feel safe. She jabbed her foot down on the accelerator and left the town of Glenwarra as fast as she could, spurned by its people because she sought justice.

It was a gruesome foretaste of what she could expect when the case went ahead but she steeled herself to withstand it. Ed Stenning had obliterated Larapinta's last hope of survival. The ranch into which Tom Hannon had poured his love and his labour would now have to be sold.

It was a heinous crime. Kate was going to exact due punishment.

The courtroom was packed to capacity for the committal hearing. It was a large, functional room, with tables set out facing each other and a dais in the central position. The public gallery was crammed with Outback people, their blank faces hiding the outrage they felt at a stranger who dared to accuse the person who was foremost among them. All of them felt the intense heat and many fanned themselves, setting up an ominous rhythm that seemed to accentuate their deep collective disapproval.

Auntie Deir and Ralph were tucked on one of the benches with Zoe and Emmie alongside them. All four looked down into the well of the court with anxiety. They admired Kate's bravery in taking on Ed Stenning but they all knew exactly what she was up against.

Kate herself sat behind a table with Tina and Dingwell.

The lawyer was dressed in a more formal suit now. He was troubled by the stifling heat and patently not relishing his task. In representing the Hannons, he would automatically alienate the Stennings and that could have a serious effect on his business.

Ed Stenning himself, a stoic figure in a lightweight suit and an open-necked shirt, sat opposite behind another table. Nick and Meg were close to him, circumstances uniting them for the first time in years. Though they sat next to each other, they were strangely unconnected. Taking part in a family charade.

The presiding magistrate was a big, florid man who was already dabbing at his bald head with a handkerchief. Familiarity with the Stenning family made his job an unenviable one and he was in a lather of discomfort up on his dais.

A court clerk and various other officials were in their appointed places. Uniformed policemen stood in front of the door.

Frank Austin, the defence lawyer, was in the middle of cross-examining Marty and he was giving the boy a torrid time. Tall, sleek and sharp-featured, Austin had a look of unassailable self-confidence.

'But there *was* smoke,' he probed. 'Lots of smoke. You said so yourself.'

Sensing a trap, Marty hesitated and shot a glance at Kate.

'Was there smoke, son – or wasn't there?'

'Yes – but the wind blew it away.'

'Just like that?'

'Yes.'

'And how far was Mr Stenning from you?'

'Fifteen or twenty yards, I guess. I don't know.'

'You don't know?' mocked Austin with easy sarcasm. 'You can remember that the smoke cleared suddenly but you don't know how far away he was?'

'I couldn't tell *exactly*,' Marty explained. He was flustered, feeling the heat and the strain.

'Was that because the sun was in your eyes?'

'Objection, Your Worship!' declared Dingwell, standing up. 'That's not been established. Defence counsel is leading the witness on.'

'He's right, Mr Austin,' the magistrate agreed.

Austin nodded his head respectfully towards the bench and changed his tack slightly. He moved in close to Marty and smiled.

'Your mother doesn't like the Stennings, does she?'

'Mom doesn't hate them all,' he blurted out.

'Oh?' Pretending the information was new to him, the lawyer stepped back in surprise. 'And which one does she like?'

'Nick,' the boy muttered uneasily.

'A lot?'

Marty looked at Kate in mild panic then replied with a nod. Austin's next statement was so flat and calm that it produced jeering laughter in the public gallery.

'Kate Hannon likes Nick Stenning . . . a lot.'

The magistrate pounded his gavel above the disturbance.

'Order! Order!' he shouted.

'Objection!' urged Dingwell, on his feet again.

'Explain your line of questioning, Mr Austin,' the magistrate demanded with measured severity.

The defence lawyer used a manicured hand to indicate the people whose names he mentioned. His manner was as calm and plausible as ever.

'If my client were gaoled, his son, Nick Stenning, would take over Cutta Cutta. That would be a blessing for Mrs Hannon. Her own ranch is in trouble. She needs a "friendly neighbour" to help her out.'

'No, that's not true!' yelled Marty.

'Isn't it?'

Before Dingwell could stop her, Kate was on her feet to howl above the turmoil in the court.

'That's enough! He's only a boy!'

But Austin had already done enough damage.

The revelation about a friendship between Nick and Kate had caused an uproar. Austin gazed around serenely then went back to his seat. The gavel banged impotently.

'Order! Order!'

Kate could not raise her eyes from the table in front of her. She was mortified. It was harrowing enough to be reminded of her involvement with Nick, but it was unbearable to have it used against her in a public courtroom. Even worse was the fact that her own son had, unwittingly, helped to create the minor sensation. Kate began to question her wisdom in putting Marty into the witness box.

'Order! Order!'

The excitement gradually died down.

But the commotion in Kate's heart did not abate.

The long, hot day took its toll of everyone and Ed Stenning was no exception. When he took the witness stand himself, he was grey-faced and glistening with perspiration. Dingwell's cross-examination made him feel more uncomfortable.

'Did you buy dynamite?' the lawyer pressed.

'We all keep dynamite, for clearance work. Gouging out dams and so on.'

'Please answer the question,' Dingwell insisted. 'Did you or did you not buy dynamite just a couple of weeks before the Larapinta bore was blown up?'

A pregnant pause. Ed looked to Austin for guidance. A nod came.

'Yes,' the old man admitted softly.

'The person who sold it to you remembers it clearly. He's given us a statement.' Dingwell held a paper aloft. 'He says he thought it was strange that you were buying so much dynamite and he asked why you needed it. What did you tell him, Mr Stenning?'

'To clear some rock?'

'And did you clear rock?'

'I hadn't gotten around to it,' Ed muttered, shifting in his seat and evidently in some pain.

'You kept that dynamite for *weeks* and never used it?'

'That's right.'

'Is that unusual?'

'There were more important things to worry about.'

Dingwell pounced. 'Or were you saving it for something else?'

'Objection!' Austin cried.

But the magistrate's concern for Ed Stenning won out over formal proceedings. He had turned white and he was breathing with obvious difficulty. He seemed to be almost on the point of collapse. Nick and Meg watched him in alarm and even Kate was worried for him.

'Ed?' asked the magistrate. 'You all right?'

'Yeah.'

'If you'd like an adjournment to . . .'

'Let's get it over with,' the old man decided wearily.

Dingwell took his cue and threw down a document in front of Austin with a dramatic flourish.

'Our scientific report,' he said triumphantly. 'It proves that the dynamite bought by Ed Stenning was used to blow up the Hannon well!'

A murmur of disbelief went round the court.

Ed Stenning was shaken to his very soul.

Nick was dazed. He looked first at his father then across at Kate. Further denial was pointless. He had to accept that Ed *had* been involved in the sabotage. His father had lied to him.

He lowered his head in defeat.

Reporters and photographers ringed the court-house in droves as they waited for news. Unable to get a seat in the public gallery, dozens of people hung about outside with ghoulish interest. Word about the dynamite had spread. Everybody was shocked. They were in a state of absolute suspense as they awaited the verdict.

Inside the courtroom, the tension was extraordinary. One of the most prominent figures in the whole Territory seemed to have been caught out in a criminal action.

The silence was profound as the magistrate read out his decision.

'I have considered the evidence that has been placed before this Court. And it is my determination that a prima-facie case against Edward Clive Stenning *has* been established . . .'

Commotion ensued. The magistrate wiped rivulets of sweat from his forehead and put in some strenuous work with the gavel.

'Order, please!'

Ed Stenning was utterly crushed and in real distress. Meg was seething with rage. Nick was stunned. Austin was quietly furious. Kate and her children enjoyed the thrill of success. Dingwell smiled.

When the noise subsided, the magistrate continued.

'I shall therefore recommend to the Director of Public Prosecutions that Mr Edward Stenning be charged under Section . . .'

His voice trailed off as he looked at the old man. Ed Stenning had clutched his heart, let out a gasp, and pitched forward.

'Dad! Dad!' cried Meg in apprehension.

'Someone get a doctor!' shouted Nick.

New uproar added to the confusion as everyone clustered round the stricken man. Nick waved them back so that his father would have room to breathe, then supported Ed in his arms. Meg was stroking the old man's face and trying to soothe him.

Kate came over anxiously to see what was happening.

'Is there anything I can do?'

Meg rounded on her. 'You've done enough already! Look at him! You've almost killed him! I hope you're satisfied!'

Kate was thunderstruck. There was an element of truth in the accusation that she could not escape: it was the strain and humiliation of the trial that had provoked the heart attack. In seeking to bring Ed Stenning to justice, she had helped to cut him down. Remorse ran through her.

She knew that they were all blaming her, and recoiled from the general hostility. When she caught Nick's eye and saw the dull hatred in it, she wanted to turn and run away.

Her mind kept coming back to one refrain.

I wish I'd never come here and I wish I'd never met him.

Another nightmare had started.

— 20 —

A new day brought the same old round of jobs at the Larapinta homestead. Even though they would soon have to leave, Kate and the children went on with their chores. Marty fed the chickens as usual then went back into the kitchen. He found his mother cleaning the cooker.

The boy was still trying to come to grips with his traumatic experience in court. He had never realised that a cross-examination could be so harrowing and he was still jangled. Consideration for his mother's feelings now prompted him to apologise to her.

'Mom?'

'Yes, honey?'

'I'm sorry about yesterday. I let you down.'

'No, you didn't, Marty,' she reassured him.

'What I said about you and Nick . . .'

'It was tricked out of you. Forget it.'

'I feel lousy.'

Kate looked at him and saw the self-doubt in his eyes. She crossed over to enfold him in her arms and hug him tight.

'I was proud of you in court. Very proud.'

'And we won!' he reminded her, rallying slightly.

'Only after a fashion,' she admitted.

'Yeah – we still have to sell up.'

'They beat us, Marty. The Stennings finished us off.'

This time it was the boy who hugged her. The embrace was foreshortened by the sound of a car outside in the yard. Kate was surprised.

'Who can it be this early?' she wondered.

She hurried out on to the verandah to investigate.

'Good morning, Kate!'

'Hi there, Henry.'

He got out of his car and came over to shake hands with her. 'Another beautiful day.'

'Unfortunately,' she replied, glancing up at the blue sky. 'We need rain. Isn't there someone you can sue for breach of promise?'

'That's not a bad idea,' he joked. Then looked at her more closely. 'How're you feeling?'

'Pretty groggy.'

'That figures.'

'Yesterday was tough on us all. Marty, especially.'

'You could have spared him all that, Kate. And yourself.'

'I'm not going back on my decision,' she affirmed. 'Still, what brings you out here? Long drive. Must be something important.'

'It is,' he conceded. 'A cup of that American coffee you make.'

'And what else?'

He clicked his tongue then waded in with what he had to say.

'Nick's a mate of mine,' he explained. 'We go back a long way. None of this is his fault. Don't blame him.'

'I don't know who to blame,' she confessed. 'I'm just totally bewildered, Henry. Why did we come to this place? They hate us.'

'Nick doesn't. He loves you.'

Kate was torn between anger and interest.

'Did he send you out here to say that?'

'Nope. And he'd kick my backside from here to Darwin if he ever found out. But I just wanted to set the record straight. Kate Hannon comes first in his book. Doesn't that please you?'

'It's too late, Henry,' she whispered. 'Nothing pleases me now.'

'Just give the man a chance, will you?'

But Kate had no wish even to discuss Nick. It was his father who occupied the forefront of her mind.

'How's Ed Stenning?'

'Not so good.'

'It was dreadful to see him collapse that way.'

'When he's well enough, he'll have to face trial.'

Kate digested the information slowly and remorse touched her. Anguish suddenly showed in her face.

'I know I shouldn't,' she said. 'And I'm annoyed at myself, but . . . I feel so guilty!'

'You've no need to.'

'It's so unfair!' she insisted. 'So damned unfair! I mean, here's a guy who blows up my well so that he can put me out of business and I end up feeling *sorry* for him. It's crazy! What sort of a country is this, Henry? Just let me get out!'

The bedroom was vast. It was superbly furnished and had a slightly unreal air. Dominating the room was a huge oak bed. Ed Stenning was sitting up in it. Pale and weak from his heart attack, he stared into space with watery eyes. Time had no meaning for him.

The door opened quietly and Nick peeped in.

'I'm not asleep,' murmured the old man.

'How're you feeling, Dad?'

'I'll live.'

Nick came into the room and crossed to stand by the bed.

'That's good news,' he said.

'Will you be staying around for a while, son?'

'Yeah. I think I might.'

Ed gave a contented sigh and beckoned him closer. 'I didn't dynamite that bore, Nick. I swear it.'

'I know that now, Dad.'

'Have you figured out who was behind it?'

'I think so.'

'It was Meg. When you hit that lake at Larapinta, she

just couldn't handle it. Festered inside her. So she grabbed herself some of that dynamite and rode over there.'

'How come you showed up at the site?'

'Phil told me she'd gone,' the old man remembered. 'I rode off after her but I wasn't quick enough. Whole place went up with a bang. No sign of Meg. I arrived in time to find that loose stick of dynamite.'

'And that's when Marty saw you,' Nick guessed.

'Caught red-handed. Circumstantial evidence.'

Nick put a hand on his father's shoulder and squeezed it. 'I knew that you were covering for somebody, Dad,' he said. 'It wasn't difficult to work out who it was. I was shocked to think that you might have been capable of it. I'm not shocked about Meg.'

Ed gave a crooked smile of resignation. 'Story of my life,' he decided. 'Making excuses for my womenfolk. I covered up for your mother all those years. Now I have to do it for my daughter.'

'Only because she won't come forward herself,' Nick argued, his anger surfacing. 'She let you go through with that court case. It was Meg who helped to put you in bed.'

'Forget her for the moment. What're *you* gonna do, Nick.'

He shrugged. 'Depends.'

'On Kate Hannon? She's quite a woman.'

'I know.'

'Good luck, son.'

With Nick's hand still on his shoulder, Ed dozed off peacefully into a deep slumber. He had no dream and no consciousness of the passing of time. When he awoke, there was still a hand on his shoulder and he expected it to be his son's.

Instead, it belonged to Meg and she was shaking him.

'Wake up, Dad,' she said. 'We have to talk.'

'What's going on?' he mumbled, taking a while to adjust.

He had gone asleep in daylight and awoken in darkness. He had left a son with whom he had at last been reconciled to find a daughter from whom he was becoming estranged.

Meg had brought an oil lamp with her and set it on the bedside table. In its flickering glow, her father looked pallid and in pain. She sat beside him and gazed down.

'I felt I owed you an explanation,' she began. 'It's been on my conscience ever since ... what happened in court.'

'Go on,' he invited, watching her carefully.

'I did it for you, Dad – to get Larapinta.'

'Don't give me that nonsense!'

'It's true.'

'You'd have let them send me to gaol for something I didn't do.'

'No,' she argued. 'If it'd gone to trial, I'd have owned up. I couldn't stand by and see you take the punishment.'

'You saw me take enough punishment in court,' he accused.

His hand went to his chest as a severe ache troubled him.

'I had to do it, Dad. Don't you understand? It was the only way to get our hands on Larapinta.'

'All I understand is that you disgust me, Meg. As a result I've made Nick my heir.'

Meg reacted to the news as if she had been punched.

'But your will appointed *me*.'

'I changed my will.'

'You can't do that!' she exclaimed. 'I've spent my whole life looking after you and taking care of this place. What the hell has Nick done?'

'He's my son.'

'That's not an answer, Dad!' she railed. 'I want what's mine.'

'Marry Phil,' he advised. 'You could do a lot worse. I may be old but I'm not blind.'

But Meg was not even listening. Having waited all those years to inherit Cutta Cutta, she was now going to lose it to her brother. Vitriolic rage surged up in her. She stood up and waved her arms about in the air. Taking no account of her father's frail state of health, she howled at the top of her voice: 'This place belongs to me!'

'You blew your chances when you dynamited that bore,' he told her. 'I'm not leaving Cutta Cutta to someone as rotten as that. Even if you are my daughter. What you did was unforgivable.'

'Nobody can prove I did it,' she challenged. 'Not even you!'

Enough of his old spirit returned for his eyes to blaze. 'Get out!' he roared. 'I've finished with you! I never want to see you again!'

Even before the last words were out he began to choke. Fear covered him like a shroud as he clutched at his throat.

'Meg!' he gasped. 'Jesus . . . I don't want to die . . .'

Ed Stenning went still as if he had fallen into a catatonic trance. Filled with horror, his eyes remained on his daughter. She let out a cry and fell to her knees beside the bed, clutching at him in a last desperate bid to hold him there.

'No, Dad . . . no!'

'Man is born of woman, is of few days, and full of trouble. He comes forth like a flower and withers. He passes like a shadow and does not stay. In the midst of life we are in death . . .'

The voice of the Reverend Metcalf was intoning at the funeral of Ed Stenning. A large crowd had gathered for the momentous occasion. Friends and enemies alike had come to pay homage to a man who had been a legend for decades. Ed had ruled his empire with a stern authority that all had been forced to respect.

Now he was lying in his coffin beside an open grave.

A great presence had passed out of the Territory.

'The days of man are but as grass: he flourishes like a flower of the field; when the wind goes over it, it is gone: and its place will know it no more.'

Kate and the children came hurrying into the cemetery and made their way to the back of the crowd. Like the other mourners, they were all in traditional grey or black but there the resemblance ended. The newcomers were immediately set apart from the rest by a muted hostility. Dark looks and black thoughts were aimed at them.

It wounded Kate and it took all her self-possession to withstand it. She glanced around surreptitiously to see if there was any friend at the graveside. She collected a brief, supportive smile from Dingwell, a nod from Auntie Deir and a vague wave from Ralph Shackleton.

For the rest, it was subdued enmity. They blamed her. If Kate Hannon had not brought a court case against Ed Stenning, then he would still be alive. The question of his guilt was somehow passed over. He had died and she was the scapegoat.

Kate was made to feel like his killer.

'Friends, we are gathered here to commit the body of our brother, Edward Stenning, to the ground . . .'

The words floated unheard into Kate's ears. She was looking at Nick's expressionless face and Meg's white mask of suffering. Whatever hatred she felt for the Stenning family, it was muffled now beneath an overriding sympathy.

She thought of the proud, imperious, arrogant man whom she had first met at a barbecue. Ed had rattled her immediately but she had been impressed by the deference everybody else had shown him. To achieve such pre-eminence in a world as tough as the Outback was a supreme compliment. At the height of his powers, she now realised, he must have been an extraordinary man.

His salient qualities were reflected in his children. Nick had his inner strength and his refusal to compromise, while Meg evinced his ruthlessness and unscrupulousness. Both of them had their father's single-mindedness.

Kate remembered the Camel Cup in which Ed had pitted himself against someone much younger and stronger than himself. That said a lot about the essence of the man. He was not just the acknowledged king of the Territory. He was ready to prove it against anybody.

271

Nick turned his gaze in her direction for a second. He was surprised but grateful that she had come, knowing how difficult it must be for her. Beyond that, his feelings were contradictory. Preoccupied with his grief, he could not begin to sort them out.

She read the confusion in his eyes and it matched her own. Instinct drew her to him but harsh fact pulled her away. Their intimacy had been cancelled out by his return to Cutta Cutta. In siding with his father, he had declared war on her. Kate still could not understand why.

All she knew was that she responded to his suffering and wished she could do something to allay it. Her heart stirred as the coffin was lowered into the earth.

'Earth to earth, ashes to ashes, dust to dust . . .'

Brushing aside helping hands, Meg scooped up a handful of red soil and let it fall into the grave. It was her last, symbolic farewell to her father before she was led away by Nick.

The mourners began to drift away towards the main gate in small groups. A reverential silence hung over the cemetery. It was not every day that a man of Ed Stenning's stature was laid to rest. They had witnessed the end of an era.

Kate and the four children moved between the gravestones, studiously ignored by everyone they passed. Zoe and Emmie faltered. They stood for a moment in a state of indecision, wondering whether to stay where they were or to approach old friends. The antagonism was directed at Kate and her children but not at them. They were free to choose sides.

The two sisters exchanged a glance and acted in consort. They ran to catch up the woman who had been their mother for all those long, difficult weeks. Emmie took Kate's hand and she strolled by her side. The final commitment had been made.

In the dining room at Cutta Cutta, the three of them sat around the table in an unnatural tableau, eating very little of the food that was set out before them. Nick occupied his father's seat at the head of the table. Meg faced him and Phil was between the two of them. A strained silence was broken by the sound of Meg pouring herself some more wine.

She glared at her brother and a sneer brushed her lips.

'Go on. Say it, Nick. It's all my fault.'

'You hated Kate Hannon from the moment she got here,' he asserted.

'Yes, I did!'

'Because of Tom.'

'A jumped-up waitress with a nose for a dollar. That's all she was. He picked her up in a restaurant. She had no right to him.'

'Did you?' he asked pointedly.

'Of course,' she declared with a defiant tilt of her head.

'How do you make that out?'

Carried away by high emotion, Meg completely forgot that Phil was sitting there. Her words tumbled out with a fierce pride.

'I loved Tom Hannon,' she boasted. 'He's the only man I've ever loved properly. If he'd married me, I'd have been a real wife to him and helped to run his ranch. I'd have been mistress of Larapinta.'

'When that failed,' Nick pointed out, 'you tried to be mistress here instead. Whatever it took.'

'I only failed because of her,' screamed Meg. 'She took Tom Hannon from me. That was the start of it. Then Dad turned against me. She's to blame for everything!'

'You dynamited her well!'

'And I'd do it again!' yelled Meg, flailing her arm and knocking over her glass of wine. 'I'll be glad when that bitch is gone for good. The sooner she gets out of my life, the better!'

Phil had heard enough. He rose abruptly and stalked out.

'Hey . . .' She was taken aback. 'Wait!'

273

Nick flung the truth at her from the other end of the table.

'There's something in you that men can't stomach. They all walk out on you in the end because you drive them away. Tom Hannon was the first to go. Then Dad himself turned his back on you. Now it looks as if Phil is doing the same.'

'Shut up!' she screeched, hitting the table with both fists.

'Then, of course, there's me. I wrote you off years ago.'

She got to her feet and stood there quivering for a second before racing out of the door. Fear lent extra speed to her feet as she raced out into the middle of the yard. It was deserted.

'*Phil!*'

There was no answer. Meg raced on down to the bunkhouse and found a saddled horse waiting outside. Phil emerged through the door with a pack containing all his belongings.

'What d'you think you're doing?' she demanded.

'Leaving.'

'But I need you, Phil.'

'I wish that was true,' he said with genuine sadness. 'I thought it was at first. That's why I stayed.'

'Don't leave me,' she begged, grabbing his arm.

'You're sick, Meg. Hate eats you away like a cancer. I wish I could help you but I don't think anyone can do that now.' He lifted her hand away, threw his pack across the horse then mounted. 'Tell Nick I said goodbye. Cutta Cutta's in good hands.'

Her disappointment quickly converted to malice.

'Go on!' she jeered. 'I was getting bored with you anyway! You'll never get a job around here! I'll see to that!'

He tipped his hat to her and rode off across the range with her threat pursuing him like an angry wasp.

She shouted until he was well out of earshot, then she rested against the bunkhouse. She had lost everything.

Her father, her lover, her right to inherit Cutta Cutta. Kate was responsible. She had stolen Tom Hannon away and the rest had followed from that. Meg was now totally isolated.

She had nobody and nothing left.

Except a chance of revenge.

'Marty? What's Aunt Molly like?' asked Zoe with forced interest.

'Nice,' he replied, trying to sound encouraging. 'A bit like Tom. But kind of American. A mixture. You'll like her. Really.'

'Are there any horses in San Diego?'

'Well, maybe not right in the middle,' he said. 'But out a bit . . . sure. Lots of horses.'

Dressed in their night things, they were out on the verandah together. The three girls were sprawled together in an old hammock while Marty sat on the step and rested his back against a post.

Their mood was sombre. None of them was really looking forward to a future in California. Zoe and Emmie did not want to leave their own home. Marty hated the feeling that they were going in disgrace with their tails between their legs. And even Tina, who had been the person most anxious to return to America, now wavered.

Adversity had welded them into a proper family now. She did not want it to be broken up. The irony of the situation depressed her. At the very moment they started to like Larapinta, it was being taken away from them.

Tina made an attempt to cheer the girls up.

'You'll be able to go to Disneyland.'

It did not make up for having to emigrate from Australia.

Kate appeared in the doorway, conscious of their mood and sharing it herself. She looked around them with sorrow.

'Time for bed,' she announced.

The children wished her good night and trooped off to

their respective bedrooms. Kate locked up then retired to her own room. It was late and they were all tired. They were soon fast asleep.

None of them heard the Jeep driving up to the homestead. Or the sound of petrol cans being unloaded on to the ground. Or the slurp of petrol itself as it was poured over the verandah.

Meg Stenning went swiftly and stealthily about her work.

Nick searched the house with growing unease. His sister was nowhere to be found. He went into the yard to check the barn and the outbuildings, calling her name aloud but getting no response. When he saw the garage door open, he rushed across to it. The Jeep had gone.

So had several cans of petrol.

'Oh, no . . . Meg! Not that!'

He sprinted to his helicopter in a surge of panic.

Meg lit the match and dropped it into the petrol. It ignited at once and a blue flame darted along the trail to the house. With a resounding hiss, the Larapinta homestead exploded into a ball of fire, turning night into day and illuminating the plain for miles.

She stood well back and admired her handiwork.

It was the ultimate vengeance.

Kate awoke to find flames leaping in through her window. She put her hand to her throat as the smoke attacked her, then she jumped straight out of bed. Shouts and screams from other parts of the house told her that the children were roused as well. Dashing to the door, she flung it open so that she could get to them but she was confronted by a wall of flame.

'Oh, my God!'

The heat made her move back and shield her face.

A hysterical cry came from the room at the far end of the passageway. Zoe's voice rose above the roar of the flames.

'Kate! Help! Please – someone! Help!'

Kate responded without delay. Keeping her head down and her hands over her mouth, she ran straight through the flames that blocked her path and on down the passageway. She pushed open the bedroom door to be greeted by billowing smoke.

'Over here!' called Zoe. 'Quick!'

Coughing and spluttering, Kate stumbled through the gloom to the bed. Zoe had thrown a blanket over Emmie, who was screaming her terror underneath it. The older girl was crouched beside her sister as flames ate their way through the curtains and up through the floor. The heat and the smoke were almost overpowering. Zoe stared at the flames, mesmerised.

'Come on!' ordered Kate. 'Get out!'

'Emmie's under the blanket.'

'I'll bring her.'

She snatched up girl and blanket and turned back towards the door, which was now a savage rectangle of fire. A loud crash startled them and they turned to see that Gillie had just smashed the window in. Retching from the smoke, he waved frantically to them.

'This way, missus.'

'Thank God!' Kate exclaimed with relief, handing Emmie through the window in the blanket.

'I got her,' said Gillie. 'Jamie – he's got young Tina.'

'Where's Marty?'

'I haven't seen 'im.'

Kate helped Zoe through the window then went off in search of her son. She got no further than the door. It was blazing so fiercely that she was knocked back as if by an invisible hand. Her eyes streamed with tears and her whole body was roasting.

'Marty!' she yelled in anguish.

'Help!' came a distant shout. 'Mom! I'm in here!'

'Come on, missus!' implored Gillie at the window. 'Before it's too late. This is the only way out.'

Racked by the agony of not being able to reach her son,

277

Kate swung on her heel and darted to the window. Gillie pulled her through it without ceremony and led her clear of the flames.

They gathered in front of the burning verandah and watched Larapinta being consumed by the inferno. The noise was so ear-shattering that they did not hear the Jeep driving away — or even the landing of the helicopter. The first they knew of that was when Nick came racing up to them.

Jamie was now having to hold Kate back by force.

'Let me go, Jamie! My son is in there!'

'It's hopeless, missus,' he argued. 'You kill yourself.'

'Where is he?' asked Nick, stepping forward.

Kate broke away to grab at his shirt as she jabbered at him, 'Nick — Marty's still inside . . . in his room at the back.'

'Don't go in there!' pleaded Gillie.

But Nick ignored the advice. With a hand over his mouth, he dived straight in through a front door that looked like the burning mouth of hell. Once inside, he found himself in a chaos of flame and smoke, wood crackling noisily all around him and ferocious heat closing in on him every second.

He ran across the room and into the passageway, pushing aside a spar of timber that fell in his way then kicking away a small rug that was burning with yellow flame. When he got to the door of Marty's room, he found that it was stuck; the heat had caused it to expand. The brass doorknob was red hot and thick black smoke was gusting everywhere.

Nick acted quickly. Hunching his shoulder, he hurled himself at the door and knocked it clean off its hinges. Marty's room was a furnace and the boy himself, overcome by fumes, was lying on the floor. Curled up beside him and whimpering pitifully was Bluey the dog.

Before Nick could reach them, there was a cracking sound and the roof began to cave in. A section of the beam came down and hit the unconscious boy with brutal unconcern. Nick leaped forward and grabbed hold of the beam, burning his fingers as he did so but not letting go until he had thrown the timber aside.

Lifting the boy over his shoulder, he ran back towards the door with the dog at his heels. The smoke was darker and denser than ever now and his lungs were full of it. Marty's weight slowed him down and made it more difficult to clamber over fallen beams. But the memory of Kate's suffering face impelled Nick. To help her, he would walk through anything.

When he got to the front door, he was almost dropping with exhaustion and the legs of his jeans were smouldering. The exit was a sheet of white flame that defied him to pass through it. Gathering up all his remaining strength, he literally flung himself through the doorway and out into the night.

Kate came rushing over as he laid Marty on the ground and beat out the tiny flames on his jeans.

'How is he?' she gasped, her eyes filled with dread.

'He's alive. We'll have to get him to the hospital.'

Willing him to survive, Kate touched her son's face.

'Come on, Gillie,' said Nick. 'Help me carry him to the helicopter. Every minute is vital.'

The prostrate body was borne off to the waiting machine.

In the background, Larapinta continued to blaze away and send a column of black, avenging smoke all the way up to heaven.

The intensive-care ward had all the latest equipment but it still did not guarantee Marty's recovery. Connected to a life-support machine, he lay on his bed in a coma. Kate and Tina sat near him and kept their vigil. Both of them had been treated for minor burns but their injuries were negligible beside Marty's condition.

'Mom . . . is he going to die?'

'I hope not, honey.'

They went into each other's arms and let their tears

flow. Of all the horrendous things that had happened to them since they had been in Australia, this was the worst. Marty's life was hanging on a single thread. All they could do was to watch and pray.

When Tina had stopped crying, she let herself out of the room and went off to join Zoe and Emmie, who were sitting in the waiting room with Auntie Deir. The sisters comforted her all they could and the old woman soothed her with words of quiet hope.

Kate remained by the bedside. An oppressive stillness hung in the air. Marty seemed hardly to be breathing. He was bandaged all over and looked ridiculously small and frail.

Nick came up outside and watched through the glass window. His own burns had been treated now and both his hands were bandaged. Though he was in considerable pain, he forgot his own injuries as he looked at the stricken boy and his mother bending over him. There had been moments when he thought he hated Kate Hannon for what she had done to his father. All that was over. Love and compassion came flooding back.

He longed to be in the room with her, providing comfort, sharing her anguish, lifting her hopes. But there was no place for him. He was convinced that Kate did not want him any more.

Unaware of Nick's presence, Kate was talking to her son. Her eyes were glistening and her heart was full to overflowing. She tried to reach across the chasm of unconsciousness and touch him.

'Marty,' she whispered. 'I don't know if you can hear me but if you can . . . don't quit on us. Please – we need you. You're the man of the house. We've been through some tough times but we've always made it somehow, haven't we? Don't leave us now. Try, Marty. Please. Try hard . . . I love you so much . . .'

She remained perfectly still as the first rays of sun hit the window, turning the room from grey to mellow gold and bathing Marty's head in yellow light.

Kate saw it as a sign. Her optimism flickered. Somehow, she believed, they would survive.

'The only way from here on in is up,' she murmured.

As hope resurfaced, she looked to the future and started to make plans. The time in Australia had not been one of unrelieved failure. There had been many small triumphs. They had grown together as a family and discovered qualities in themselves that they had not even suspected were there. Larapinta had educated them. They should be thankful for that.

Everything would be better in the future. More secure. The twins would go back to a familiar American world and they would all do their best to help Zoe and Emmie adapt to it with the minimum of difficulty.

And what of Nick Stenning? He had saved Marty's life. There had been a moment in his bedroom at Alice Springs when she had felt that he might save her life as well, but it had come to nothing. Regret coursed through her. She had an impulse to see him and thank him for what he had done for Marty. It became a compulsion and she went swiftly out of the room, her face glowing. When she got to the waiting room, Auntie Deir read her thoughts.

'Nick's not here, dearie. Left a few minutes ago.'

Mid-morning brought a change of treatment. Two order-lies carried a two-way radio and set it up near Marty. The nurse explained.

'Just following doctor's orders, Mrs Hannon.'

She checked her watch and switched on. Dotty Phillips spoke.

'Hello, everyone. This is a very special broadcast on School of the Air. Children from cattle stations and farms right across Central Australia are standing by their radios at this very minute to say a cheerio to a friend and fellow pupil . . . Marty, this is for you.'

Kate was profoundly moved. She listened as the teacher struck a few notes on her portable keyboard, then the discordant voices of many children swelled in a rendering of 'The Star-spangled Banner'.

It was a glorious, heart-wrenching cacophony.

> Oh! Say can you see by the dawn's early light
> What so proudly we hail at the twilight's last gleaming?
> Whose broad stripes and bright stars thro' the perilous
>   fight,
> O'er the ramparts we watched, were so gallantly streaming?

Kate took her son's hand as she listened to the Australian voices singing her country's national anthem. Tears gushed.

> And the rockets' red glare, the bombs bursting in air,
> Gave proof through the night that our flag was still there.
> Oh! Say does that star-spangled banner yet wave
> O'er the land of the free and the home of the brave?

As the singing continued, Marty's eyelids flickered. Very slowly, he began to respond to the words that he knew so well. His eyes came fully open and he looked up at his mother. She squeezed his hand hard and he gave her a pale smile of recognition.

It was enough. Marty would pull through.

The Larapinta truck rolled along the road to Cutta Cutta with its driver humming the tune of 'The Star-spangled Banner'. It was dusk. Now that her son was through his crisis, Kate felt able to leave him so that she could go and thank the person who had saved his life. Nick had taken an enormous risk in charging into the burning house. She wanted to tell him just how much she appreciated what he had done.

When she reached the turn-off to Cutta Cutta, the impossible happened. Spots of rain started to fall on her windscreen. Kate could not believe it. The spots became a steady drizzle and she braked to a halt at once, jumping out to look up at the sky.

It opened properly to let a deluge fall. Rain slanted down in torrents and soaked her within seconds. Kate held up her hands in thanks. She whooped for joy and let the water cascade down her for several minutes, luxuriating in its feel and taste, knowing what it would mean to the parched land.

The drought was over.

Happily drenched, she got back into the truck and drove on towards Cutta Cutta, enjoying the novelty of using her windscreen wipers. Kate was ecstatic. Two miracles in one day. Marty's recovery. And now, the rain.

As she drove along a winding track, she saw a figure ahead of her in the middle of her path. She got closer and spotted the rifle that was being pointed at her. Kate stopped at once and alighted.

Meg Stenning trained the gun on her chest.

'I've been waiting for you,' she said with malevolence.

'Meg, hasn't there been enough death and destruction already?'

'I thought the fire would do the job for me,' Meg explained. 'I don't like leaving things unfinished.'

Kate was aghast. '*You* started the fire?'

'I blew your precious bore up as well,' boasted Meg. 'It wasn't Dad at all. It was me. Yes – and I paid Simmo to wreck the first one.'

Kate reeled from the shock. It was mind-blowing.

'What on earth made you do it, Meg?' she gasped.

'*You* did!'

'Me?'

'Yes!' raved Meg, consumed with bitterness. 'If it hadn't been for you, Tom would have married me. You only knew him for two weeks whereas I knew and loved him all my life. When his wife died, I was glad. It gave me my chance at last. But I wanted to give Tom some time. And so I waited.'

'Meg, I'm sorry. Tom never said anything.'

'Would it have made any difference if he had?'

Kate shrugged. 'Who knows?'

283

'You stole Larapinta from me by marrying Tom. Now you want to take Cutta Cutta as well through Nick.'

'That's not true.'

'It belongs to me!'

'I don't want it . . . you have it . . .'

Kate backed away a step as Meg raised the rifle to point it at her face. Cold fear gripped her. Though the rain was still pouring down to soak them to the skin, her mouth was dry.

She tried to plead with Meg. 'Don't do this . . . I'm going back to America . . .'

'You left it too late.'

'If you kill me, everyone will know who did it.'

'Will they?' asked Meg with a sneer. 'You're not very popular in these parts. Nobody will miss you when you go. Nobody will bother much about what happened – as long as they've got rid of you.' She used the tip of the weapon to motion Kate to the left. 'Over there.'

They walked across to a waterhole that was already half-full. Kate had never been so terrified in all her life. This was worse than the fire, worse even than sitting at her son's bedside and praying for his recovery. The sheer helplessness of her position appalled her.

'It'll be months before they find your body,' said Meg with grisly satisfaction. 'There's hundreds of waterholes around here.'

'Stop it, Meg. *Please!*'

'Did you stop the things you did to me?'

'You've got it all wrong.'

'Goodbye, Mrs Hannon . . .'

It was now or never. If Kate did not do something she would be shot down at point-blank range. She relied on instinct. Backing towards the waterhole, she deliberately stumbled to the ground, grabbed a handful of mud and hurled it into Meg's face. Then she flung herself at the other woman with all her force.

Caught off guard, Meg was momentarily blinded by the mud and knocked flat by the tackle. The rifle went off but

284

the bullet screamed harmlessly across the plain. Kate got her hand to Meg's wrist and twisted hard. With a yelp of pain, Meg dropped the rifle.

Crazed with anger, she went for Kate's throat.

'I'll kill you! I'll murder you with my bare hands, you bitch!'

Meg got a firm grip and began to throttle her. She was a powerful woman. Kate's eyes bulged, her throat was on fire and her lungs felt as if they were about to burst. She could not hold out much longer. With a sudden upward thrust of her knee, she dislodged her attacker and sent her slithering down the muddy bank. Kate went after her with a vengeance.

She knew that Meg would never give in. She might be stopped by physical force, but not by reason. The only logic an irrational woman would understand was superior strength.

The downpour continued. The women were soaked to the skin. As they grappled with each other again, their hands slipped and their feet failed to grip in the thick mud.

'Tom Hannon was mine!' Meg howled.

'Then why didn't he ask you to marry him?'

The taunt spurred Meg on. She was fighting like a maniac, punching, scratching and biting wildly. But Kate had much more than hatred to sustain her. She had a family and a future and a man she now realised she loved. So much had been taken away from her since she had come to Australia. She was not going to yield up her life.

As Meg tried to gouge out her eyes, Kate ducked and pulled her forwards, rolling over at the same time. They slid into the water and it almost covered them. Meg did her best to kick herself free, but Kate at last had the upper hand. Holding the other woman down with all her strength, she slowly forced her head beneath the surface.

Meg struggled violently, but could not escape. Gradually the resistance drained from her. When she began to go limp, Kate hauled her up and delivered a swing punch to her jaw. Meg was knocked cold.

Kate took a few seconds to gather herself before catching hold of Meg's feet and dragging her up the bank to safety. Slowly, Meg opened her eyes.

'Don't move!' Kate snapped. Meg looked at the rifle in her hand and was silent. It was over.

The nightmare was finally at an end.

Nick stood on the summit of his hill and surveyed the landscape all around him. Freshened by the rain and lit now by the sun, it had more desolate grandeur than ever. He had come back to his silence and his isolation. He was at home.

A scraping noise made him turn round.

Sweating and panting, Kate Hannon was hauling herself up to him on the guide chain. She reached the summit, paused to get her breath back, then shot him a friendly smile.

'I thought you were going back to America,' he said.

'Changed my mind.'

Hope flowered. 'You're staying?'

Kate walked right over to him and spoke with feeling.

'Am I always going to have to climb this damn hill when I need you?'

Nick took her in his arms and they sealed their love with a long kiss. High above the plain, their souls united as one at last.

In the deep silence, they seemed to hear the murmur of Wanabi, the Rainbow Serpent, guardian of the last frontier.

He was bestowing his blessing.